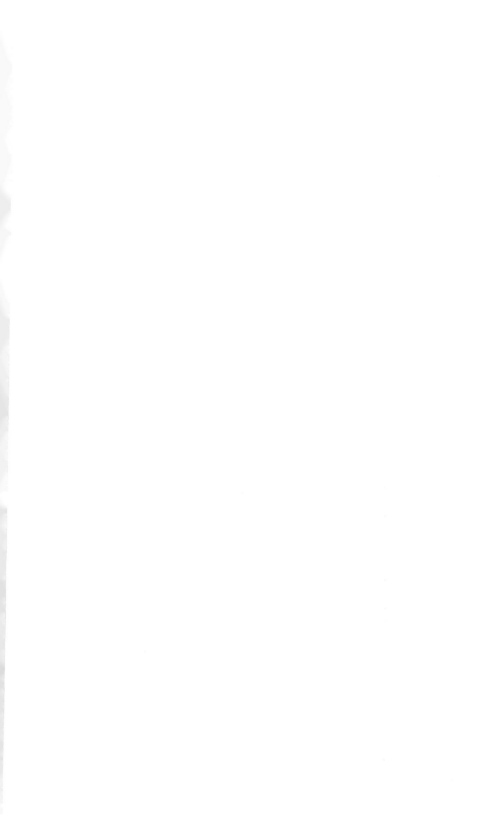

Interpretation of The Book of Revelation

Pastor Bob Stidham

WESTBOW
P R E S S®
A DIVISION OF THOMAS NELSON
& ZONDERVAN

This book is a work of non-fiction. Unless otherwise noted, the author and the publisher make no explicit guarantees as to the accuracy of the information contained in this book and in some cases, names of people and places have been altered to protect their privacy.

Scripture taken from the King James Version of the Bible.

WestBow Press books may be ordered through booksellers or by contacting:

WestBow Press
A Division of Thomas Nelson & Zondervan
1663 Liberty Drive
Bloomington, IN 47403
www.westbowpress.com
1 (866) 928-1240

ISBN: 978-1-9736-6746-9 (sc)
ISBN: 978-1-9736-6745-2 (hc)
ISBN: 978-1-9736-6747-6 (e)

Library of Congress Control Number: 2019908722

Print information available on the last page.

WestBow Press rev. date: 07/17/2019

Interpretation
Of The Book Of Revelation
By Pastor, Bob Stidham

Everything in this book is taken from the
King James version of the Bible

Written in the year of (1611)

The interpretation of the book of Revelation, is interpreted by
Pastor Bob Stidham, as he is led by the Holy Spirit of God. The
author of this book use these scriptures to guide him. [James, 1: 5]
[Mat. 7: 7,8] [Rom. 8: 14] [Heb. 11: 6]. The prayer of faith is the key
of all understanding.

About the Author of this Book

Pastor Bob Stidham, was called, and added to the church in the year
of 1977 January, 1. He is speaking of this church [Mat. 16: 18] [Acts,
2: 47]. Baptized July 24th. 1977, in a running stream of water Mitchell
Creek in Crawford County, near Eckerty, Indiana. By Pastor Louis
Adams, and Elder Darrel Stidham. On this date July 24th. 1977 his
wife LaVania Raleigh Stidham, also was baptized. They both took
membership in the Community Chapel Church at Eckerty, Indiana.
They were baptized with these words in the Bible [Mat. 28: 19].

Called to Minister the Gospel of Jesus Christ

In less than (24) hours after Pastor Bob, was baptized. Jesus, called
him into the Ministry to preach the Gospel of Jesus Christ, the
Heavenly Kingdom. Pastor Bob, was called the same way Jesus,
called the Twelve Apostles "Come and follow me". Pastor Bob, was
shown many, many things by Jesus, and his Holy Angels. These
scriptures Pastor Bob, works from [Gal. 1: 11, 12] [Rom. 8: 14].

Pastor Bob, was set aside under the Arm of Grace, and the watch care of the church, and given full privilege to use his calling into the field of Ministry of Jesus Christ. He worked three years in the field of ministry under the Arm of Grace, and the watch care of the church. Ordained to preach the Gospel of Jesus, July 20th. 1980. By the Presbytery Elders of the Community Chapel Church. Pastor Louis Adams, Elder Joe Combs, Elder Barry Adams, Deacon Jess Adams, Deacon Densil Polin. Pastor Bob, worked several years in the Community Chapel Church, and traveled a lot.

By the grace of God, Pastor Bob, is the founding Pastor, of the Freedom Gospel Church where the Book of Revelation is the Foundation (Jesus). Established April 19th. 1986, near the town of Lexington, Indiana.

Where The Spirit of the Lord is There is Liberty, [2nd. Cor. 3: 17].

PREFACE

The book of Revelation is very simple it starts in the book of Genesis. You will find references all through the bible to help us understand the interpretation. If we don't prove what we are saying, then we are not teaching anything. I am Alpha, and Omega, The Beginning, and the Ending. The First, and the Last. This is Symbolic Language, all six names are the same. They represent Jesus. Which indicates Jesus, is with mankind from the beginning to the end. To simplify Jesus, is the beginning of man, and the ending of man. Because there is no end to Jesus. The beginning of Jesus, see [Pro. 8: 22, 23] [Col. 1: 15] [Rev. 3: 14]. The beginning of man see [Gen. 1: 26]. The ending of man see [Rev. 1: 7,8] [Rev. 20: 11-thru-15].

Revelation is full of symbolic language. This Symbol (S/L) will be used for Symbolic Language. Everything (S/L) will be explained. These brackets Example, [John, 3: 16] will be used for Bible Reference, all through this book.

All the Signs, Seals, Beast, Great Red Dragon, Seven Heads, Ten Horns, Bottomless Pit, Sharp Two Edge Sword, (Each Edge Has a Name) The Mark of the Beast, The Number (666), All will be explained there are so much to learn.

The Book of Revelation, isn't written that anyone can read it chapter, verse, page, and line, for line, and understand it. Example [Rev. 1: 6] this Dominion was given to Jesus, in the book of [Dan. 7: 14] also this [Mat. 28: 18]. We can see there are long spans of time between these events.

I need to share something with you. The word Many is used all through the bible. I wanted to know why. Here is what the Holy Spirit brought to me. Many is a untold number see [Gen. 22: 17] [Mat. 22: 14] [Rev. 7: 9]

These word <u>See</u>, and <u>Hear</u> are both the same; A <u>Spiritual Mind</u> to understand see [Mat. 13: 13, 14, 15].

Jesus, told Peter, to feed my Sheep, and my Lambs, this is (S/L) people. Here is what Jesus, wanted his sheep, and lambs fed [Jer. 3: 15] <u>Knowledge, and Understanding.</u>

This book is not written to, Harm, Deceive, Persuade, or Offend anyone. Let every man be fully persuaded in is own mind [Rom. 14: 5]. This book is a tool used for learning, helping, and teaching others.

When I use the word <u>We</u> I am talking to the person reading this Great Book of Interpretation of Revelation everything is proven in the good Old Bible.

May God, Bless You
Where The Spirit of The Lord is; There is Liberty.
2nd. Cor. 3: 17

Pastor, Bob Stidham
2716 Sunset Trail
Charlestown, In 47111

INTERPRETATION OF THE BOOK OF REVELATION

By
Pastor, Bob Stidham

Everything in this book is taken from the
King James version of the Bible

Written in the year of (1611)

The interpretation of the book of Revelation, is interpreted by Pastor Bob Stidham, as he is led by the Holy Spirit of God. The author of this book use these scriptures to guide him. [James, 1: 5] [Mat. 7: 7,8] [Rom. 8: 14] [Heb. 11: 6]. The prayer of faith is the key of all understanding.

CHAPTER 1

1. The Revelation of Jesus Christ, which God gave to him, to shew unto his servants things which must shortly come to pass; and he sent and signified it by his angel unto his servant John;

Let's interpret, Revelation is an act of revealing making known the divine truth. Only God, can reveal his son Jesus. [Mat. 11: 27]. Which God, gave to him; [Mat. 28: 18] Power.

To shew unto his servants; This is righteous people living on earth today, and the future. Things which must shortly come to pass. This is events coming upon the earth the world of mankind. Jesus, is carrying out God's, plan. He Jesus, sent and signified it by his angel. Jesus, has an <u>Angel</u> [Rev. 22: 16]. Unto his servant John. This is the apostle John. [Mat. 10: 2].

2. Who bare record of the word of God, and of the testimony of Jesus Christ, and of all things that he saw.

Let's interpret, The pronoun Who, is (John) bare record of the word of God. This record that John, bare of the word of God, started here [Mat. 4: 21] called to the ministry.

And of the <u>Testimony</u> of <u>Jesus Christ.</u> We know the Testimony of Jesus, is the <u>Spirit</u> of <u>Prophecy</u>, see [Rev. 19: 10]. And of all that he saw. This goes back to when John, was called to ministry the gospel of Jesus, through the <u>Book</u> of <u>Revelation.</u>

Record is to put in writing an authentic official copy. John, wrote <u>Five Books,</u> <u>Saint John,</u> <u>First,</u> <u>Second,</u> and <u>Third John,)</u> and <u>Revelation.</u> We can see John, has <u>Documented</u> a perfect <u>Record,</u> of the word of God. The word of God, is Jesus, Here is the record

John, bare [John, 1: 1] [1ˢᵗ John, 5: 7, 8]. And of all things that he saw.

Here are some of the things John, saw that Jesus, did. <u>Miracles, Raising</u> of the <u>Dead, Deaf Hear, Blind see, Jesus, Crucified, Jesus Raised From The Dead.</u> John, saw Jesus, Ascend in to heaven [Acts, 1: 8, 9, 10, 11] see also [John, 21: 25] Plain isn't it?

3. Blessed is he that readeth, and they that hear the words of this prophecy, and keep those things which are written therein; for the time is at hand.

Let's interpret, Look at the three promises, <u>Blessed</u> is he that <u>Readeth,</u> and they that <u>Hear</u> the <u>Words</u> of this prophecy, and <u>Keep,</u> those things which are written therein.

We have three things we must do.(<u>Readeth, Hear, Keep</u>). I will interpret these words for you. <u>Read</u> this is Seek [Mat. 7: 7]. <u>Hear</u> The preached word, and understand it [Rom. 10: 14, 15]. <u>Keep</u> Is Faith [2ⁿᵈ. Tim. 4: 7]. To guide us through this see [James, 1: 5].

<u>Blessed,</u> is <u>Enjoying Happiness</u>. For the time is at hand; this is now (Present Time). Jesus, wants us to study the bible see [2ⁿᵈ. Tim. 2:15]. The Blessing is <u>Eternal Life</u>. Plus all the good things that Jesus, Gives us through our life on earth.

4. John to the seven churches which are in Asia; Grace be unto you, and peace, from him which is, and which was, and which is to come; and from the seven Spirits which are before his throne;

Let's interpret, John, to the Seven Churches, which are in Asia. This is the first time that we have record of the <u>Seven Churches</u> in Asia, and they have been there a long time, they belong to <u>Jesus.</u>

Grace, is divine help from Jesus, to overcome temptation, and Peace, is without fear from <u>Jesus,</u> (Which is) in (Heaven); and (Which was) on (Earth); and (Which is to come) from (Heaven). All of these verbs are (S/L) of Jesus, at different places and time.

And from the seven Spirits which are before his throne. This tells us that Jesus, has a Throne, see [Rev. 3: 21] The Seven Spirits, before his throne are these [Rev. 5: 6] The Seven Horns, and Seven Eyes, Which are the Seven spirits of God. This is the Kingdom that God, appointed Jesus. [Luke, 22: 29] all Power, [Mat. 28: 18].

5. And from Jesus Christ, who is the faithful witness, and the first begotten of the dead, and the prince of the kings of the earth. Unto him that love us, and washed us from our sins in his own blood.

Let's interpret, In verse (4) Jesus Christ, is not mention by his name. It is all (S/L) Symbolic Language of him. The faithful witness. He is the Faithful Witness of God, to mankind. Faithful, is Firm in Keeping Promises. Witness, is a True Testimony.

First begotten of the dead (Raised From The Dead) [Col. 1: 18]. Prince of the kings of the earth [Luke, 1: 32] King David. Unto him that loved us and washed us from our sins in his own blood. This is a praise, to Jesus, see verse (6) also [Rev. 5: 10].

6. And hath made us kings and priests unto God and his Father; to him be glory and dominion for ever and ever, Amen.

Let's interpret, Made us (Kings) and (Priests) unto God, and his Father. You will find this praise here [Rev. 5: 10]. We are looking at the Hundred Forty Four Thousand. [Rev. 16: 12] These are the Kings and the Priests.

To him be glory and dominion for ever and ever, Amen. This was given to Jesus, here [Dan. 7: 13, 14], and [Luke, 22: 29]. The Bible proves it's self.

7. Behold, he cometh with clouds; and every eye shall see him, and they also which pierced him; and all kindreds of the earth shall wail because of him. Even so Amen.

Let's interpret, These clouds are the Glory of God, that surround Jesus. [Mat. 24: 30] [Dan. 7: 13]. Every eye shall see him. This goes back to <u>Adam</u>. They also which pierced him. This is another generation of people. Thousands, of years from <u>Adam,</u> And all kindred of the earth; shall wail shall wail because of him, This is all nationality on earth Shall wail because of him, this is sinner people. The word <u>A Men,</u> is an agreement with what was said.

8. I am Alpha and Omega, the beginning and the ending, saith the Lord, which is, and which was, and which is to come, the Almighty

Let's interpret, I am; this is Jesus, Alpha, and Omega, <u>Alpha,</u> is the first letter in the Greek, alphabet. <u>Omega,</u> is the last letter in the Greek alphabet. The beginning and the ending Saith the Lord, all four of these are (S/L) of Jesus.

<u>Jesus,</u> wants the world to know he is the first of all things; including man. [Pro. 8: 22, 23]. Jesus, was at the beginning of Adam, [Gen. 1:26,27] the ending of the way of life on earth; [Rev. 1:7] [Mat. 24: 30] proves this. Saith the Lord, This is Jesus, doing the talking, look close at this.

These verbs; (<u>Which is</u>) (<u>Which was</u>) (<u>Which is to come</u>). Are (S/L) of Jesus, at different times and places. Let's take a look; at these verbs. <u>Which</u> is <u>Present Tense</u> (In Heaven). <u>Which Was</u> is <u>Past Tense</u> (On Earth) <u>Which</u> is to <u>Come</u> is <u>Future Tense</u> (From Heaven). The Almighty, This is <u>Jesus</u> he has all <u>Power</u> see [Mat. 28: 18].

9. I John, who also am your brother, and companion in tribulation, and in the kingdom and patience of Jesus Christ, was in the isle that is called Patmos, for the word of God, and for the testimony of Jesus Christ.

Let's interpret, Notice! In verse (8) <u>Jesus,</u> identified himself. Here John, is doing the same thing. Notice! I John, This is the apostle John, of the <u>Original Twelve Apostles</u> [Mat. 10: 2].

Who also am your brother, and companion in tribulation, and in the kingdom.

Who am your <u>Brother</u>; this is acceptance. And <u>Companion,</u> in <u>Tribulation,</u> This is I am with you in good times, and bad times, and in the <u>Kingdom.</u> This is the Kingdom that John, helped <u>Jesus,</u> build here on earth. [Luke, 22: 28, 29, 30], And patience of Jesus Christ. This is trying of our faith, [James, 1: 3] [James 5: 7, 8].

Was in the isle that is called Patmos; for the word of God, and the testimony of Jesus. This shows us the people of Asia Minor didn't was to hear John, preaching the word of God, nor using the Spirit of Prophecy <u>Testimony</u> of <u>Jesus.</u> This is why John, was Exiled to the Isle of Patmos.

10. I was in the Spirit on the Lord's day, and heard behind me a great voice, as of a trumpet,

Let's interpret; I was in the Spirit on he Lord's day. We can see John, remembered the Sabbath to keep it Holy. [Ex. 20: 8]. [Lev. 26: 2]. We understand the Seventh Day; is called the Lord's day; because God, Blessed it and Sanctified it, and rested from all his work [Gen 2: 2, 3]. The great voice belongs to Jesus, The Trumpet has a distinct sound; so does the voice of Jesus.

11. Saying, I am Alpha and Omega, the first and the last: and, What thou seest, write in a book, and send it unto the seven churches which are in Asia; unto Ephesus, and unto Smyrna, and unto Pergamos, and unto Thyatira, and unto Sardis, and unto Philadelphia, and unto Laodicea.

Let's interpret; Saying I am Alpha and Omega, the First, and the Last. This is (S/L) of Jesus. Alpha, and Omega, are the first, and last letters in the Greek Alphabet.

<u>First,</u> and the <u>Last,</u> is <u>Jesus,</u> The <u>First</u> Begotten <u>Son</u> of <u>God,</u> and the <u>Last.</u>

They all represent Jesus, which is this; Jesus, is with mankind form the beginning to the end. Proof, [Heb. 13: 5] "I will never leave thee nor forsake thee" [Heb. 13: 8] "Jesus Christ, the same yesterday, and today, and for ever".

What thou seeth, write in a book This is the Angel, talking to John; for Jesus, the book is Revelation. Proof see chapters, (2, 3) And send it to the seven churches; which are in Asia. There is a reason Jesus, chose these seven churches. Ephesus, Smyrna, Pergamos, Thyatira, Sardis, Philadelphia, and Laodicea. They are Guide Lines; or Instructions for all churches on earth today, to help themselves when things don't go well with us.

12. And I turned to see the voice that spake with me. And being turned, I saw seven golden candlesticks;

Let's interpret, John, heard the voice behind him, and turned to see who it was. The only thing he saw was, Seven Golden Candlesticks. John. Didn't know he was looking at the New Faith Covenant see [Heb. 10: 8, 9]. These Seven Golden Candlesticks, have names. They are the Seven Churches verse (20) shows this. These Golden Candlesticks are Spiritual.

The Old Law Covenant, Candlesticks, were made of pure gold from the earth. Notice they didn't have names then!! But God, and Jesus, had a plan. All of these Represent the Old Church; Which the name Church. Is not mentioned. The first time Church is mention is here [Mat 16: 18], and Jesus, doing the talking.

13. And in the midst of the seven candlesticks one like unto the Son of man, clothed with a garment down to the foot, and girt about the paps with a golden girdle.

Let's interpret, Jesus, is in the midst of all churches on earth today. The Seven Churches in [Rev. Chapter-2] and [Rev. Chapter-3] Prove this. One like unto the son of man. John, is looking at the

Glorified Flesh Body of Jesus, John, has seen Jesus, in his glorified body, on earth. [Mat. 17: 2,3] [Luke, 24: 38-thru-43] [John, 21: 7,12]. What John is looking at now is [John, 17:5] The Glory of God, covering the Flesh Body of Jesus.

The Golden Girdle; is what is known today as a vest. The Garment that Jesus, is clothed with is a Heavenly Garments, Eternal.

14. His head and his hairs were white like wool, as white as snow; and his eyes were as a flame of fire.

Let's interpret, This is the prayer that Jesus, ask God, to do for him, while he was on earth [John, 17: 5] Notice!! Glorify thou me with thine own self, with the glory which I had with thee before the world was.

What we are looking at here is the (Image of GOD).see [Dan. 7: 9] [Heb. 1: 3]. Now Jesus, is the (Express Image) of God. John, had never see this image of Jesus, before.

His eyes were as a flame fire; The Fire Is God, [Heb. 12:29] also [Mat. 3: 11]. We don't know what color this flame of fire is. We can't add to or take from.

15. And his feet like unto fine brass, as if they burned in a furnace; and his voice as the sound of many waters.

Let's interpret, His feet like unto fine brass. This is glowing or brightness in color as highly polished see [Dan. 10: 5, 6] This is Jesus.

His voice as the sound of many waters. Many waters is (S/L) people of all Nationality. When Jesus, speaks; All mankind understand him in their own tongue.

Form Adam, through all generations of people. Both in heaven, on earth, under the earth, and in the sea. See [Mat. 12: 40] and [1st. Peter, 3: 19]

The Many Waters, are here. [Rev. 17: 15] People, of the earth. If all the people of the earth praise Jesus, it would be one Voice,

"Spirit". Let's simplify, hearing one voice Jesus, speaking with many "Languages" To help us understand this better; See [Acts, 2: 4,5,6,7,8] I pray this has opened a door of understanding for all of us.

16. And he had in his right hand seven stars: and out of his mouth went a sharp two-edged sword: and his countenance was as the sun shineth in his strength.

Let's interpret, And he had in his right hand seven stars. The seven stars is (S/L) of the Seven Angels, of the seven churches, see verse (20).

And out of his mouth went a <u>Sharp Two Edged Sword.</u> The Sword is (S/L) of the word of <u>Jesus.</u> See [Is. 49: 1, 2] The two edges, or two sides, have names <u>Life,</u> and <u>Death.</u> Proof see [Mat. 25: 32, 33, 24] This side or edge is <u>Life.</u> [Mat. 25: 41, 46] This side or edge is <u>Death. Jesus,</u> is the <u>Word</u> of <u>God,</u> For the <u>Word</u> of <u>God,</u> is <u>Quick,</u> and <u>Powerful,</u> and <u>Sharper</u> than any <u>Two Edged Sword.</u> [Heb. 4: 12] proof.

His countenance was as the sun shineth in his strength. This is the Glory of God, shining through the Glorified Body of Jesus, [John, 17: 5]. This is the first time John, has seen Jesus, in his Glorified Heavenly Body. John, didn't know who Jesus, was.

And his countenance was as the sun shineth in his strength. This is the <u>Glory</u> of <u>God,</u> shining through the Glorified Flesh Body of <u>Jesus,</u> [Rev. 21: 23].

17. And when I saw him, I fell at his feet as dead. And he laid his right hand upon me, Saying unto me, Fear not; I am the first and the last:

Let's interpret, When John, saw Jesus, he fell at his feet as dead. This strongly Suggest John, did not recognize Jesus. There is no doubt it scared John. When he saw Jesus, with the Glory of God, shining through Jesus. And I fell at his feet as dead. In other words John, couldn't move he could still hear what Jesus, said. Like Paul on the road to <u>Damascus</u>

When Jesus, laid his right hand upon John, saying fear not; This fear is (Phobe). Jesus, is assuring John, or comforting him.

I am the first and the last. [Pro. 8: 22,23] proves this. Jesus, is the only begotten son of God, The first, and the last there is no other.

18. I am he that liveth, and was dead; and, behold, I am alive for evermore, Amen; and have the keys of hell and of death.

Let's interpret, Jesus, is assuring John, that he was dead; in the (Flesh Body) on earth, and alive forever more in his <u>Glorified Flesh Body</u> in Heaven. He is telling the whole world the same thing.

And have the keys of hell and of death. These <u>Keys</u>, are <u>Power</u>. <u>Hell</u>, is a place of confinement. [Luke 16; 22,23,26] <u>Death</u>, is sin see [Rev. 6: 8] and [Rev. 20: 14]. The Bible explains its self.

19. Write the things which thou hast seen, and the things which are, and the things which shall be hereafter.

Let's interpret, These verbs; (Hast seen) is past tense, (Which are) is present tense, (Hereafter) is future tense. This makes the complete book of Revelation. The Past, Present, and the Future. What thou hast seen are in these verses (11-thru- 18). The things which are; is in verse (20) and the Seven Churches Chapters Two, and Three. The things hereafter begins in Chapter Four.

20. The mystery of the seven stars which thou sawest in my right hand, and the seven golden candlesticks. The seven stars are the angels of the seven churches: and the seven candlesticks which thou saweth are the seven churches.

Let's interpret, What the Angel in verse (1) is showing us, and John, is writing it for us; is the <u>Faith Covenant</u> notice where it is, in the <u>Right Hand </u>of Jesus see [Heb. 10: 9]. This verse is self explanatory, It Interprets it's self. All of this chapter are the words of the Angel in verse (1) speaking for Jesus.

CHAPTER 2

—————•◦•—————

1. Unto The angel of the church of Ephesus write; These things saith he that holdeth the seven stars in his right hand, who walketh in the midst of the seven golden candlesticks;

Lets interpret, Unto the Angel, of the Church of Ephesus. This is the Faith Covenant this is why the Angel, Is at the Ephesus Church, see [Heb. 1: 14]. They are Ministering Spirits, to minister for them that shall inherit salvation.

Saith he that holdeth the seven stars in his right hand, and walketh in the midst of the golden candlesticks; this is <u>Jesus.</u> We need to understand this is the Angel in [Rev. 1: 1] doing the talking and showing John, these things of Jesus. It is the same angel here [Rev. 22: 16], and [Mat. 2: 2,9,10].

He that holdeth the Seven Stars, in his right hand; This shows that Jesus, has power and control of these angels. Who walketh in the midst of the seven golden candlesticks. This shows us that Jesus, walks in the midst of the churches on earth today that are his, proof [Mat. 18: 20].

2. I know thy works, and thy labour, and thy patience, and how thou canst not bear them which are evil: and thou hast tried them which say they are apostles, and are not, and hast found them liars.

Let's interpret, I know thy works, and thy labour, and thy patience. Let's analyze These word. <u>Works</u> is the choice of mind <u>Good,</u> or <u>Evil</u> "Thoughts".

The word <u>Labour</u> is the physical action of the choice of Mind. [James, 2: 18, 20] [Mat. 9: 20, 21,22].

The word <u>Patience,</u> Is the ability to bear trials without complaining. [James, 1: 2,3,4]

Here are some of the trials; the Ephesus Church, had. Thou Canst not bear them which are evil. Evil in mankind brings, Sorrow, Trouble, and Destruction. Here are some of them. Tried them which say they are apostles; and are not. These are (EVIL) Here they are, [Acts, 20: 29,30,36,37,38] [2nd. Cor. 11: 13] [2nd. Peter, 2: 1] And has found them liars. [1st. John, 4: 1]. The Bible is full of them.

3. And hast born, and has patience, and for my name's sake hast laboured, and hast not fainted.

Let's interpret, And hast <u>Borne.</u> this is to show exceptional endurance in difficult times. And hast <u>Patience,</u> This is the ability to bear trials without complaining. And for my name's sake this is <u>Love</u> hast <u>Laboured,</u> This is you have continued. And hast not <u>Fainted,</u> This is you have not <u>Quit.</u> This is their <u>Reward,</u> see [Mat. 24: 13] very plain.

4. Nevertheless I have some-what against thee, because thou hast left thy first love.

Let's interpret, <u>Nevertheless,</u> is however in spite of all that you have done for my name's sake. I have somewhat against thee. Because thou hast left thy first love. Their first love is here [Acts, 20: 28-thru-38]. The love of the gospel that Apostle Paul, Preached to them.

5. Remember therefore from whence thou art fallen, and repent, and do the first works; or else I will come unto thee quickly, and will remove thy candlestick out of his place, except thou repent.

Let's interpret, Remember from whence thou art fallen, and repent, and do the first works. This is you have quit preaching the

Gospel, and taking care of the church as you were instructed by the Apostle Paul. See [Acts, 20: 17,18,28,29,30,31]. Apostle Paul, is working for Jesus. [Acts, 22: 21]

The word repent; is ask for forgiveness, of the error, or mistake we all make. All sins are pardonable except the blasphemy against the Holy Ghost. [Mat. 12: 31,32].

And do the first works. This is follow the instructions The Apostle Paul, gave you. See [Acts, 20: 28].

Or else I will come unto thee quickly, and remove thy candlestick out of his place. This would be a building with people in it; Without the Holy Spirit, in them. See [Rom. 8: 9, 27]. Except thou repent. Repent is you are sorry for what you have done; you owe Jesus, an Apology. Repent is the most Valuable word for Christian People, on earth; use it!

6. But this thou hast, that thou hatest the deeds of the Nicolaitans, which I also hate.

Let's interpret, But this thou hast, that thou hatest the deeds of the Nicolaitans. The Nicolaitans, are a sect of people that teach loose moral standards. Example; "Just any old way will do" "It doesn't matter" "No one will notice" "Who cares" "Bad Hygiene Habits".

Which I also hate. If Jesus, hates these loose moral ways; take heed.!!

Jesus, said I am the way, [John, 14: 6, 15] If you love me keep my commandments.

Jesus, has set a standard that all mankind can live with, and not be ashamed, plain and simple.

Jesus, said this thou hast, thou hatest the deeds of the Nicolaitans; which I also hate. We can see some of the people in the Ephesus Church, have the Spirit of Jesus, in them see [Rom. 8: 14, 27].

7. He that hath an ear, let him hear what the Spirit saith unto the churches; To him that overcometh will I give to eat of the tree of life, which is in the midst of the paradise of God,

Let's interpret, He that has and ear, this Ear, is a Spiritual Ear, In the Spirit Mind, of mankind. [Eph. 4: 23] Blind Bartimaeus, Had this Spiritual Ear. [Mark, 10: 46-thru-52].

Let him hear what the Spirit, saith to the churches. The Spirit is the Holy Ghost see [Acts, 2: 4] This is instructions to the Angel of the church of Ephesus.

The Angel, of the Ephesus Church; knows the mind of each member. Whether it be a (Spirit Mind) or a (Carnal Mind). Spirit Mind Belongs to God, and Jesus, [John, 10: 3, 4, 5]. Hear means to understand. God, controls all things by his Spirit [Zach. 4: 6].

The Tree of Life is Jesus, Paradise, is the Second Heaven under the altar of God. [Rev. 6: 9, 10, 11]. This is where the souls of mankind are kept till the day of Resurrection .

To eat of the Tree of Life; is to be fed with the Holy Spirit., see [Ps. 23: 5] Thou anointest my head with oil my cup runneth over. The Holy Ghost; The Spirit of Truth, is the one that speaks of the Rewards to him that covercometh this is in all Seven Churches.

8. And unto the angel of the church in Smyrna write; These things saith the first and the last, which was dead, and is alive.

Let's interpret, And unto the angel of the church in Smyrna. Notice the first (Greeting) to all the Seven Churches is to the (Angel) of that church, and not to the church. These Angel, are responsible for what the church is doing see [Heb. 1: 14]. We are led by the Spirit.

The first and the last, is (S/L) Jesus, [Rev. 1: 11] Which was dead, this is on earth crucified [John, 19: 30. 33]. And is alive, [Mat. 28: 5,6,7]. [Rev. 1: 18]. Jesus, has showed us we can live on earth, and believe in him, and when we die have Everlasting Life [John, 3: 16] also [John, 11: 26] very plain isn't it

9. I know thy works, and tribulation, and poverty, (but thou art rich) and I know the blasphemy of them which say they are Jews, and are not, but are the synagogue of Satan.

Let's interpret, I know thy works, tribulation, and poverty, (but thou art rich) Let's analyze this. (Works) is the choice of <u>Mind.</u> (Tribulation) is <u>Distress,</u> and <u>Suffering.</u> (Poverty) is the state of <u>Being Poor.</u> (But thou art rich) the Smyrna Church, is (Rich) in <u>Faith.</u>

I know the blasphemy of them which say they are Jews and are not. This is sin, these people are (Liars) (Hypocrites) (Tares among the wheat). But are the Synagogue Satan. These are people that are <u>Satan Worshipers.</u>

10. Fear none of those things which thou shall suffer; behold, the devil shall cast some of you into prison, that ye may be tried; and ye shall have tribulation ten days: be thou faithful unto death, and I will give thee a crown of life.

Let's interpret, Fear none of those things which thou shall suffer. [Heb. 13: 5,] I will never leave thee, nor forsake thee. [Heb. 13: 6] I will not fear what man shall do unto me. This is "Faith" Fruit of the Spirit proof see [Gal. 5: 22].

The devil shall cast some of you into prison. The devil is, a <u>Evil Spirit</u>. The synagogue of Satan are Hypocrites (People) Tares among the wheat. These are the ones that are going to cast some of the Smyrna Church Members into prison; falsely accused.

To help us understand, (Devil, Satan) and the synagogue of Satan, are all one. See [John, 6: 70, 71] [John, 13: 2, 26, 27] [John, 8: 44].

That ye may be tried, This is <u>Fruit</u> of the <u>Spirit</u> (Faith). [Dan. 12: 9, 10]. Ye shall have <u>Tribulation Ten Days</u>. This is <u>Suffering</u>, and <u>Distress</u> Fruit of the Spirit. Be thou faithful unto death. Fruit of the Spirit is, <u>Faith</u>. To open a <u>Door</u>, for us see [Rev. 6: 9,10,11]. I will give thee a <u>Crown</u> of Life this is life <u>Eternal</u>. You will find the Fruit of the Spirit here see [Gal. 5: 22, 23].

11. He that hath an ear, let him let him hear what the Spirit saith unto the churches; He that overcometh shall not be hurt of the second death.

Let's interpret, He that hath an ear let him hear, this is instruction to the angel of the Smyrna Church. Let him hear what the Spirit saith unto the churches. Here is what the Spirit said, He that overcometh shall not be hurt of the second death. This is Judgment Day. The Spirit is the Holy Spirit of God. [John, 14: 16, 17]] [Eph. 4: 6]. Jesus, didn't find any <u>Fault</u>, with the Smyrna Church. He found all of the <u>Fruit</u> of the <u>Spirit</u> in it [Gal. 5:22, 23, 25].

12. And to the angel of the church in Pergamos write; These things saith he which hath the sharp sword with two edges;

Let's interpret, And to the angel of the church in Pergamos write; These are the words of the Angel, in verse (1) instructing John, to (Write), here is where the angel got his instructions from. Saith he which hath the Sharp Sword, with Two Edges, this is Jesus.

The Sharp Sword with Two edges is (S/L) It is not made of anything. It is the power of God, Put in the mouth of Jesus. see [Is. 49: 1,2] [Is. 11:4] [Rev. 19: 13, 15, 21]. When Jesus, speaks things happen. Example: (Rebuked the Stormy Sea) [Mark, 4: 39] (Raised the Dead) [John, 11: 43,44]

The Two Edges, or sides if you will have it; have names. One side is <u>Life</u> [Mat. 25: 31.32.33.34] the other side is <u>Death.</u> [Mat. 25: 41,46]. This Sharp Two Edged Sword is the Power of God, given to Jesus. [Mat. 28: 18]. Now we know what the Sharp Sword with Two Edges are, and their names. Also The two edges represent: The <u>Right Hand</u>, and the <u>Left Hand</u> of Jesus, See [Mat. 25: 34,41]. We can see Life, and Death here. (Heaven or Hell).

13. I know thy works, and where thou dwellest, even where Satan's seat is; and thou holdest fast my name, and hast not denied my faith, even in those days wherein Antipas was my faithful martyr, who was slain among you, where Satan dwelleth.

Let's interpret, I know thy works, and where thou dwellest, we know the word (Works) is the choice of mind of the <u>Pergamos Church.</u> We see where the <u>Works</u> of the Pergomas Church is.

Thou holdest fast (My Name) and hast not denied my (Faith). And where thou dwellest, This is to keep attention directed on their mistake. You dwell on things in your mind.

Even where Satan's seat is. This is the seat of (Power) to direct or vote on business matters in the Pergamos church. These are hypocrites in the church. They are the ones that slew Antipas.

And thou holdest fast my name, and hast not denied my faith, even in those days wherein Antipas was my faithful martyr. This shows us in the (Face of Death) the Pergamos Church kept the faith.

Who was slain among you This happen in the Pergamos Church. Where Satan dwelleth, these are (Hypocrites) in the congregation of the Pergamos Church. These Hypocrites are here see [Jude, 1: 4] [Mat. 13: 37, 38, 39] [Mat. 7: 15] [John, 8: 44] they all belong to Satan. The children of God, and Jesus, don't kill one another.

14. But I have a few things against thee, because thou hast there them that hold the doctrine of Balaam, Who taught Balac to cast a stumblingblock before the children of Israel, to sacrificed unto idols, and to commit fornication.

Let's interpret, But I have a few things against thee. Jesus, searches the mind of mankind.

Because thou hast there them that hold the doctrine of <u>Balaam.</u> When Jesus said I know where Satan's seat is. He was talking about the people that hold the doctrine of Balaam, verse (13).

Who taught Balac to cast a stumbling block before the children of

Israel, to eat things sacrificed unto idols, and to commit fornication. Here is where Balaam, taught Balac, to cast the stumbling block before the children of Israel. [Num. 25: 1, 2, 3] (Whoredom with the daughters of Moab) They ate things sacrificed unto their gods, and bowed down to their gods.

The Doctrine of Balaam, is False Doctrine. Commit Fornication is willfully turning from God, and worship of Idols. This shows us the Pergamos Church is (SPLIT) it has the Spirit of God, in it, and the spirit of Satan in it.

Balaam, became a False Prophet here he tuned from the Lord. Balaam, did this for Silver, Gold, and Wealth of the World see [Jude, 4, 11] The Children of Israel Slew Balaam, With the Sword see [Num. 31: 8] also [Josh. 13: 22].

15. So hast thou also them that hold the doctrine of the Nicolaitans, which thing I hate.

Let' interpret, The doctrine of the Nicolaitans; Are a sect of people that teach, Loose Moral Standards. Examples, (That's alright) (Just any old way will do) (Code of dress) and (Hygiene) (No one will notice) (Loud mouth) [James, 1: 26] see [James, 4: 4]. Any one a Friend of the World is the enemy of God. This is why Jesus, hate these things of the Nicolaitans.

Jesus, set a standard for mankind to go by. Keep your self unspotted form the world see [James, 1: 27] "Pure and Clean" If you love me keep my commandments [John, 14: 15]. See [Lev. 20: 7] [Lev. 11: 44] be ye Holy for I am Holy.

Summary: (Verse-13) I know where Satan's seat is, here they are. The people that hold the (Doctrine of Balaam) and the (Doctrine of the Nicolaitans) These two are the ones that martyred Antipas, who was slain among the members of the Pergamos Church. Where Satan, dwelleth. Satan is an Evil Spirit that get into the minds of people see [Luke, 22: 3] "A Destroyer"

16. Repent; or else I will come unto thee quickly, and will fight against them with the sword of my mouth.

Let's interpret, Repent; Jesus, is talking to the Pergamos Church members that are his. Or else I will come unto thee quickly, and will fight against them with the sword of my mouth. This is the (Sharp two edge Sword). Jesus, is talking about these (Reprobates) that hold the Doctrine of (Balaam, and Nicolaitans).

The Elders of the Pergamos Church, knew about the False Doctrine in it. They need to set their house (Church) in order. They can do this by what Jesus, said <u>Repent.</u>

17. He that hath an ear, let him hear what the Spirit saith unto the churches; to him that overcometh will I give to eat of the hidden manna, and will give him a white stone, and in the stone a new name written, which no man knoweth saving he that receiveth it.

Let's interpret, He that hath an ear, Notice this (Ear) is single it is Spiritual inside of man. So he, and him only can hear what the Spirit saith unto the churches. Hear means to <u>Understand.</u> These scriptures [Heb. 1: 14] [John, 10: 4, 16, 27] will help us understand this, also [Rom. 8: 14].

To him that overcometh (Repent) will I give to eat of the hidden manna, This is the Holy Spirit hidden in the Glorified Flesh Body of Jesus, see [John, [16; 13, 14, 15] And will give him a white stone; This <u>White Stone</u> is the <u>Soul</u> of <u>Man</u>, washed in the <u>Blood</u> of <u>Jesus</u>, [Is. 1: 18] [Ps. 51: 7] [1st. Peter, 2: 5].

And in the stone a new name written, which no man knoweth saving he that receiveth it. Here is the scripture that opens our door of understanding this. [Rev. 3: 12] [Rev. 14: 1]. [Rev. 22: 4]. Only you, and Jesus, know this [John, 10: 27].

18. And unto the angel of the church in Thyatira write; These things saith the Son of God, who hath his eyes like unto a flame of fire, and his feet are like fine brass;

Let's interpret, We know who the son of God, is Jesus. His eyes like unto a flame of fire. This is color; with no indication of hue. Mankind does not know what color. We know God, is a consuming fire [Heb. 12: 29] but no color known also the Burning Bush, that Moses, saw on fire but not consumed still no color given.

And his feet are like fine brass. This is bright or glowing in appearance. This is the same body Jesus, had before the world was. [John, 17: 5] [Heb. 1: 3] The Brightness of his glory; this shows us his feet like unto fine brass. Jesus, is the express image of God. God, is a Spirit; [John, 4: 24] Jesus, is not a Spirit [Luke, 24: 39]. The body of Jesus, now is a Glorified Flesh Body; of God, proof [John, 17: 5] And now, O Father, Glorify Thou Me with thine own self with the glory which I had with thee before The World Was.

19. I know thy works, and charity, and service, and faith, and thy patience, and thy works; and the last to be more than the first.

Lets interpret, I know thy works. (Works is the choice of mind) Here is the physical action of the choice of mind. (Charity, Service, Faith, Patience,) And the last to be more than the first. We can see the last is Faith, and Patience. See [James, 1: 2.3.4] Let Patience, have her Perfect Work that ye may be perfect. This is a Pure Mind. This is the real Thyatira Church.

After Jesus, cast out Jezebel. We can see the last to be more than the first. (More Charity, Service, Faith, Patience).(Charity, is Love) (Service, is help) (Faith, is pure) (Patience, is perfect).

20. Notwithstanding I have a few things against thee, because thou sufferest that woman Jezebel, which calleth herself a prophetess, to teach and to seduce my servants to commit fornication, and to eat things sacrificed unto idols.

Let's interpret, Notwithstanding; I have a few things against thee. The word, sufferest; is permit or allow. That woman Jezebel, which calleth herself a prophetess.

Jesus. didn't call this woman Jezebel she is a pagan, idol worshiper. The dogs ate Jezebel [1st. Kings, 21: 23] Jesus, knew Jezebel, then so did the prophet Elijah.

The false doctrine of Jezebel, came to the Thyatira church, the same way the doctrine of Balaam, came to the Pergamos church through the synagogue of Satan, which are these people see [John, 8: 44].

To teach and seduce my servants (Seduce) is to persuade to be (Disloyal) This is the Evil spirit in Jezebel, false doctrine To commit fornication. This is willfully turning from God, to idol worship. And to eat things sacrificed unto idols. This is animals that God, said thou shall not eat. [Lev. 11: 4,5,6,7,8]. This is also (Idol Worship).

21. And I gave her space to repent of her fornication; and she repented not.

Let's interpret, Jesus, gave Jezebel time to repent, of her fornication; which is turning from God, to idol worship. She repented not. [Gal. 6: 7] God, is not mocked; whatsoever a man soweth, that shall he also reap, see [Rev. 20: 15] We can see where Jezebel, is going plain to see isn't it?

22. Behold, I will cast her in a bed, and them that commit adultery with her into great tribulation, except they repent of their deeds.

Let's interpret, I will cast her in a bed. We can see Jesus, cast Jezebel, out of the Thyatira Church.

Behold is to keep in View, Mind, or Remember. This bed is (S/L) Symbolic Language, a False Church. Them that commit adultery with her; these are members of the False Church . The pronoun Them depicts the whole world of mankind.

And will cast them that commit adultery with her; into Great Tribulation. This Great Tribulation, is distressful suffering of body and mind. The word great depicts severe. Jesus, gave the members of this false church a chance to repent; if not see [Rev. 20: 15] very plain.

23. And I will kill her children with death; and all the churches shall know that I am he which searcheth the reins and the hearts: and I will give unto every one of you according to your works.

Let's interpret, And I will kill her children with death. We know death is sin. Here is how Jesus, is going to do it. [Rev. 6: 8] The Pale Horse, and his name that sat on him (Was Death) and (Hell) followed with him see [Rev. 20: 13, 14, 15] this is very plain.

And all the churches shall know I am he that searcheth the Reins; This is the Controlling or Directing Power; of a Governing Body. See [Eph. 4: 10,11,12] the Elders of the church.

We know the Hearts of mankind is the Mind of mankind see [Heb. 10: 16] [Eph. 4: 23] tells us this. The mind of man, is the Spirit of man. God, and Jesus, does not work with the flesh of man. And I will give unto every one you according to your works. Works is our choice of Mind, Good or Evil. This is judgment, Jesus, has two things to give, Live in heaven; or Death in hell.

24. But unto you I say, and unto the rest in Thyatira, as many as have not this doctrine, and which have not known the depths of Satan, as they speak; I will put upon you none other burden.

Let's interpret, But unto you I say, This is speaking directly to the Thyatira Church, and unto the rest in Thyatira. We know Lydia a seller of Purple lived in Thyatira. [Acts, 16: 14] and heard Apostle Paul, Praying and Preaching, and was baptized [Acts, 16: 15]. We can see Jesus, is speaking to those that are his. (Lydia), is one that we know of lived in Thyatira.

We know what this Doctrine is Pagan worship, of Idol. Which have not known the depth of Satan, as they speak. The Pronoun They, is speaking of the followers of Jezebel's, (False) (Doctrine).

The depths of Satan, see [Mat. 24: 24]. This shows us how strong Satan, and his followers are.

The depths of Satan, as they speak. This is the teaching, and preaching of false doctrine. I will put upon you none other burden; this is Hold Fast Till I Come; keep the faith.

25. But that which ye have already hold fast till I come.

Let's interpret, Here is what they have. Charity, Service, Faith. Patience see verse (19). Hold fast till I come, this is Jesus, see [John, 14: 3] Plain, and simple.

26. And he that overcometh, and keep my works unto the end to him will I give power over the nations;

Let's interpret, And he that overcometh, this is "Victory" [1st. John, 5: 4]. And keep my works unto the end. This is Charity, Service, Faith, Patience this is Fruit of the Spirit [Gal. 5: 22]. Also If you love keep my commandments. [John, 14: 15]. Unto the end; this is our life on earth see [Mat. 24: 13].

To him will I give power over the nations. This is sinner people on earth. This power is authority and to ruler see [Rev. 5: 10].

27. And he shall rule them with a rod of iron; as the vessels of a potter shall they be broken to shivers; even as I received of my father

Let's interpret, And he shall rule them with a rod of <u>Iron</u>. This is power, strength, and <u>Strong</u>. As the vessels of a potter shall they be broken to shivers; This is small pieces broken by sudden violence force. Even as I received of my father; this is Power, see [Mat. 28: 18].

28. And I will give him the morning star.

Let's interpret, I will give him the morning star. This is Jesus, he is the morning Star. See [Rev. 22: 16]. Also [2nd, Peter, 1: 19] and [Mat. 2: 2] Very plain isn't it? Remember all these Spiritual Gifts is given by the Holy Spirit of God. Notice, he that hath an ear let him hear what the Spirit saith unto the churches.

29. He that hath an ear, let him hear what the Spirit saith unto the churches.

Let's Interpret, He that hath and ear, let him hear. This is the Holy Spirit, talking to the Angel, of the church in Thyatira. This Ear, is a <u>Spiritual Ear.</u> Let him hear, is to understand what the Spirit, saith to the churches. The Angel in [Rev. 1: 1] is in control.

CHAPTER 3

---

1. AND UNTO the angel of the church in Sardis write; These things saith he that hath the seven Spirits of God, and the seven stars; I know thy works, that thou hast a name that thou livest, and art dead.

Let's interpret, And unto the angel of the church in Sardis. The Angel, in [Rev. 1: 1] is doing the talking and John, doing the writing.

Write these things saith he that have the seven Sprits of God. This is <u>Jesus</u>, [Rev. 5: 6]. And the seven stars, this also is Jesus, [Rev. 1: 20] these are Spirits [Heb. 1: 14].

I know thy works; Works, is the choice of mind of mankind. Whether (Good) or (Evil) Jesus, knows.

Thou hast a name that thou livest, and art dead. This name is Jesus, [Rom. 8: 10] tells us the name is <u>Jesus,</u> and Explains it. That thou <u>Livest,</u> This is <u>Spirit.</u> Because of righteousness. And art <u>Dead,</u> this is the flesh body because of sin, see [John, 11: 26] also [John, 14: 20] plain isn't it?

2. Be watchful, and strengthen the things which remain, that are ready to die; for I have not found thy works perfect before God.

Let's interpret, Be watchful, is continual without interruption, and Strengthen, is to make strong.

The things which remain, are Faith, Love, Holy Spirit, and the Preached Gospel of Jesus. Things; is a (Plural Noun) <u>State of affairs,</u> an <u>Improving Situation.</u> [2nd. Tim. 1: 13,14] "That are ready to die" The Sardis Church, is <u>Starving</u> to <u>Death,</u> For the Preached Word of The Gospel of Jesus. Proof see [Amos, 8: 11, 12]. We can see some of the Sardis Church, Has drifted away from Faith, Love and the Holy Spirit see [John, 14: 15, 23, 24].

They have gone to Formality, or customary rules and ceremony see [1st. Tim. 6: 20, 21]. A few of the Sardis Church, are worthy. This is why Jesus, said I have not found thy works perfect before God. Repent, and Forgiveness is the key to the Kingdom of Heaven.

3. Remember therefore how thou hast received and heard, and hold fast, and repent. If therefore thou shall not watch, I will come on thee as a thief, and thou shall not know what hour I will come upon thee.

Let's interpret, Remember therefore how thou hast received and heard. Received is the Preached Gospel, of Jesus, and heard, this is understand, the Preached Gospel of Jesus. Hold fast, this is keep the Faith, Repent, this is Godly Sorrow; Worketh Repentance [2nd. Cor. 7:10].

If therefore thou shall not watch, this is continually; I will come on thee as a thief. This is you will not know, what hour, Day, or Night I will come. Jesus, is talking to them that are ready to die. This is why the word Repent was used. These people in the Sardis Church, have Formalism; Having a form of godliness but denying the power thereof, [2nd. Tim. 3: 5]. See also [Mat. 7 : 13, 14], and [2nd. Tim. 1: 13], [Rom. 8: 9

4. Thou hast a few names even in Sardis which have not defiled their garments; and they shall walk with me in white; for they are worthy.

Let's interpret, This entire verse is here see [Mat. 7: 14]. The key word is, (FEW). This Garment which is White is a Heavenly Garment see. [Rev. 4: 4] [Rev. 6: 11] [Rev. 19: 8] very plain, the Bible proves it's self.

5. He that overcometh, the same shall be clothed in white raiment; and I will not blot out his name out of the book of life, but I will confess his name before my Father, and before his angels.

Let's interpret, He that overcometh this is the sins of the world by (Faith) see [1ˢᵗ John, 5:4]. Shall be clothed in white raiment. This is a Heavenly Garment. [Mat. 28: 3] [John, 20: 12], also [Rev. 4: 4] [Rev. 6: 11]. I will not blot out his name, out of the book of life. The book of Life is Jesus, see [John, 14: 6] also [Rev. 20: 15].

As long as mankind is on earth, regardless of their age, and have not turned the Holy Spirit, away; They still have a chance to (Repent) of their sins.

Everyone that is born on earth ; Their name is written in the Lamb's Book of Life from birth. When mankind, refuses to accept, (The Holy Spirit, Jesus, and God). During their life time on earth; their name is Blotted out of the (Book of Life) which is Jesus. [Rev. 20: 15].

I will confess his name before my Father, and before is angels. This is at the day of Judgment. No man cometh unto the Father but by me-(Jesus) [John, 14: 6].

6. He that hath an ear, let him hear what the Spirit saith unto the churches.

Let's interpret. He that hath an ear this is a Spiritual Ear, inside of mankind let him hear what the Spirit saith to the churches. See this Ear, [Mat. 10: 27] These are the sons of God, see [Rom. 8: 14] The Spirit is the Holy Ghost talking to the churches, and the church members.

7. And to the angel of the church in Philadelphia write; These things saith he that is holy, he that is true, he that hath the key of David, he that openeth, and no man shutteth; and shutteth and no man openeth;

Let's interpret, All of this verse is about Jesus. He that is Holy, is Jesus, see [Luke, 1: 35] he that is true, is Jesus, [John, 10: 41] [Rev. 3: 14] [Rev. 19: 11]. He that hath the key of David, <u>This is Power</u>, see [1st. Sam. 16: 1, 11, 12, 13] [Luke, 1: 32,33]

He that openeth and no man shutteth; This is <u>Jesus,</u> opens our Spiritual Ear, and no man can shut it!! And shutteth and no man openeth this is <u>Jesus,</u>

Shuts, the door of mankind's understanding because they have no interest, in the Kingdom of Heaven. See [Mat. 13: 14, 15]. This is the power of Jesus; [Mat. 28: 18] he controls the mind of mankind see, [Mat. 13: 9, 11, 13, 14]. The open mind of mankind is <u>Receptive,</u> to the Preached Gospel of Jesus. The <u>Closed Mind,</u> is <u>Rejective</u> to the Gospel of Jesus, [2nd. Thess. 2: 11, 12,13, 14].

8. I know thy works: behold, I have set before thee an open door, and no man can shut it: for thou hath a little strength, and hast kept my word, and hast not denied my name.

Let's interpret, I know thy works; Works is the choice of mind of mankind.. Jesus, knows what is on the mind of mankind whether, (Good-or Evil), see [Gen. 3: 22].

Behold I have set before thee an open door. Behold is to remember, or keep in mind. These are open doors [John, 3:16] [Rev. 22: 17] [Mat. 10: 1-thru-8] [Mark, 16: 16] Peter, and Cornelius [Acts, 10: 44-thru-48], Philip, and the Eunuch, [Acts, 8: 35-thru-39]. All of these are open doors; sent by Jesus. See [John, 14: 6]

For thou hath a little strength; Here is this little strength <u>Faith</u> as a <u>Grain</u> of <u>Mustard Seed</u> [Mat. 17: 20] [Luke, 17: 6]. Kept my word; [John, 14: 15, 23]. And hast not denied my name see [Luke, 12: 8, 9]. We can see <u>Jesus,</u> knows all things it was spoken by <u>Jesus,</u> before it was written in the book of <u>Revelation</u>.

9. Behold, I will make them of the synagogue of Satan, which say they are Jews, and are not, but do lie; behold, I will make them to come and worship before thy feet, and to know that I have loved thee.

Let's interpret, The synagogue of Satan, (S/L) are people that belong to Satan. [John, 8: 44]. [Mat. 7: 15] Wolves in Sheep Clothing. [2nd Peter, 2: 1,2] False Prophets, and False Teachers the list is endless.

Which say they are Jews, and are not, but do lie this shows us these people are of Satan, [John, 8: 44] there are no truth in him or these lying people. This shows us Jesus, knows the mind of everyone, whether Good, or Evil.

I will make them come and worship before thy feet. This teaches us; Greater is he that is in you than he that is in the world. [1st John, 4: 4]. And to know that I have loved thee. This shows us this, Vengeance belongeth unto me, I will recompence, saith the Lord. [Heb. 10: 30].

The Philadelphia Church, no doubt had some, trials, and tribulation. They kept the words of Jesus, and did not deny his name. Here is how they did it. [1st. John, 5: 4] The Victory that overcometh the world is our <u>Faith.</u> Without <u>Faith</u> it is impossible to please him, God, and Jesus.

10. Because thou hast kept the word of my patience, I also will keep thee from the hour of temptation, which shall come upon all the world. To try them that dwell upon the earth.

Let's interpret, Because thou hast kept the word of my patience. This word <u>Patience,</u> is off Great Value, to the children of God, and Jesus. [James, 1: 1, 2, 3, 4] this is Divine Guidance.

The Philadelphia Church, according to the words we have to work with, they had different temptation. But the trying of their <u>Faith </u>worketh <u>Patience. </u>[James, 1: 4] But let patience have her perfect work that ye may be perfect, and entire <u>Wanting Nothing</u>.

I also will keep thee from the hour of temptation, which shall come upon all the world. To try them that dwell upon the earth.

Here is the hour of Temptation; and also the Temptation [Rev. 13: 15, 16, 17].

verse (17) mankind gives up everything; that belongs to them; for the Mark, Name, or Number of the Beast. Also Worship the Beast, or his Image. This subject will be explained in Detail, In [Rev. Chapter-13].

This temptation is world wide; to try them that dwell upon the earth. This is righteous and unrighteous. We find this in the prophesy of [Dan. 12: 10]. The Philadelphia Church, has no fault they have kept the faith.

11. Behold I come quickly; hold that fast which thou hast, That no man take thy crown.

Let's interpret, Behold I come quickly; see [Mat. 24: 27] [1st Cor. 15: 52]. Hold that fast which thou hast, this is keep the faith, and endure to the end see [Mat. 24; 13]. That no man take thy Crown, is let no man deceive you. [Mat. 24; 4]. This Crown is Eternal the Crown of Life see [Rev. 2: 10].

12. Him that overcometh will I make a pillar in the temple of my God, and he shall go no more out; and I will write upon him the name of my God, and the name of the city of my God, which is new Jerusalem, which cometh down out of heaven from my God; and I will write upon him my new name.

Let's interpret, Overcometh, is our Faith, [1st John, 5: 4]. I will make a pillar in the temple of my God. Pillar is a person who is a main support of an institution.

For instance Noah, Abraham, Isaac, Jacob, Joseph, Moses. And he shall go no more out; This is eternal in heaven, their work on earth is finished.

I will write upon him the name of my God, Jehovah. [Ex. 6: 3]. The name of the city of my God, New Jerusalem, [Rev. 21: 2] Which cometh down out of heaven from my God.

And I will write upon him my new name. JESUS, [Luke, 1: 31], [Luke, 2: 21], [Mat. 1: 21].

13. He that hath an ear, let him hear what the Spirit saith unto the churches.

Let's interpret, This Spirit, is the Holy Ghost, speaking to the Philadelphia Church. This ear is a Spiritual Ear, on the inside of the mind of mankind their Spirit. When mankind are Born Again [John, 3: 3, 5, 6] they receive this Spiritual Ear see [Rev. 3: 20]. Without it no man can hear what the Spirit is saying.

Example see, [Rev. 1: 10, 11] John, had this Spiritual Ear. Jesus, found no fault with the Philadelphia Church. They are led by the Spirit of God, See [Rom. 8: 14].

14. And unto the angel of the church of the Laodiceans write; These things saith the Amen, the faithful and true witness, the beginning of the creation of God;

Let's interpret, Write these things saith the Amen; this is Jesus, The Faithful, and True Witness, this is Jesus, The Beginning of the creation of God. This is Jesus. See [Prov. 8: 22,23] all of this verse is Jesus.

15. I know thy works, that thou art neither cold nor hot: I would thou wert cold or hot.

Let's interpret, We know that work, or works is the choice of mind of man. Jesus, could have said; I know what is on your mind.

Which he did notice, thou art neither cold nor hot. The word Cold, is Unfriendly, The word Hot is a Fiery Temper. This is Double Minded see [James, 1: 8]. I would thou wert cold or hot. This is one or the other. If a person is (Cold) unfriendly, Jesus, can help them.

If they are (Hot) fiery temper, Jesus, can help them. The Laodicean Church, is <u>Double Minded,</u> <u>Unstable in all Their Ways</u>. [James, 1:8].

16. So then because thou art lukewarm, and neither cold nor hot, I will spew thee out of my mouth.

Let's interpret, Lukewarm; this can be <u>One Person,</u> or a <u>Group</u> of <u>People</u>. We are looking at the Laodicean Church that is double minded, [James, 1: 8]. I will spew thee out of my mouth. We see the, <u>Sharp Two Edges Sword</u> in <u>Action</u> here. [Rev. 1: 16] [Rev. 2: 16] [Heb. 4: 12] [Is. 49: 2]. Spew thee out of my mouth is depart from me ye workers of Iniquity see [Mat. 7: 23].

17. Because thou sayest, I am rich, and increased with goods, and have need of nothing; and knowest not that thou art wretched, and miserable, and poor, and blind, and naked;

Let's interpret, Because thou sayest, I am rich, increased with goods, and have need of nothing. This shows a <u>Haughty Spirit.</u> [Pro. 16; 18] (Arrogant) See also [Gal. 5: 19, 20 21] (A corrupt tree); See [Mat. 7: 17, 18] see this scripture also [Luke, 12: 16-thru-21] worldly goods.

And knowest not, let's analyze this. Thou art wretched is <u>Very Miserable,</u> <u>Unhappy</u>. Miserable is <u>Great Discomfort,</u> Poor is <u>Not</u> of <u>Good Quality.</u> Blind is <u>Lack</u> of <u>Good Judgment.</u> Naked is <u>Sin.</u> [Gen. 3: 7].

Let's summarize; take a close look!! The Laodicean Church, Is <u>I Am Rich,</u> increased with goods. This is things of this <u>World.</u> Yet (POOR)!! Consider the <u>Great City Babylon;</u> Destroyed.

Smyrna Church, <u>Tribulation, Poverty.</u> (But Thou Art Rich) <u>FAITH!!</u>. Be thou faithful unto death, and I will give thee a <u>Crown</u> of <u>Life.</u> This is very plain.

By Their Fruits (Good) and (Evil) ye <u>Shall Know Them</u> see

[Gal. 5: 19, 20, 21] (Evil Fruit) [Gal. 5: 22, 23] (Good Fruit) Simple. A great book could be written here.

18. I counsel thee to buy of me gold tried in the fire, that thou mayest be rich; and white raiment, that thou mayest be clothed, and that the shame of thy nakedness do appear; and anoint thine eyes with eye salve, that thou mayest see.

Let's interpret, This <u>Gold</u> tried in the <u>Fire</u>, is <u>Faith</u>. [Dan 3: 13-thru-30] [1st. Peter, 1: 7] See [Heb. 11: 6]. That thou mayest be <u>Rich</u> this is heavenly treasures.

[Rev. 2: 9] Smyrna Church, their <u>Rich,</u> is <u>Faith</u>. We see it here [Rev. 2: 10] <u>Faithful,</u> unto death. This <u>Rich</u>, was bought in <u>Prison.</u> The Smyrna Church, bought themself a <u>Crown</u> of <u>Life</u> while they were in prison with their <u>Faith</u>. Jesus, is counseling, the Laodiceans church to do the same thing.

White raiment that thou mayest be clothed. This white raiment is a Heavenly Garment see [Rev, 3:4] [Rev. 4: 4] [Rev. 6: 11] [Rev. 7: 9].

That the shame of thy <u>Nakedness</u>, do not appear nakedness is <u>Sin</u> [Gen. 3: 7, 8, 10, 11]. And anoint thine eyes with eye salve that thou mayest see. This is the <u>Holy Spirit</u>, [Eph. 1: 17,18] see is to understand, and hear is to understand.

19. As many as I love, I rebuke and chasten: be zealous therefore, and repent.

Let's interpret, As many as I love, this is Jesus, talking. I rebuke. This is <u>Disapprove</u> and <u>Criticize Sharply.</u> Chasten, Is to correct by <u>Punishment</u> see verse (16). Be zealous therefore, and repent see verse (17) all of verse (19) is good counsel, from Jesus.

20. Behold, I stand at the door, and knock: if any man hear my voice, and open the door, I will come in to him, and will sup with him, and he with me.

Let's interpret, Behold is to look or view. The door is the mind of mankind. Knock are the ministers that are called and sent by Jesus, to preach the everlasting Gospel [Rev. 14: 6] [Mark, 16: 15, 16] [Rom. 10: 14, 15, 17].

If any man hear my voice, this man has a <u>Spiritual Ear.</u> and open the door, this is (His Mind). Notice what Jesus, said "I will come in to him, and will sup with him and him with me. They rejoice in fellowship with each other see [John, 14: 20, 23].

<u>Sup</u> with him, and he with me. This is Fellowship one with another, [1st, John, 1: 7]. This man heard the <u>Gospel</u> of his <u>Salvation.</u> [Eph. 1: 13] And <u>Sealed</u> with the <u>Holy Spirit</u> of <u>Promise.</u>

The closed door, (Mind of mankind) is a rejective mind, You can find this all through the Bible, see [John, 1: 11] he came to this own and his own received him not.

21. To him that overcometh will I grant to sit with me in my throne, even as I also over came, And am set down with my Father in his throne.

Let's interpret, To him that overcometh; This is our <u>Faith</u>. [1st. John, 5: 4]. Will I <u>Grant</u>, to sit with me in my throne. We need to understand something here. <u>God</u>, said <u>Heaven</u> is my <u>Throne. Earth</u> is my foot stool [Is. 66: 1].

The <u>Throne</u> of <u>Jesus;</u> Starts here [Is. 65: 17] Prophecy; [Dan. 7: 13, 14] Prophecy; [2nd, Peter, 3: 13] Faith; [Rev. 21: 1, 2] <u>The Real Thing.</u>

All of these are the <u>Kingdom,</u> that God, appointed Jesus. [Luke, 22: 29,30].

Here is proof, [Mat. 28: 18, 19, 20].

Even as I also overcame, [John, 16: 33]. And am set down with my father in his throne. See [Heb. 1: 3] [Ps. 110: 1] [Acts, 1: 9, 10, 11] [Acts, 7: 55, 56]. We can overcome also [1st. John, 5: 4] we see [John, 3: 16] here.

22. He that hath an ear, let him hear what the Spirit saith unto the churches.

Let's interpret, All <u>Seven Churches</u>, got the same Instructions. This Spirit, is the Holy Ghost, that rules the world of mankind today, under the direction of <u>Jesus.</u>

[John, 16: 7-thru- 14] Notice, [John, 16: 13] See also [Rom. 8: 14] a perfect connection.

This is the end of the <u>Seven Churches.</u> I will make a <u>Summary</u> of the <u>Seven Churches</u>.

Summary of The Seven Churches

This Angel, [Rev. 1: 1] Is doing the Talking.
John, is doing the writing.
All of Revelation if under the direction, of Jesus Christ.
All Seven Churches are Instructions For
All Churches on Earth Today.

CHAPTER 4

1. After This I looked, and, behold, a door was opened in heaven: and the first voice which I heard was as it were of a trumpet talking with me; which said, Come up hither, and I will show thee things which must be hereafter.

Let's interpret, After this; Is after writing all the instructions to the Seven Churches; Which are in Asia. John, was in the Spirit. [Rev. 1: 10,11]. Now we see John, in his natural state of mind at this time he is not in the Spirit, but has a Spiritual Ear to hear with.

I looked and behold a <u>Door</u> was <u>Opened</u> in <u>Heaven</u>. The first voice, which I heard, was as it were a <u>Trumpet</u> <u>Talking</u> with me. John, has heard this Trumpet Voice before [Rev. 1: 10].

Which said, Come up hither, and I will show thee things which must be hereafter. We know the <u>Voice</u> of a <u>Trumpet</u>, is <u>Jesus,</u> from [Rev. 1: 10, 11]. Come up <u>Hither</u> is in <u>Heaven</u>. I will show thee things which must be hereafter this is future. Jesus, is speaking of the book of Revelation. He is showing John, and us how he is building his Kingdom that God, appointed unto him. The earth has run out of time [Rev. 10: 6].

2. And immediately I was in the Spirit: and, behold, a throne was set in heaven, and one sat on the throne.

Let's interpret, And immediately I was in the Spirit, This is the same Spirit, John, received in [Acts, 2: 4] The Holy Ghost.

And behold a throne was set in heaven, behold is to look upon. And one sat on the throne, this is God.

3. And he that sat was to look upon like a jasper and a sardine stone: and there was a rainbow round about the throne, in sight like unto an emerald.

Let's interpret, And he that sat is God, was to look upon like a Jasper and a Sardine stone. This is color John, doesn't tell us of a image on the throne Ezekiel, gives us a good picture of what we are looking at see [Ezek. 1: 26, 27, 28] Ezekiel, describes, as the appearance of a man sitting upon the throne. We know God, has the appearance of man because we are made in his image.

God, is light, [1st John, 1: 5]. God, sitting on the <u>Throne</u>, with his <u>Glory</u>, shining through these two Translucent Stones; The <u>Jasper</u> and the <u>Sardine</u>, is a Magnificent Sight to behold.

The rainbow is the Glory of God, light shining round about the throne like unto an emerald. The Emerald is a Brightly Rich Green Gem. [Ezek. 1: 28]. It is the same Rainbow, that God, set in the cloud after a rain. A token of a covenant between God, Noah, and the earth. Gen. 9: 12,13].

John, describes the Jasper, and Sardine stone. We know John, saw a book in the right hand of him that sat on the throne, this shows us there was an image on the throne.

4. And round about the throne were four and twenty seats: and upon the seats I saw four and twenty elders sitting, clothed in white raiment; and they had on their heads crowns of gold.

Let's interpret, We need to understand something here. What we are looking at is the building of the Kingdom that God, appointed Jesus, [Luke, 22: 29, 30] [Rev. 3: 21]. The Kingdom of Jesus, are people of the earth that are saved by Grace. And the <u>Transition</u> of <u>Power.</u> from God, to Jesus. [Mat. 28: 18]. The <u>Kingdom</u> of <u>Jesus,</u> is the <u>New Heaven, New Earth,</u> and the <u>Holy City New Jerusalem.</u> Wherein Dewlleth Righteousness, [2nd. Peter, 3: 13].

Round about the throne this is the Throne of God, were four and twenty seats. These are thrones [Rev. 20: 4]. They are for the chosen ones of God, and Jesus.

And upon the seats I saw four and twenty elders sitting, clothed in white raiment. This is a <u>Heavenly Garment</u> see [Acts, 1: 10] [Rev. 6: 11]. And they had on their heads crowns of gold. This represents <u>Power</u>, and <u>Authority.</u> These are the only ones that have the Golden Crown upon their heads that we know of. Notice these crowns. <u>Crown</u> of <u>Life</u> [Rev. 2: 10], <u>Crown</u> of <u>Righteousness</u> [2nd. Tim. 4: 8] a crown is the height of anything.

Sitting upon these seats, John, saw four and twenty, elders. We know who twelve of these Elders, are. <u>The Twelve Apostles</u> of <u>Jesus.</u> [Mat. 10: 1-thru-24] [John, 6:70,71] (Judas, Iscariot fell by transgression). <u>Matthias</u>, took his place see [Acts, 1: 23, 24, 25,26]. Jesus, appointed this position to the Apostles, while he was on earth with them [Luke, 22: 29, 30]. This is what Jesus, was speaking of in [John, 14: 2, 3] I go to prepare a <u>Place </u>for you. Place is a position (Throne). Now we know who twelve of these Elders are.

The other twelve we don't know who they are or their names. We do know God, started his Royal Priesthood; with Abraham, Isaac, and Jacob. No where in the scriptures can we find the names of the other twelve Elders, that God, chose to sit around his throne. We can't prove anything by the scripture; But we can, accept it, and that we will do.

5. And out of the throne proceeded lightnings and thunderings and voices: and there were seven lamps of fire burning before the throne, which are seven Spirits of God.

Let's interpret, Heaven is God's, throne [Is. 66: 1]. The Lightning, depicts the power of God, [Job, 38: 35]. The power of lightning can not be measured by any means neither can the power of God.

The Thundering, depicts the voice of God. This is also powerful no man can measure it. We have a record of the voice of God, that sound like thunder [John, 12: 28,29,30]. Here are the voices that proceeded out of the throne. [Mat. 3: 17] [Mat. 17: 5] [Luke, 3: 22]. The voice of God, is all through the Bible.

The Seven Lamps, of fire burning before The throne; this depicts Active or Ready. Which are the Seven Spirits of God. We find these Seven angels here also, [Rev. 8: 2] and [Rev. 5: 6].

We find God, is a Spirit from Genesis [1:2] to Revelation. We are looking a the mighty power of God, ready to be given to Jesus.

6. And before the throne there was a sea of glass like unto crystal: and in the midst of the throne, and round about the throne, were four beast full of eyes before and behind.

Let's interpret, The Sea of Glass, is (S/L) the Glory of God, Clear as Crystal see [Rev. 22: 1] Pure River of water of "LIFE" Clear as Crystal. This is the Glory of God, Flowing out from God, toward mankind on earth today.

Notice!! In the Midst of the Throne. We need to understand; Heaven is God's, throne. [Is. 66: 1] this is taking place in the Center of Heaven. Notice! Round about the throne. In Heaven, there are no directions; As East, West, North, and South.

The Four Beast full of Eyes full of eyes before, and behind this is (S/L). they are not Beast at all. They are the Hundred Forty, and Four Thousand. Full of Eyes Before, and Behind. This is Before the Throne and Behind the Throne Every eye is looking at the one sitting on the Throne, God.

7. And the first beast was like a lion, and the second beast like a calf, and the third beast had a face as a man, and the fourth beast was like a flying eagle.

Let's interpret, These beast are not beast at all they are four sons of Jacob.

Chosen by God, to be set in order round about the tabernacle see [Num. 2: 3, 10,18, 25].

these same four sons of Jacob, are in Heaven around the throne of God.

What we are looking at are, <u>Flags</u>, or <u>Ensign</u>. Of the four sons of Jacob, chosen by God. The first beast, like a Lion is Judah. His Flag or Ensign is a Lion. The second beast like a Calf, is Reuben. His Flag or Ensign is a Calf. The third beast had a face as a Man, is Ephraim, (Son of Joseph) his Flag or Ensign is, Face as a Man. The Fourth Beast was like a Flying Eagle, this is Dan, His Flag or Ensign is a Flying Eagle.

There four sons of Jacob, with their brother tribes are the hundred forty four thousand, around the throne of God, in heaven see [Rev. 7: 4]

This is the army in heaven [Rev. 19: 14] also [Rev. 14: 4]. They follow the Lamb whithersoever he goeth. This is the <u>First Resurrection</u> [Rev. 20: 5].

8. And the four beasts had each of them six wings about him; and they were full of Eyes within; and they rest not day and night, saying, Holy, holy, holy, Lord God Almighty, Which was, and is, and is to come.

Let's interpret, The four beast, we know who they are and what they are. The six Wings; are what we call in our army today; Flanker, units, which are on each side, of the center movement. Example, Judah, The Lion; is on the East side of the tabernacle. His Wings are <u>Issachar</u>, and <u>Zebulon</u> (2) His wings are on the South. <u>Simeon</u>, and <u>Gad</u>. (2).

His wings on the North are <u>Asher</u> and <u>Naphtali</u> (2) this makes (6) Wings. This holds true all around the tabernacle. Now they are in Heaven, around the throne. The same four sons of Jacob; with their <u>Brother Tribes</u>. See [Rev. 7: 4] also [Mat. 27: 52,53] [Rev. 14: 1] the (144000).

They were full of eyes within. This is all eyes were looking at Jesus, on the throne.

These words Lord God Almighty, Which was, and is, and is to come; is Jesus. [Rev. 1:8]. They rest not day and night, saying, Holy, holy, holy, Lord God. Almighty, this means continually for there are no day, and night in heaven.

9. And when those beast give glory and honor and thanks to him that sat on the throne, who liveth for ever and ever,

Let's interpret, We know who those beast are, the four sons of Jacob. Judah, Reuben, Ephraim, Dan, with their brother tribes. At this time a Hundred Forty Four Thousand see [Rev. 7: 4].

These words glory, honor, thanks given by the four beast is a high quality of Praise to Jesus, who liveth for ever and ever. This is Jesus, sitting on the throne in his Glorified Flesh Body see [Rev. 1: 18]. I am he that liveth.

10. The four and twenty elders fell down before him that sat on the throne, and worship him that liveth for ever and ever, and cast their crowns before the throne, saying,

Let's interpret, We see the elders worship Jesus, now sitting on the throne. We need to understand God, is in the Glorified Flesh Body of Jesus, sitting on the Throne.

See [John, 10: 30] also [John, 14: 10, 11]. Worship him that liveth for ever, and ever.

This shows us Jesus, [Mat. 28: 18] [Rev. 5: 6] for God, never was dead.

Cast their crowns before the throne. This shows total Submission, to power and authority, Humble.

11. Thou art worthy, O Lord to receive glory and honour and power; for thou hast created all things, and for thy pleasure they are and were created.

Let's interpret, Thou art worthy, O Lord, this is a unanimous praise from the Four and Twenty Elders To receive glory, honor, power. The word receive indicates some one gave it, which is God, [Mat. 28: 18].

For thou hast created all things. [John, 1: 3, 10] [Eph. 3: 9]. And for thy pleasure they are, and were created. God, created all things by Jesus, and gave them to him.

This is the kingdom of Jesus, we are looking at.

CHAPTER 5

1. And I saw in the right hand of him that sat on the throne a book written within and on the backside, sealed with seven seals.

Let's interpret, And I saw in the right hand of him that sat on the throne. This is God, the book is Revelation of <u>Jesus Christ,</u> [Rev. 1: 1] proves this.

Written within and on the backside this is; both sides of the page front and back. Nothing can be added to or taken from this book.

<u>Sealed</u> with <u>Seven Seals,</u> The Seals, are long spans of time in God's, plan. Jesus, is the only one that can open these Seals, and put God's, plan in Action.

Revelation, is the end of time for earth, and all the things that are on the earth. See [2nd. Peter, 3: 10] also [Rev. 10: 6]

Jesus, is the one that <u>Sealed,</u> this Book in the days of the <u>Prophet Daniel</u> see [Dan. 12:4,9]. Jesus, sealed it and put it in God's, hand until he finished the work that God, gave him to do on earth see [John, 17: 4, 5]. This is establish his Kingdom [Mat. 16: 18]

2. And I saw a strong angel proclaiming with a loud voice, Who is worthy to open the book and loose the seals thereof?

Let's interpret, The <u>Strong Angel,</u> John, saw is here. [Rev. 1: 1] This <u>Angel,</u> is still in charge of revealing <u>Jesus,</u> whether in heaven or on earth even to [Rev. 22: 21].

Notice the pronoun <u>Who,</u> indicates man. The book of Revelation**,** is not of man. It is of <u>Jesus Christ,</u> [Rev. 1: 1]. Revelation is a book of <u>Prophecy</u> [Rev. 1: 3] which is <u>Future</u>. No man can open the Book of the Future Nor to loose one <u>Seal</u>. Because man can not see the Future.

The word <u>Worthy</u> Is A person of <u>Outstanding</u> and of <u>Importance,</u> <u>Jesus</u>, has this qualification amen, <u>Jesus,</u> can open the book and loose the seals see [Mat. 28: 18] plain isn't it?

3. And no man in heaven, nor in earth, neither under the earth, was able to open the book, neither to look thereon.

Let's interpret, In (Verse-2) This Strong <u>Angel,</u> is looking for a <u>Righteous man</u>. He started in <u>Heaven</u> where <u>Righteous Men</u> are, Then on <u>Earth</u> where <u>Righteous Men</u> live. He searched <u>Under</u> the <u>Earth</u> where <u>Righteous Men</u> are buried.

No man was found <u>Able</u> to open the <u>Book</u>, of the <u>Future</u>, of things to come. Only Jesus, can do can do it.

Neither to look thereon this is the <u>Glory</u>, and the <u>Power</u> of God, To much power for man. These scripture helps us to understand why man cannot open the book; neither to look thereon. [Is. 40: 13] [1st. Cor. 2:16]. [Job, 21: 22]. No man knows the mind of God

The word <u>Able</u> Is having much; <u>Power</u> of <u>Mind Skill</u> and <u>Talented</u> to do something. <u>Jesus</u>, has this qualification <u>Amen.</u> It is his book [Rev. 1:1]. No man can <u>See</u> <u>Know</u>, or understand the <u>Future</u> only <u>Jesus</u>, knows [Read Proverbs, Chapter-Eight].

4. And I wept much, because no man was found worthy to open and to read the book, neither to look thereon.

Let's interpret, Notice! John, saw the <u>Book</u>, verse (1) It was written within and on the back side, <u>Sealed</u> with <u>Seven Seals</u>. John, knew this book was of <u>Great Importance</u>; for God, had it in his right hand. We can see John, was disappointed when he wept much because no man was found worthy to open and to read the book, neither to look there on.

These words (I will shew thee things which must be hereafter) [Rev. 4: 1] this is why John, was called up to heaven. To see these things which must be here after, future.

This goes all the way from [Rev. 4: 1] to [Rev. 22: 21] We understand these words Point Toward the Future. John, knew the Future was in the book, in God's right hand, Revelation.

We need to understand we are looking at the Kingdom that God, appointed Jesus, while he was here on earth [Luke, 22: 29, 30].

5. And one of the elders saith unto me, Weep not: behold the Lion of the tribe of Judah, the Root of David, hath prevailed to open the book, and loose the seven seals thereof.

Let's interpret, This Elder, is one of the Four and Twenty Elders sitting around the Throne [Rev. 4: 4]. This is (S/L) Lion of the tribe of Judah, the Root of David, both of these are Jesus, (S/L) Lion, Is the Ensign or Flag of the tribe of Judah, the Fourth Son, of Jacob, Jesus, came from this Tribe so did David. The Root of David, this is the Lineage or the family of David [Luke, 1: 32] [Mark, 10: 46, 47]. Jesus, is of Royal Blood from the beginning.

Hath prevailed to open the book and to loose the Seven Seals thereof. Prevail, is to overcome proof [John, 16: 33]. To open the book is time to start the End of Time on earth of mankind.

To loose the Seven Seals; These Seals, are Long Spans of Time in God's, plan of his creation of the Earth, and the things therein. The Seals being Loose have a place to go the (Earth) All of (Verse-5), are the words of the Elder, he knew all about Jesus.

6. And I beheld, and lo, in the midst of the throne and of the four beast, and in the midst of the elders, stood a Lamb as it had been slain, having seven horns and seven eyes, which are the seven Spirits of God sent forth into all the earth.

Let's interpret, And I beheld, and lo, in the midst of the throne and of the four beast, and in the midst of the elders. All of these are the Kingdom of Jesus. They are in their Glorified Flesh Body.

Stood a Lamb this is (S/L) Jesus, as it had been slain, this points to the <u>Scars</u> on the body of Jesus. John, saw these scars on Jesus, on earth [Luke, 24: 39]. Jesus had been standing there all the time. John, didn't recognize him with the Seven Horns, and Seven Eyes, these are Self Explanatory which are the Seven Spirits of God, sent forth into all the earth. These Seven Spirits of God, are going through the earth today.

7.   And he came and took the book out of the right hand of him that sat upon the throne.

Let's interpret, The pronoun he is <u>Jesus,</u> The book is Revelation. Him that sat upon the throne is God. This is a <u>Transition</u> of <u>Power,</u> from God, to Jesus. Now Jesus, has all Power These scriptures are fulfilled, [Rev. 1:1] [Dan. 7: 13, 14] [Matt. 28:18]. [John, 16: 15] [John. 3: 35] [Luke, 15: 31] [Prov. Ch. 8].

8.   And when he had taken the book, the four beast and four and twenty elders fell down before the Lamb, having every one of them harps, and golden vials full of odours, which are the prayers of the saints.

Let's interpret; And when he <u>Jesus,</u> had taken the book this is a transition of power from God, to Jesus.

Notice, the Four Beast, and Four, and Twenty Elders, fell down before the Lamb. We see now the Worship is to Jesus. Having every one of them Harps and Golden Vials full of Odours. Which are the prayers of the Saints.

This shows us something. The Four Beast, and The Four, and Twenty Elders, are offering up our Prayers to Jesus, in Golden Vials, full of Odours. We find this odours to be much (Incense). A pleasant sweet smelling perfume when burnt see [Rev. 8: 3, 4]. We see the prayers of the Saints offered with much Incense upon the Golden Altar, Which was before the theone.

We understand now the Four Beast; which are the Hundred Forty Four Thousand, and the Four, and Twenty Elders. Are helping us here on earth, with our prayers.

9. And they sung a new song, saying, Thou art worthy to take the book, and to open the seals thereof; for thou was slain and hast redeemed us to God by thy blood out of every kindred, and tongue, and people, and nation;

Let's interpret, What makes this <u>Song</u> a <u>New Song</u> is they are the <u>First</u> people to be <u>Redeemed</u> from the <u>Earth</u>, by the Blood of <u>Jesus</u>. [1st. Peter, 1:18,19]. These people knew all about Jesus, on earth, and they know by the blood of Jesus, they are before the throne of God, see [Rev. 14: 1-thru-4].

The last part of this verse is <u>Self Explanatory</u> Thou art worthy to take the book, and to open the seals thereof; For thou was slain and hast redeemed us to God, by thy blood, out of every kindred, and tongue, and people, and nation.

We need to look at these words. Out of every <u>Kindred Tongue People</u>, and <u>Nation.</u> The children of <u>Israel,</u> were captured and taken to different countries; before Jesus, came. [Ezek. 1: 1, 3] In the country of <u>Babylon</u>, Daniel, Shadrach, Meshach, and Abednego. In the country of <u>Babylon.</u> Consider the children of Israel, in the land of <u>Egypt</u>, Four Hundred, and Thirty Years [Ex. 12: 40] [Gal. 3: 17]. This is just to name a few.

The children of Israel you can find all through the Old Testament. They were carried away to different countries many times. Jesus, knew where they were, and he got them from every tongue people, and nation. We are looking at the Hundred Forty Four Thousand. The word <u>Redeemed</u> shows us that [Rev. 14: 3, 4].

This tells us the Four Beast, and their brother tribes are the

Hundred Forty Four Thousand. As mention in Verse (8). There are a lot of hidden Mysteries in the Bible. Here are a few see [Mat. 13: 10, 11] [Rev. 10: 7].

10. And hast made us unto our God kings and priests: and we shall reign on the earth.

Let's interpret, This is the (144,000) [Rev. 7: 1,2,3,4] [Rev. 14: 1]. They came from here [Mat. 27: 52. 53]. These have Glorified Flesh Bodies, like Jesus, see [Luke, 24: 39] They will live for ever, and ever. This is the First Resurrection [Rev. 20: 5, 6].

Made us unto our God, Kings, and Priests. This is a double honor. Kings, are given Power, and Authority. Priests, delivers Messages, from people of the earth to the throne of God, and Jesus. This is the (144000) doing the talking.

These same Kings, and Priests Are the same ones here see [Rev. 16: 12]. And we the 144000, shall reign on the earth. Reign, is Power, and Authority see [Rev. 19: 14, 19,20,21]. We see here [Rev. 19: 16] JESUS, KING OF KINGS, AND LORD OF LORDS. See [Rev. 16: 12] [Rev. 16: 16]. These are the ones that will fight the battle of Armageddon with Jesus. These are the Army in Heaven, [Rev. 19: 14]. This is where they will Reign on Earth. The Great River Euphrates, was dried up for them. They are the ones that followed the Lamb, whithersoever he goeth [Rev. 14: 4].

11. And I beheld, and I heard the voice of many angels round about the throne and the beasts and the elders; and the number of them was ten thousand times ten thousand, and thousands of thousands;

Let's interpret, Notice John, isn't talking about people. "I beheld, and heard" Is I saw the angels, and heard their voices round about the Throne, Beast, and the Elder. What a Blessing this is. Totally Embraced, by the Holy Angels of God, and Jesus. With all of these "Thousands of Angels" that John, saw is here an <u>Innumerable Company</u> of <u>Angels</u> see [Heb. 12: 22] very plain isn't it?

12. Saying with a loud voice, Worthy is the Lamb that was slain to receive power, and riches, and wisdom, and strength, and honour, and glory, and blessings.

Let's interpret, We see all of this is <u>Praise</u> from the <u>Angels.</u> These angels knew all about Jesus, [Luke, 2: 13] Notice!! What they praise him for <u>Worthy</u>, to receive <u>Power, Riches</u>, <u>Wisdom</u>, <u>Strength</u>, <u>Honour</u>, <u>Glory</u>, and <u>Blessings</u>. They also called Jesus the Lamb. Here is why the angels praise Jesus, [Heb. 1: 6], [Phil. 2: 9,10]. All the blessings of God, are given to Jesus.

13. And every creature which is in heaven, and on the earth, and under the earth, and such as are in the sea, and all that are in them, heard I saying, Blessings, and honor, and glory, and power, be unto him that sitteth upon the throne, and unto the Lamb for ever and ever.

Let's Interpret, (S/L) <u>Creature</u> Is <u>Man</u> in heaven <u>Eternal</u>. [Rev. 14: 1-thru-5]. On the <u>Earth</u> righteous men living by faith in a flesh and blood body. [1st. Thess. 4:16,17] Under the <u>Earth</u> righteous man. [Rev. 14: 13] In the <u>Sea</u> righteous man, [Rev. 20: 13]. Notice!! And all that are in <u>Them;</u> This is all the <u>Places Mentioned</u>.

We can see this entire verse (13) is Jesus, and all the <u>Angels</u> in heaven, and all of mankind where ever they are; <u>Worship</u> and <u>Praise</u>, Jesus. All of these are <u>Righteous People.</u> They have the Spiritual Ear. Only God, has these <u>Blessings</u> to give. The word <u>Power</u> proves this [Matt 28:18]. [Dan. 7: 13,14]. <u>JESUS,</u> is worthy, of all things.

These words, unto (Him that sitteth upon the throne), and unto the (Lamb). This looks like two (God, and Jesus), these two are one see [John, 10: 30]. This scripture helps us understand this see [2nd. Tim. 2: 15] "Rightly dividing the word of truth".

14. And the four beast said, Amen. And the four and twenty elders fell down and worshipped him that liveth for ever and ever.

Let's interpret, (S/L) The Four Beast; are the Four Sons of Jacob, which are Judah, (Lion), Reuben, (Calf), Ephraim-"Joseph", (Face as a Man), Dan, (Flying Eagle).

See [Num. 2: 3, 10, 18, 25]. We are looking at these see [Rev. 7: 4] [Rev. 14: 1] the 144000.

They said "Amen" which is "I agree with what you said" they agree with all the Angels, and all of mankind that Praise and Worship Jesus, wherever they are.

The Four and Twenty Elders, fell down and worshipped him that liveth for ever and ever. This is Jesus, they are worshipping now. This phrase That liveth for ever and ever is Jesus, [Rev. 1: 18] God, never was dead; and never will be Amen .

WE NEED TO UNDERSTAND SOMETHING HERE ESTABLISHED DOCUMENT

From Revelation Chapter One Verse One; Has been Established, and Documented, Both in Heaven, and on Earth in the first Five Chapters, of Revelation

By it being Established, and Documented; is why today mankind on the earth can read the True Document, That John, wrote, of Jesus, while on the Isle that is called Patmos. It is God's, plan fulfilled in his son Jesus, The Book of Revelation.

The first Three Chapters, the Seven Churches; Are Established, and Documented on earth forever they will not be changed. They are given by Jesus, instructions, and guidelines, for all churches on earth today to Govern themselves by. They are true and will not change.

Revelation, Chapters Four, and Five. These two chapters were Established, and Documented, in Heaven forever. [Rev. 4: 1] "Come up hither, and I will show thee things which must be hereafter" This is why we can read this "Document" That was "Established" in Heaven. Documented by The <u>Apostle John</u>, as he saw, and heard it.

These <u>First Five Chapters</u>, of <u>Revelation;</u> have been fulfilled of <u>God's</u>, plan in his son <u>Jesus</u>.

We have this <u>Document</u>, of <u>God's, Plan</u>, fulfilled; with us today. <u>Noah</u>, and the <u>Flood</u>. The Bible will not fail us, it is written; by <u>Holy Men</u>, of <u>God</u>, as they were moved by the <u>Holy Ghost</u>. See [2nd. Peter, 1: 21] [Rev. 1: 10] [Rev. 4: 2].

We now see <u>Jesus</u>, has all <u>Power</u>, Both in <u>Heaven</u>, and in <u>Earth</u> [Mat. 28: 18]. We see this scripture fulfilled, [Col. 2: 9, 10]. For in him (Jesus), dwelleth all the fullness of the Godhead, (BODILY) this is the <u>Glorified Body</u> of <u>Jesus</u>, [1st. John, 5: 7]. These three are one in the Glorified Body of Jesus, now. See [John, 10: 30] God, is in the Glorified Body of Jesus.

From chapter (1) to chapter (5) Jesus, has got his Kingdom set up and God, has given him all Power, in heaven and in earth [Mat. 28: 18].

We are now ready to go into the future; From Revelation, Chapter-Six, to Revelation Chapter-22: 21 Look close. Whatever is fulfilled I will bring it to your attention; and show you where it is in the Holy Bible.

MAY GOD, AND JESUS, BLESS YOU
AS YOU SEE YOUR LIFE IN THIS GREAT BOOK
REVELATION

CHAPTER 6

1. And I saw when the Lamb opened one of the seals, and I heard, as it were the noise of thunder, one of the four beast saying, Come and see.

Let's interpret, And I saw when the Lamb (S/L) is (Jesus) open one of the seal. And I heard as it were the noise of thunder this is a loud clear voice.

One of the four beast saying, Come and see. This is a span of time in God's, plan that no man could put in action, until Jesus, got his Kingdom established, on earth, and in Heaven.

The beast having the voice as a noise of thunder. Points to the First Beast like a Lion [Rev. 4: 7] Judah, the son of Jacob, Come and see, this is what is in the seal, sealed up for a long span of time.

2. And I saw, and behold a white horse: and he that sat on him had a bow; and a crown was given unto him: and he went forth conquering, and to conquer.

Let's interpret; White is Pure, Horse, is Power; He that sat on him is the Holy Ghost, the Spirit of Truth. [John, 14: 16, 17, 26] The Bow is the Glory of God. [Rev. 4: 3] [Rev. 10: 1] [Gen. 9:13].

The Crown given to him " Is Power and Authority" These words he went forth Conquering and to Conquer. Show the power and the authority of the Crown given to him. Conquering is action; [Acts, 5: 3-thru-10] To Conquer is a Purpose. [Eph. 1: 13]. The Holy Ghost is working for Jesus. [John, 16: 7-thru-14]. Crown is the height of anything. There is no higher power then God, and Jesus.

Jesus, told the Apostles tarry ye in the city of Jerusalem, until ye be endured with power from on high [Luke, 24: 49]. Jesus, is speaking of these scriptures. [John, 15; 26] [John, 14: 16,17,20] [John, 16: 7, 13]. Now we know the Holy Ghost, is working for Jesus.

These words, he went forth, here is where the Holy Ghost went. [Acts, 1:26] [Acts, 2: 1-thru-8]. This is the Holy Ghost, in action The First Seal. It is still with the world of mankind today, and forever, [John, 14: 16]

It is the first thing Jesus, did for mankind on earth when he ascended up to the Father, Send the Comforter which is the Holy Ghost [John, 14: 26]

Jesus, fulfilled the promise of his Father [Luke, 24:49]. We see the Holy Ghost busy here, [Acts, 6: 3, 4] also working in the Seven Churches, Which are in Asia, He is here also [Rom. 8: 14]. For as many as are led by the Spirit of God, they are the Sons of God. The first Seal The Holy Ghost, Has control of the entire earth, with the instructions of Jesus [John, 16: 13, 14, 15] [Zech. 4: 6].

We know now the First Seal, is the Holy Ghost, sent back to the Kingdom of Jesus, on Earth. The Twelve Apostles, were the first to receive the Holy Ghost. [Acts, 2: 1-thru-9] The Holy Ghost is all through Revelation.

3. And when he had opened the second seal, I heard the second beast say, Come and see.

Let's interpret, We understand in verse one the voice of one of the four beast indicates the tribe of Judah "Lion" there are no number given in verse (1) as First Beast.

Here we have the second beast, which is specific the tribe of Reuben, [Rev. 4: 7]. (S/L) "Like a calf" This is his Ensign or Flag. These words "Come and See" indicates John, was taken to anther location, or into another span of time. Which these Seals, are long spans of time in God's, plan for mankind on earth.

4. And there went out another horse that was red: and power was given to him that sat thereon to take peace from the earth, and that they should kill one another: and there was given unto him a great sword.

Let's interpret; The <u>Horse</u> is <u>Power</u>: <u>Red</u> depicts <u>Anger</u>, Suggest a desire to gain or revenge. Power was given to him that sat thereon to take peace from the earth this is a <u>Evil Spirit</u>. And that they should kill one another this is mankind on the earth.

The <u>Great Sword</u> is that <u>Evil Spirit.</u>

We are looking at a <u>Twofold Picture</u> One is War, <u>Take peace from the earth</u>.

The Other is; Individual people, that <u>Kill one another</u>.

Consider our Work Places, Schools, Highways, Suicide, and many other. <u>The Great Sword</u> is a Evil Spirit; That get into the mind of mankind on earth and it is: (KILL KILL, KILL). From the youngest to the oldest, both male, and female. People want to know what is going on now they <u>Know.</u> This <u>Evil Spirit</u> is trying to destroy the; <u>Image</u> of <u>God</u>, From the earth.

These scriptures prove the <u>Evil Spirit</u>, Is the Great Sword; It over powers the mind of mankind It started here [Gen. 4: 8] [John, 6: 70,71] see [1st. John, 3: 12].[John, 13: 2, 26, 27] Jesus, cast Satan, from the earth [John, 12: 31]. He was cast here [Rev. 20: 1,2,3]. See also [Luke, 8: 29, 35] [Luke, 9: 39, 42]

Children are afraid to, go to school. Many things could be mentioned here. This Evil Spirit, works on the mind of mankind. [Luke 8: 29, 35]. The Evil Spirit is on earth today among mankind. See [Mat. 12: 45] evil mind, see [Luke 22: 3] plain isn't it?

THESE TWO SEALS ARE FULFILLED;
YET ACTIVE ON EARTH TODAY.

The first Seal, White Horse and he that sat on him had a Bow, the <u>Glory of God.</u> The <u>Crown</u>, given unto him; is <u>Power</u>, and

Authority. This is the Holy Ghost which is with us today, and for ever [John.14:16] This is the first thing Jesus, did for mankind on earth when he ascended up to heaven to his eternal kingdom. [John, 16: 7]. We find the White Horse, and he that sat upon him here [Acts, 2: 1-thru-8]. In the <u>Mind</u> of <u>Man.</u>

The second Seal, Red Horse and power was given to him that sat thereon to take peace from the earth, <u>THIS</u> is <u>WAR</u>, Nation against Nation; Kingdom against Kingdom.

[Mat. 24: 7,8]. (That they should kill one another) this is individual people. The Great Sword, is a <u>Evil Spirit</u> from him that sat upon the Red Horse, that get in the mind of mankind to kill one another. The great sword can be anything to kill some one with see,

[Acts, 7: 59, 60] Deacon, Stephen, killed by (STONED) [Acts, 12: 2]. Apostle James, killed by the (SWORD) of king Herod Today we have, Guns, Knives, Home made bombs, Cars, Poison, Consider Concentration Camps Starvation. The list is endless.

The First Two Seals; are <u>Good,</u> and <u>Evil. Kingdom Against</u> Kingdom [Mat. 24: 7]

They are at <u>War,</u> over the <u>Image</u> of <u>God,</u> <u>Mankind,</u> 0n Earth, <u>You, and I.</u>

5. And when he had opened the third seal, I heard the third beast say, Come and see, And I beheld, and lo a black horse; and he that sat on him had a pair of balances in his hand.

Let's interpret; The third beast is the tribe of <u>Ephraim</u>, the son of <u>Joseph</u>, [Num. 2:18]. [Rev. 4:7] (S/L) Face as a man. "This is the Image of God.

<u>Come</u> and <u>see</u> this is another <u>Span</u> of <u>time</u> in God's, plan. <u>The Black Horse</u> is <u>Power</u> it depicts <u>Future.</u> He that sat on him had a pair of balances in his hand. This indicates <u>Judgment</u> see [Dan. 5: 26, 27]. Notice the <u>Black Horse,</u> and he that sat on him didn't go anywhere.

6. And I heard a voice in the midst of the four beast say, A measure of wheat for a penny, and three measures of barley for a penny; and see thou hurt not the oil and the wine.

Let's interpret; I heard a voice in the midst of the four beast say, The voice <u>John</u>, heard in the midst of the four beast is Jesus, see [Rev. 5: 6] Jesus, is talking to the <u>Rider</u> on the <u>Black Horse</u>. And here is what Jesus, said.

A measure of <u>Wheat</u>, for a <u>Penny</u>, the wheat is <u>Christians,</u> [Mat. 3: 12] The <u>Penny</u>, Represents <u>Jesus</u>, [Mat. 20: 2, 16].

Three measures of <u>Barley</u>, for a <u>Penny</u>, The three measures of <u>Barley</u>, are the <u>Heart, Soul</u>, and <u>Mind</u>, of mankind. [Mat. 22: 37,38] also [Mat. 13: 33]. The <u>Penny</u> is <u>Jesus</u>, He doesn't change [Heb. 13: 8]. We are bought with a price [1ˢᵗ. Cor. 6: 20] also [1ˢᵗ. Peter, 1: 18, 19]. [Acts, 20: 28] the <u>Blood of Jesus,</u> the (Wine).

And see thou hurt not the <u>Oil</u>, and the <u>Wine</u>. The <u>Oil</u>, is the <u>Hoy Spirit of God.</u> [Ps. 23: 5] also [1ˢᵗ. Sam. 16: 1, 12,13]. The <u>Wine</u>, represents the shed blood of <u>Jesus.</u> [Mat. 26: 27, 28, 29].

The <u>Heart, Soul,</u> and <u>Mind</u>, are the <u>Spirit</u> side of Man, when God, made Adam, and breathed into his nostrils, the breath of Life, and man became a Living, Soul.

[Gen. 1: 26, 27] [Gen. 2: 7].

All of verse (5, and 6) Are <u>Righteous People.</u> The Balances represent Judgment, the <u>Second Death.</u> Here are the Righteous People, A measure of Wheat for a <u>Penny</u>, and three measures of Barley for a <u>Penny.</u> The penny is (S/L) of <u>Jesus.</u> We are bought with the shed <u>Blood</u> of <u>Jesus.</u> We shall not be hurt of the <u>Second Death,</u> [Rev. 2: 11].

7. And when he had opened the fourth seal, I heard the voice of the fourth beast say, Come and see.

Let's interpret, We know the fourth beast is the <u>Tribe</u> of <u>Dan</u>. [Num. 2: 25] and [Rev. 4: 7] <u>Flying Eagle</u>. (S/L) The Flying Eagle, is the Ensign or Flag, of the Tribe of Dan. Come and see, we know Dan, is talking to John, This is another span of time in God's, plan for mankind. All these Beast, are talking to John, say Come and see.

8. And I looked, and behold a pale horse: and his name that sat on him was Death, and Hell followed with him. And power was given unto them over the fourth part of the earth, to kill with the sword, and with hunger, and with death, and with the beasts of the earth.

Let's interpret, The Pale Horse is Power. His name that sat on him was Death. He is the one that does the "KILLING".

We know death is Sin. [Rom. 5: 12] [Gen. 2:17] We know Hell. is a place of confinement a Lake of Fire. Where the wicked people of the earth are cast into.

We can start here see [Luke, 16: 22-thru-28] [Rev. 20: 13,14,15]. We also know where the Righteous People go. [Luke, 16: 22, 25] [Luke, 23: 42,43]. Many things could be written about this subject.

We can see the purpose of the Pale Horse, and his rider Death is to kill. Let's look at it. Power was given unto them over the fourth part of the earth. This is the fourth part of the entire earth; not just one location.

Example a fourth part of the East, West, North, South. Let's look at his weapons. To Kill with the Sword, this is an Evil Spirit that gets in the mind of mankind, and destroys him. Also man will kill one another, today they call it Insanity. Kill with Hunger this is evil people against one another; Example in prisons, Concentration Camps, and many more. Kill with Death, This is Sin, and Sickness, Which destroys the body and mind [Matt 17: 15,17,18] [Mark, 5: 2-thru-20]. Kill, with the Beast, of the earth.   This is twofold, The First Beast is Man, Apostle Paul, fought with beast at Ephesus. [1st. Cor. 15: 32] also [2nd. Peter, 2: 12] [Tit. 1: 12]. The Second Beast is a Natural Beast. Example, Animal trainers, Wild animals, and

Pets. The Evil Spirit can get in the mind of any animal, and it will destroy, or kill. [Mat. 8: 30,31,32].

Summary The Pale Horse and his name that sat upon him was <u>Death</u>, and <u>Hell</u> followed him. All that are in these <u>TWO,</u> as they go through the earth seeking whom they can devour; are <u>Sinner People.</u>

Lets prove it! [Rev. 20: 13, 14,]. Death and Hell delivered up the dead which were in them. This is plain Let the Dead Bury Their Dead. This is a sinner man alive, and a sinner man dead see [Matt. 8:22]. So Death is Sin. A righteous man is not dead see [John, 11: 11]. Notice the Pale Horse, and Death, and Hell; Are Equivalent, to the Second Seal, The Red Horse, The Great Sword, that they should Kill one another.

THIS FOURTH SEAL IS FULFILLED; YET ACTIVE ON EARTH TODAY.

9. And when he had open the fifth seal, I saw under the altar the souls of them that were slain for the word of God, and for the testimony which they held.

Let's interpret, We need to understand this is <u>Paradise</u> we are looking at. Under the altar is; under the third heaven where God's, throne is [Is. 66: 1]. There is a Golden Altar before his throne. There is no Altar in Paradise no need for it. [Rev. 8: 3].

These <u>Souls</u> are in <u>Paradise</u> if you will receive it; <u>The Second Heaven.</u> See [Luke, 23: 43] [Rev. 2: 7].

These "Souls" under the Altar came from here. [Mat. 12: 40] also [1st. Peter, 3: 18, 19, 20] also [1st. Peter, 4: 6] [Is. 42: 7]. These <u>Souls,</u> are from <u>Adam,</u> to <u>Moses.</u> And from Moses, to <u>Jesus.</u> Jesus, <u>Preached</u> the <u>Gospel</u> of the <u>Heavenly Kingdom</u> and <u>Salvation,</u> to them that all mankind will be <u>Equal</u> on the day of <u>Judgment.</u> There will be <u>One Fold</u> and <u>One Shepherd</u> "JESUS" see [John, 10: 16] plain isn't it?

Let's look at these heavens. The <u>First Heaven.</u> God, made for the earth, and man. The <u>Second Heaven,</u> is Paradise. [Luke, 23: 42,

43] [Rev. 2: 7] Where the souls of mankind are kept until the day of resurrection. Then these souls will be given their own Glorified Flesh Body [1st. Thess. 4: 14-thru-18].

The Third Heaven, is where God's, Throne is. Apostle Paul, said I was caught up the Third Heaven. [2nd. Cor. 12: 2]. These two Apostles; "Paul, and John", are the only ones that we have record of that lived on earth and caught up into the Glorious Kingdom of God, and Jesus. Then came back to the earth and Preached the Gospel of the Kingdom of God, and Jesus. Paul, and John, wrote several books of the New Testament.

These Souls, that were slain for the word of God, and the testimony which they held. The word of God, is his Commandment, and he that does his will. [Mat. 7: 21].

The Testimony which they held is their Faith. Read the entire chapter, [Heb. 11]. Which Is a "Perfect Picture" of their Testimony.

We have a record of some of these souls. Abel, [Gen. 4;8] John, the Baptist, [Mark, 6; 24, 25, 26, 27] Stephen, [Acts, 7: 8, 59] Apostle James, [Acts, 12; 2]. I am sure there are many more see [Rev. 2: 10] Smyrna Church; also [Mat. 24: 9].

10. And they cried with a loud voice, saying, How long, O Lord, holy and true, doth thou not judge and avenge our blood on them that dwell on the earth?

Let's interpret, These Souls were slain for the word of God, ad the testimony which they held verse (9). Notice! When Jesus, opened the Fifth Seal these souls saw him and knew him.

They had a question for him; How long O Lord, holy and true doth thou not judge, and avenge our blood, this let's us know they knew they were slain, and they knew where.

Avenge our blood on them that dwell on the earth. Here is where Jesus, avenged their Blood see [Rev. 19: 2] plain isn't it?

Here is how they knew; Jesus, Preached, to some of them Three Day, and Three Nights, while he was with them in the Heart, of the

<u>Earth.</u> [Mat. 12: 40] [1st. Peter, 3: 18,19,20] [Rom. 12: 19] also [John, 10: 16] They also knew they lived on earth in a <u>Flesh Body</u>, and their blood kept them alive.

These souls are Wanting to be clothed with their <u>Own Flesh Body</u>. [2nd Cor. 5: 1, 2, 3]. We see here [1st. Thes. 4: 14,15,16,17] where these <u>Souls</u>, will be reunited with their own flesh body they lived in on earth

We need to understand the children of God, and Jesus, are scattered all over the entire earth. From Generation to Generation.

11. And white robes were given unto every one of them; and it was said unto them, that they should rest yet for a little season, until their fellow servants also and their brethren, that should be killed as they were, should be fulfilled.

Let's interpret, The <u>White Robe</u>, is a <u>Heavenly Garment</u>. [Rev. 3: 4]. [Matt. 28:3].

We can find this all through the <u>Bible.</u> [Rev. 7: 13,14] We understand the souls under the altar didn't have anything on them until Jesus, clothed them with a <u>Heavenly Garment</u>. A White Robe, see [Mat. 17: 2] [Acts, 1: 10].

The little season is a span of time on earth. Because there is no time in <u>Heaven</u>.

Notice! Until their fellow servants, these are <u>Gentile People</u> [Rev. 7: 13, 14] and their brethren these are the children of <u>Israel.</u> This is both <u>Jew</u> and <u>Gentile</u> people.

Notice! Until their fellow servants also and their brethren, that should be killed as they were, should be fulfilled.

Jesus, said some of us will be <u>Killed</u> as the souls under the altar were. We must be like the <u>Apostle Paul</u>, fought a good fight, finished my course (I have kept the faith) [2nd. Tim. 4: 7].

12. And I beheld when he had opened the sixth seal, and, lo, there was a great earthquake; and the sun became black as sackcloth of hair, and the moon became as blood;

Let's interpret, And I beheld when he had opened the sixth seal, and lo, there was a great earth quake. The word lo, is Wonder, or Surprise. This earthquake is the entire earth this is shaking the earth. And the sun became black as sackcloth of hair, this is the Light of the Sun has been turned off, and the moon became as blood. This is Shaking the Earth, and the Heaven also. We find this prophesy here [Heb. 12: 26]. John, is looking at the end of Time from heaven. Remember these words (Come up hither, and I will show the things which must be hereafter see [Rev. 4; 1] we are looking at it, this is soon.

All of the (Six Seal), is pointing at the End, of Time, For the Earth, and Mankind. This is the Future Prophecy Jesus, told us of the (Sixth Seal) see [Mat. 24: 29, 30, 35] [Rev. 1: 3] [Rev. 16: 18, 20, 21] [Dan. 12: 1, 2, 3, 4]. We can find it all through the Bible, see [Luke, 21: 25, 26,27].

The word Lo is Wonder or Surprise; John, is looking at the, End of Time, Total destruction of the Heaven and Earth, as we know it, look a verse (14).

Look at what God, and Jesus, did for us! [Is. 65: 17] [Rev. 21: 1] [2nd. Peter 3: 13]. Let's, Interpret these scriptures so we can understand them. [Is. 65: 17] This is (Prophecy) [2nd. Peter, 3: 13] This is (Faith) [Rev. 21 : 1] This is the real thing; John, saw it, and it belongs to us.

13. And the stars of heaven fell unto the earth, even as a fig tree casteth her untimely figs, when she is shaken of a mighty wind.

Let's interpret, And the stars of heaven fell unto the earth. Jesus, told us that when he was on Earth, [Mat. 24: 29].

The rest of (Verse-13), is a parable of a Fig Tree on earth shaken by a <u>Mighty Wind</u>, and the figs fell unto the earth. This is the power of God, shook heaven, and the stars fell unto the earth.

The <u>Mighty Wind</u>, and the power of God, and Jesus, are the <u>Same</u>. Look at this [Acts, 2: 1. 2, 3, 4] In our term, or way of understanding this awesome power is; (Dynamic Power) a force of energy that can't be seen but felt. We can see the things (Moved by this Great Power). Let's prove it.

[Gen. 8: 1] The Flood, [Ezek. 37: 9, 10] Valley of dry bones, [John, 3:5] Any one born again. I will show you a mystery; We feel the wind, we see the movement of it, we breath it; but we can't see it. Neither can we see God, He is "Invisible" How close is God, and Jesus, to their (CREATION? They are in it see [John, 14: 20].

14. And the heaven departed as a scroll when it is rolled together; and every mountain and every island were moved out of their places.

Let's interpret, And the heaven departed as a scroll when it is rolled together. This is, it is <u>Gone</u>. And every mountain and every island were moved out of their place <u>Gone.</u> We see this here [Rev. 21: 1]

This is a good indication that God, is preparing a place for the New Heaven, and a New Earth, [Rev. 21: 1] Gives us a good understanding of this. This is also the fulfilling of this prophecy [Is. 65: 17] [Heb. 12: 26]. God, has totally destroyed the old world, and the sinner people with it see [Rev. 20: 11, 15] We need to understand <u>God,</u> and <u>Jesus,</u> are <u>One</u> see [John, 10: 30].

15. And the kings of the earth, and the great men, and the rich men, and the chief captains, and the mighty men, and every bondman, and every free man, hid themselves in the dens and in the rocks of the mountains;

Let's interpret, We can see the earth is shaken with the <u>Mighty Power</u> of <u>God.</u> With the mountains, and Islands, moved out of their places; In our term of understanding The world is falling down; a mighty (Earthquake). A good picture of what we are looking at see [Rev. 16: 17-thru-21].

We see these men, from the greatest to the least, This is both gender, male and female. Hide themselves in the dens, and the rocks of the mountains. We know all of these people are sinners. God, and Jesus will not destroy their people, consider Lot.

This brings back a picture in the beginning of sin on earth. [Gen. 3: 10] Adam, and Eve, hid from God. Notice this is both (Male, and Female). No place to hide.

16. And said to the mountains and rocks, Fall on us, and hide us from the face of him that sitteth on the throne, and from the wrath of the Lamb.

Let's interpret, And said to the mountains and rocks, Fall on us. These people are talking to the (Mountains and Rocks) that can't hear nor see; the same as <u>Idol Worship</u>.

And hide us from the face of him that sitteth on the throne. This is <u>Jesus,</u> with <u>God,</u> in his <u>Glorified Flesh Body.</u> Sitting on the throne.

And from the wrath of the Lamb. The wrath of the Lamb (S/L) is Jesus. He is using his <u>Power</u> [Mat. 28: 18]. To carry out God's plan, destroy this sinful earth.

Jesus, told us while he was on earth, this would happen to the sinful people of the earth [Luke, 23: 30] Both people and the earth are destroyed.

17. For the great day of his wrath is come; and who shall be able to stand?

Let's interpret, The great say of his wrath is come. These people are speaking about (Verses-12-13-14). They knew about this day Jesus, told the world of mankind when he was on earth this would happen [Mat. 24: 29, 30] [Rom. 10: 18].

Today the same thing is being preached, by those that have been Called, Justified, also Glorified [Rom. 8: 30]. We find the end of the Sixth Seal, here [Rev. 20: 11-thru-15]. I will Interpret Chapter 20 when we get to it.

Who shall be able to stand? These shall stand see [Mat. 25: 31, 32, 33, 34] [Rev. 7: 13, 14, 15]. These shall not stand. [Mat. 25: 41] These are Cursed into everlasting Fire. We need to understand John, is still in heaven from [Rev. 4: 1].

THE SIXTH SEAL, IS FUTURE, THE
DOCUMENT HAS BEEN ESTABLISHED.
Yet not fulfilled or come to pass

DON'T BE CONFUSED FOLLOW THE SCRIPTURES
THAT ARE GIVEN, IN THE BRACKETS, WHICH
ARE THE WORDS OF JESUS, SEE [Luke, 21: 33].

CHAPTER 7

1. AND AFTER these things I saw four angels standing on the four corners of the earth, holding the four winds of the earth, that the wind should not blow on the earth, nor on the sea, nor on any tree.

Let's interpret, After these things, John, is talking about the Seals, and the destruction of th earth, in (Chapter-6). I saw four angels standing on the four corners of the earth. The four corners of the earth have names (East, West, North, South) We understand John, is back on earth at this time.

Holding the four winds of the earth. that the wind should not blow on the earth, nor on the sea, nor on any tree. We can see there is no movement of the wind any where.

This covers the entire Earth, and Sea.

These Four Angels, can take the Four Winds, and create, Tornado, Hurricane, and Great Storms, on Land,and Sea. [Mat. 8: 26, 27] This is not a (Seal). This is a span of time at the, Resurrection of Jesus

2. And I saw another angel ascending from the east, having the seal of the living God: and he cried with a loud voice to the four angels, to whom it was given to hurt the earth and the sea,

Let's interpret, This Angel, ascending from he East, Having the seal of the Living God. This Angel no doubt is of a High Rank. As these Two Archangels .Michael, and Gabriel, which are Mighty in the Power of God.

He cried with a loud voice to the four angels, to whom it was given to hurt the earth and the sea. We see this Angel, has Power, and Authority from God. To carry out God's, plan on earth. His voice was heard from the East, to the West, North, and South.

Give this some (Thought), This Angel, ascending from he East, notice the Sun, and the Moon, ascends from the East. So does this Son Jesus, [Mat. 24: 27]. The East has a very strong Focal Point, all through the Bible.

3.   Saying, Hurt not the earth, neither the sea, nor the trees, till we have sealed the servants of our God in their foreheads.

Let's interpret, Saying, Hurt not the (Earth, Sea, nor the Trees) These words are of the Angel that ascended from the East in verse (2). He knew the Four Angels, holding the Four Winds, of the Earth was given Power to Hurt the Earth, and the Sea.

Till we have sealed the servants of our God, in their foreheads. The pronoun (WE) Suggest, the Angel Ascending from the East, and the Four Angels, to whom it was given to hurt the Earth, Sea, and trees. Are the ones going to seal the Servants of God, in their foreheads.

There are no other Angels, mention, but these (Five Angels) that are going to Seal the Servants of God, in their Foreheads.

We understand with the (Four Winds) not blowing on anything any where, The entire earth is Quiet, and Peaceful. In simple terms Time Has Stood Still.

The Angel, ascending from the East having the Seal of the Living God. Has set things in Order, to carry out God's, Plan, without any distraction.

4.   And I heard the number of them that were sealed: and there were sealed an hundred and forty and four thousand of all the tribes of the children of Israel.

Let's interpret, And I heard the number of them that were sealed. John, didn't see anything he just heard the number that were sealed an (Hundred Forty Four Thousand).

We have no way of knowing how John, heard this or any voice that spoke of the Hundred Forty Four Thousand, of all the tribes of the children of Israel that were sealed.

[Rev. 14: 1] This is the first time John, saw the (Hundred forty Four Thousand) and with the Seal of God, Written in their Foreheads his Father's Name.

Remember they got this seal here on earth, so are we that are saved by Grace here on earth, see [Eph. 1: 13] also [Eph. 4: 30] (This is WONDERFUL).

We can see where these (144000) came from [Mat. 27: 52,53] [Rev. 5: 9] Redeemed us to God, by thy blood out of every; Kindred, and Tongue, and People, and Nation.

The children of Israel, were captured and carried away to different countries, several times. Jesus, knew where every one of them were. I will share one thing with you, Jesus, called the (144000), by their name, Example, Daniel, Shadrach, Meshack, Abednego, also Lazarus, [John, 11: 43]. They followed the Lamb where so ever he goeth. This is their faith. Consider the Mother of Moses, in the land of Egypt. The (144000) is not just in the land of Israel. Without Faith, it is impossible to please God, [Heb. 11: 6].

5. Of the tribe of Judah were sealed twelve thousand. Of the tribe of Reuben were sealed twelve thousand. Of the of Gad were sealed twelve thousand.

6. Of the tribe of Aser were sealed twelve thousand. Of the tribe of Nepthalim were sealed twelve thousand. Of the tribe of Manasses were sealed twelve thousand.

7. Of the tribe of Simeon were sealed twelve thousand. Of the tribe of Levi were sealed twelve thousand. Of the tribe of Issachar were sealed twelve thousand.

8. Of the tribe of Zabulon were sealed twelve thousand. Of the tribe of Joseph were sealed twelve thousand. Of the tribe of Benjamin were sealed twelve thousand.

All of the (144000) are the children of ISRAEL, This is the First Resurrection [Rev. 20: 5, 6].

9. After this I beheld, and, lo, a great multitude, which no man could number, of all nations, and kindreds, and people, and tongues, stood before the throne, and before the Lamb, clothed with white robes, and palms in their hands;

Let's interpret, This Great Multitude, which no man could number see [Gen. 22: 17,18]. No man can number the stars of heaven or the sand of the sea, see also [Gal. 3: 7,8, 28, 29]. The entire world are the children of Abraham, by (Faith) proof see [Gal. 3: 7] see [Heb. 11: 6]. Now we understand what the Great Number that no man could number is.

This is the Second Resurrection, of the entire world these words prove it, of all Nations, and Kindreds and People, and Tongues. Stood before the throne and the Lamb. This is the entire Glorious Kingdom that God, Appointed Jesus, [Luke, 22: 29, 30], Bought by the Blood of Jesus [Acts, 20: 28] In their Glorified Flesh Bodies. [Acts, 20: 28] [Rev. 5: 9].

Stood before the throne, and the Lamb. The Lamb, is (S/L) Jesus. This is a good indication that Jesus, is sitting on the throne. We find this here [Luke, 22: 29, 30] [Mat. 28: 18] [Dan. 7: 14] [Rev. 3: 21.

Clothed with White Robes, this is a Heavenly Garment. [Rev. 3: 4] [Acts, 1: 10] [Rev. 19: 8]. [Rev. 6: 11]. And Palms in their Hands; This is a Symbol of Beauty, Righteousness, and Victory. Palms, are used all through the Bible [John, 12: 13] is one of them.

10. And cried with a loud voice, saying, Salvation to our God which sitteth upon the throne, and unto the Lamb.

Let's interpret, This <u>Great Multitude</u> of people knew that God, saved them through the shed blood of Jesus, this is a <u>Praise</u> to God, and Jesus, the Lamb. We see [John, 3:16] come to view here.

God, and Jesus, are <u>ONE</u> proof [John, 10: 30] [John, 17: 11, 22] [1st. John, 5: 7] [John, 14: 10, 11, 20]. God, is in the Glorified flesh body of Jesus; the body of Jesus is <u>Flesh,</u> and <u>Bone</u> [Luke, 24: 38, 39] We see <u>God,</u> in <u>Jesus,</u> here also [Rev. 21: 23] this is <u>The Glory</u> of <u>God,</u> Shining through the Glorified <u>Body</u> of <u>Jesus</u> the <u>Lamb.</u>

11. And all the angels stood round about the throne, and about the elders and the four beast, and fell before the throne on their faces, and worshipped God,

Let's interpret, This is in heaven, a glorious sight. All the <u>Angels,</u> stood round about the <u>Throne,</u> about the <u>Elders,</u> and the <u>Four Beast</u> notice the word <u>All.</u> WE see the same setting here as in verse (10) <u>God,</u> and <u>Jesus,</u> are still on the <u>Throne.</u>

The <u>Great Multitude</u> and all the <u>Angels, Elders,</u> and the <u>Four Beast.</u> Fell before the throne on their faces, and <u>Worship God,</u> see [John, 10: 30] [Heb. 1: 6, 8] [Phil. 2: 9, 10]

These scriptures, are fulfilled in this verse (11). <u>God,</u> and <u>Jesus,</u> are <u>One.</u> [John, 10: 30].

We know how to <u>Worship God.</u> in <u>Spirit</u> and in <u>Truth.</u> [John, 4: 23, 24]. The difference between worship, and praise is Worship is <u>Unfeigned, Love</u> Pure in Heart [Mat. 5:8].

Praise, is verbal or raising of hands, Dancing, Emotional movement of the body joyful. David, <u>Danced</u> before the <u>Lord</u> with all his might [2nd. Sam. 6: 14]. [Ps. 150: 6] David, said let every thing that hath breath <u>Praise</u> the <u>Lord.</u> Make a <u>Joyful Noise</u> unto <u>God,</u> [Ps. 66: 1]. Now we know the difference of <u>Worship,</u> and <u>Praise.</u>

12. Saying, Amen: Blessing, and glory, and wisdom, and thanksgiving, and honour, and power, and might, be unto our God for ever and ever, Amen.

Let's interpret, All of verses (11,12) is, <u>Worship</u> and <u>Praise</u> from a <u>Pure Heart.</u> Notice when the <u>Angels, Elders,</u> and the <u>Four Beast</u> Finished worshipping God,

They all said <u>Amen</u>, this is they all agree with one another. Here is the praise, <u>Blessing,</u> and <u>Glory,</u> and <u>Wisdom,</u> and <u>Thanksgiving,</u> and <u>Honour,</u> and <u>Power,</u> and <u>Might.</u> Be unto our God, for ever and ever <u>Amen.</u> This is they all have one mind and accord. This scripture [Mat. 28: 18] is fulfilled here. [Heb. 1:6] [Phil. 2: 9, 10]. Jesus, is the <u>Almighty</u> [Rev. 1: 8] with God, in his <u>Glorified Flesh Body.</u> We that are saved by Grace also have God, and Jesus, in our Flesh Body see [John, 14: 20] also [Eph. 4: 6] we know see [Rom. 8: 14] plain isn't it?

We see all the Angels, Elders, and the Four Beast, have <u>Accepted Jesus,</u> as their <u>God,</u> by this word <u>AMEN.</u> They know God, is in the Glorified Body of Jesus. See [John, 14: 7, 9, 10].

13. And one of the elders answered, saying unto me, What are these which are arrayed in white robes? And whence came they?

Let's interpret, We see the <u>Elders</u> are working for God, and Jesus, here as in [Rev. 5: 5, 11, 12, 13, 14] this is <u>Parallel, Scripture.</u> the (144000) Sealed. [Rev. 7: 4].

The questions the Elder, ask John. What are these which are arrayed in white robes, and whence came they? John, is looking at the future which he could not understand. He didn't know who they were, or where they came from this is the Great Multitude, in verse(9) future, and we know where they came from the entire world.

Notice these have not the <u>Seal</u> of the living <u>God, in their forehead yet,</u> this is the future the <u>Second Resurrection.</u> of the entire world, Both Jew, and Gentile. The <u>White Robe,</u> we know is a <u>Heavenly Garment.</u> [Rev. 3: 4] [Rev. 6: 11] [Rev. 4: 4]; The <u>Elder,</u> is one of the Four and twenty Elders, clothed in <u>White Raiment.</u> All of the children of God, will have his name in their foreheads (The Seal) of the living God [Rev. 22: 4]

14. And I said unto him, Sir, thou knowest. And he said unto me, These are they which came out of great tribulation, and have washed their robes, and made them white in the blood of the Lamb.

Let's interpret, And I said unto him, Sir, thou knowest. We see John, didn't know,

This is why he was looking at the future. But he knew the Elder, knew this is proof. These are they which came out of great tribulation. This teaches us we have help form heaven all we have to do is ask [Mat. 7: 7, 8].

We find Tribulation of the Saints all through the Bible [Acts, 14: 22] [Rom. 12: 12] [Rom. 8: 35, 36] [2nd. Cor. 7: 4]. [Eph. 3: 13] [Mat. 24: 21]. The Apostles, and Prophets Preached, and Prophesied in all the world. These three prophets were captives in foreign countries. [Elijah, Jeremiah, Daniel] there are many more. [Mat. 24: 14] [Mark, 16: 15]. Now we understand the Great Multitude, in verse Nine.

Washed their robes, and made them white in the blood of the Lamb. This is faith, and believe [John, 3: 16] [Is, 1: 18] [Ps. 51: 7] [Mark, 16: 16]. Their robes are their soul, washed in the shed blood of Jesus. Consider the Eunuch, [Acts, 8: 34-thru-40]. God's, people are all over the world. Consider Jonah, and Nineveh, capitol of Assyria. These people repented. A Great Book could be written on this subject, it goes on, and on.

15. Therefore are they before the throne of God, and serve him day and night in his temple: and he that sitteth on the throne shall dwell among them.

Let's interpret, Therefore are they before the throne of God, we know what is required of mankind to stand before the Throne of God. Our soul must be washed in the Blood of Jesus see [Is. 1: 18] [John, 3: 16] also [Ex. 12: 21-thru-30] [Ps. 51: 7] All of this is done by our Faith and Belief, in Jesus.

Notice and serve him day and night in his Temple. This temple is referring to our Flesh Body see [1st. Cor. 6: 19, 20] [2nd Cor. 6; 16] also [John, 2: 19, 20, 21]. The Body of Jesus, also [John, 14: 11]. The word Serve shows us what we are looking at.

We know there is no day or night in the Eternal Kingdom of God, and Jesus, day, and night is Continuous see [Rev. 21: 25]. This scripture shows us more about the temple,

[Rev. 21: 22]. We see God, in the flesh body of Jesus. The Temple they both made and called it (ADAM) The Image of both God, and Jesus.

He that sitteth on the throne shall dwell among them. This is Jesus, in his Glorified Flesh Body, sitting on the throne in his KINGDOM which God, appointed him see [Luke, 22: 29,30] also [Dan. 7: 14]. shall dwell among them see [Rev. 21: 3].

What we are looking at is the Kingdom of Jesus, The New Heaven, and The New Earth, and the Holy City New Jerusalem.

16. They shall hunger no more, neither thirst any more; neither shall the sun light on them, nor any heat.

Let's interpret, They shall hunger no more, neither thirst any more. We are looking at the Glorified Flesh Body of mankind. That will live forever and ever with the Spirit of God, in them the Living Water, [John, 4: 14].

Neither shall the sun light on them, nor any heat. This shows us there is no sun in heaven, and no heat this is a perfect place. This is the Kingdom of Jesus. The New Heaven, and The New Earth and the Holy City New Jerusalem [Luke 22: 29, 30].

17. For the Lamb which is in the midst of the throne shall feed them, and shall lead them unto living fountains of waters: and God, shall wipe away all tears from their eyes.

Let's interpret, The Lamb, (S/L) Jesus, which is in the midst of the throne. This is Jesus, in his kingdom. Shall feed them, Spirit [Rev. 2: 7] (The Tree of Life is Jesus).

And shall lead them unto <u>Living Fountains,</u> of <u>Waters.</u> This is the <u>Real Preacher</u> on earth today. [John, 7: 38] [Rom. 10: 14, 15] also [Rom. 8: 14]. And God, shall wipe away all tears from their eyes. This is the, Glorified Body Filled with the <u>Holy Spirit</u> of <u>God,</u> there is no moisture in this body.

CHAPTER 8

THIS ENTIRE CHAPTER IS FUTURE

1. And When he had opened the seventh seal, there was silence in heaven about the space of half an hour.

Let's interpret, And when he had opened the seventh seal. Seven is the completion in God's, plan. There was silence in heaven about the space of half an hour.

The span of time about half an hour is on the natural side of mankind an estimate because there is no time in heaven. This indicates there is some great consideration going on of what is going to happen to God's, creation the Earth, and Mankind, and the Seas.

This is the beginning of destruction to the earth, and mankind. Jesus, said in [Mat. 24: 8] these are the beginning of sorrows let's take a look.

2. And I saw the seven angels which stood before God; and to them were given seven trumpets.

Let's interpret, The Seven Angels, are these see [Rev. 4: 5] the seven Spirits of God. Jesus, has the seven Spirits now [Rev. 5: 6] God, controls the earth with his Spirit. [Zech. 4:6] Remember God, and Jesus, are one [John, 10: 30].

The seven trumpets, given to the Seven Angels, are God's, plan from the beginning of his creation. Each Angel, will carry out or put in action the plan he is given.

3. And another angel came and stood at the altar, having a golden censer; and there was given unto him much incense, that he should offer it with the prayers of all saints upon the golden altar which was before the throne.

Let's interpret, This angel with the <u>Golden Censer</u>; is full of the prayers of the saints. They came from here [Rev. 5: 8]. The Four Beast, and the Four and Twenty Elders, had them in Golden Vials. When the angel offered the <u>Incense</u> upon the Golden altar with the Prayers of the Saints. God, and Jesus, heard each prayer. We see this in verse (4).

I will share with you just a few of the Prayers of the Saints, see [Rev. 6: 10, 11] [Luke, 2: 25-thru-30] [Luke, 1: 13] [James, 5: 16, 17, 18] there are many.

Incense is a Sweet Perfume, very pleasant to smell; a confection the art of the apothecary a fine powder see [Ex. 30: 34]. Incense when heated has a very pleasant odor. It is used in worship throughout the bible see [Luke, 1: 8, 9, 10].

4. And the smoke of the incense, which came with the prayers of the saints, ascended up before God, out of the angel's hand.

Lets interpret, We understand God, and Jesus, are accepting and hearing each prayer of the saints. I use God, and Jesus, on the throne because they are one see [John, 10 : 30] God, is in the Glorified Flesh Body of Jesus, The eyes of the Lord, are over the righteous, and his ears are open unto their prayers [1st. Peter, 3: 12]. This is what is taking place in this verse.

5. And the angel took the censer, and filled it with fire of the altar, and cast it into the earth: and there were voices, and thunderings, and lightnings, and an earthquake.

Let's interpret, We understand in verse (3) this golden censer, was full of the prayers of the saints.

Now it is empty, the angel took the censer and filled it with fire of the altar. We know what this fire of the <u>Altar</u> is, <u>God</u>, see [Heb. 12: 28] Jesus, is in control of all things [Mat. 28: 18].

This angel didn't act on his own, he did what he was told to do. This is God, and Jesus's, answer to the <u>Prayers</u> of the <u>Saints.</u> Vengeance is mine, I will repay saith the Lord, [Rom. 12: 19].

The <u>Voices</u>, are unrighteous <u>People</u>, on the earth. God, knows how to deliver those that are his remember Lot, [Gen. 19: 24]. The Thundering, Lightning, and Earthquake. Is taking place on the entire <u>Earth.</u> From here to [Rev. Ch. 21] we will see <u>Great Disaster, and Suffering.</u>

6. And the seven angels which had the seven trumpets prepared themselves to sound.

Let's interpret, This is, they have got their orders of what to do and when to do it. everything is in order, according to God's, plan. They are ready for <u>Action!!</u>

We understand now the <u>Silence</u> in <u>Heaven</u> about the space of <u>Half</u> an <u>Hour</u>. God, and Jesus, answering the prayers of the Saints, and told the Angel at the altar what to do. And giving the Seven Angels, their instructions of what to do to the entire earth.

7. The first angel sounded, and there followed hail and fire mingled with blood, and they were cast upon the earth, and the third part of the trees was burnt up, and all green grass was burnt up.

Let's interpret, This is God's, plan, <u>Hail</u>, is a hard frozen rain very destructive.

God, used it in the land of Egypt, and destroyed it. [Ex. 9: 22, 23, 24, 25]. The <u>Fire</u> we know is God, [Heb. 12: 29]. The <u>Blood</u>, (S/L) is Jesus, this is the power of heaven [Ex 9: 24] We find Hail, and Fire mingled with Hail. The shed blood of Jesus, was not known at this time. Proof of the blood is Jesus, [Mat. 26: 28].

The Hail, Fire, and Blood, were cast upon the entire earth. The third part of the trees were burnt up, and all green grass was burnt up.

The third part of the trees gone, the building industry suffers a great loss. All Green Grass, totally gone we need to look close at this. All animals no food, the huge farms we get our food from is all gone. If you will have it the entire earth is one big dry dirt ball. Notice no one was killed. The first Angel, carried our his part of God's, plan.

8. And the second angel sounded, and as it were a great mountain burning with fire was cast into the sea: and the third part of the sea became blood;

Let's interpret, The second angel sounded, <u>Notice!</u> and as it <u>Were</u> a <u>Great Mountain Burning</u> with <u>Fire.</u> The <u>Scripture</u> doesn't say it was a "MOUNTAIN" it says as it were a great mountain burning with fire.

We can see the best description John, could give us in size is a Great Mountain. This indicates a Huge Fireball. This is the great power of God, and Jesus. It was cast into the sea, this was it's purpose and it hit the target nothing else.

And the third part of the sea became blood. This is the Spirit of God, at work see [Zech. 4: 6] also [Ezek. 14: 19] The same Spirit of God. that <u>Smote</u> the <u>Waters</u> of <u>Egypt</u>, and turned them to <u>Blood</u>. Is the same Spirit of God, that turned the third part of the Sea to Blood. God, don't change. This is <u>SPIRITUAL WORK</u> nothing can stop it.

Let's keep this thought (Together) The first disaster was the (Earth). The second disaster was the (Sea).

9. And the third part of the creatures which were in the sea, and had life, died; and the third part of the ships were destroyed.

Let's interpret, And the third part of the creatures which were in the sea, an had life died. These creatures died in the <u>Blood</u> the third part of the sea, from lack of oxygen.

We need to keep in mind this is world wide. This would create a <u>Great Foul Odor.</u> God, smote the waters of Egypt, [Ex. 7: 18, 21], and a <u>Great Stink</u> was in the land of Egypt.

And the third part of the ships were destroyed. At this present time, this would be a great number of ships; because every nation on earth has many ships, and there are many private Merchant Ships, Cruise Ships, Submarines, the list is Endless.

The ships being destroyed this suggest someone was aboard those ships.

10. And the third angel sounded, and there fell a great star from heaven, burning as it were a lamp, and it fell upon the third part of the rivers, and upon the fountains of water;

Let's interpret, This great star fell from heaven, the <u>First Heaven</u> God, created it from the beginning. When he created heaven, and earth [Gen. 1:16, 17] God, also named, and numbered the stars he created [Ps. 147: 4].

Burning as it were a lamp; this star was a light from the beginning [Gen. 1: 17]. John, described it as a (Burning as a lamp).

It fell upon the third part of the rivers, and fountains of waters. This covers the third part of the entire earth. The <u>Rivers,</u> and <u>Fountains,</u> of <u>Water</u> are fresh drinking water, we use to cook our food, wash our flesh bodies, and our clothes, many uses.

11. And the name of the star is called Wormwood: and the third part of the waters became wormwood; and many men died of the waters, because they were made bitter.

Let's interpret, The name of the star <u>Wormwood</u>, God, gave this star it's name when he put it in heaven [Ps. 147: 4]. And it has been there all this time and is yet to come. We must understand the Angel, in [Rev. 1: 1] Jesus's, angel. Told John, the name of the star called Wormwood. John, wrote what he heard, and saw.

The third part of the waters became wormwood which is a bitter.

Wormwood is used as a Symbol of Doom. [Deut. 29: 18] [Prov. 5: 4] [Jer. 9: 15]. Notice! Many Men died of the Waters. This shows us that these men drank the water that is wormwood, and Died.

It is accepted (Wormwood, and Bitter) is Poison. Notice many men died of the waters. The word MANY, is used because it is an Untold Number. No animals drank this Wormwood Water, and Died. Nor any Righteous People. Think about it see [Mat. 24: 8].

12. And the fourth angel sounded, and the third part of the sun was smitten, and the third part of the moon, and the third part of the stars; so as the third part of them was darkened, and the day shone not for the third part of it, and the night likewise.

Let's interpret, The third part of the Sun, Moon, and Stars was smitten. (Smitten) is to strike sharply or heavily with force, to destroy. This same mighty force of God, and Jesus, we find here [Heb. 12: 26]. We have a Parallel, Scripture in verse (9). The third part of the ships were Destroyed this indicates force.

The third part of them was darkened, this is Sun, Moon, and Stars. Mankind can see this with their natural eye. Jesus, Prophesied of these things happening while he was on earth see [Like, 21: 25, 26].

And the Day shone not for the third part of it, and the Night likewise. Mankind will know his time on earth is ending [Mat. 24: 33]. We understand the Day, will be Short, and the Night Long, or darkness will be long. This will be a Frightening Sight for mankind on earth.

13. And I beheld and heard an angel flying through the midst of heaven, saying with a loud voice, Woe, woe, woe, to the inhabiters of the earth by reason of the other voices of the trumpet of the three angels, which are yet to sound!

Let's interpret, Beheld, is to remember or keep in view. John, saw and heard what this angel said <u>Woe, woe, woe,</u> to the <u>Inhabiters</u> of the <u>Earth</u>. As we can see there are three angels, which are yet to sound and three woes. Woe is Great Suffering, and Trouble. Which is yet to sound, this is to continue.

These woes are directed to mankind of the earth world wide inhabiters is proof. All of these things we have studied in this chapter is <u>Future,</u> yet to come. We can sum this chapter up with this scripture [Rom. 12: 19] Vengeance Is Mine, I will Repay Saith the Lord.

CHAPTER 9

1. And The fifth angel sounded, and I saw a star fall from heaven unto the earth: and to him was given the key of the bottomless pit.

Lets interpret, And the fifth angel sounded, and I saw a star fall from heaven unto the earth. Star is (S/L) of an Angel. The star we are looking at is here [Is. 14: 11, 12, 13, 14, 15] His name is <u>Lucifer.</u> This <u>Fall</u> is from a <u>High Degree</u> of <u>Honor,</u> to a <u>Lower Degree</u> of <u>Dishonor</u>. See [Rev. 12: 3, 7, 8, 9] we find this same Angel, in verse (11). Here are the names of this angel. See [Rev. 20: 1, 2, 3,] Dragon, That Old Serpent, which is the, Devil, and Satan, and Lucifer. In the Hebrew tongue his name is (Abaddon) In the Greek tongue his name is (Apollyon) when you look at this don't be confused all these names are one. They came from here see [Rev. 12: 3,9].

Jesus, said I beheld Satan, as lightning fall from heaven see [Luke, 10: 18].

Notice Jesus, called this star (Satan) he was an archangel in heaven.

This star fell from heaven to the earth, and to him was given the key to the bottomless pit this key is <u>Power.</u> Now we know where the Bottomless pit is (The earth). Bottomless is anything round, and moving look at these. A round ball, Car tire, the Earth. (<u>Bottomless Pit</u> is also <u>Endless)</u>. It becomes the Lake of Fire burning with Brimstone.

2. And he opened the bottomless pit; and there arose a smoke out of the pit, as the smoke of a great furnace; and the sun and the air were darkened by reason of the smoke of the pit.

Let's interpret, And he opened the Bottomless Pit (S/L) the earth, verse (1) shows us that. And there arose a smoke out of the pit as the smoke of a great furnace. This shows us there is <u>Fire</u> in the <u>Bottomless Pit.</u> And the only way smoke goes is up.

The sun and the air were darkened by reason of the smoke of the pit. This shows us the Bottomless Pit is the Earth (Sun, and Air) is proof.

We can see by this, the smoke from the Bottomless Pit is very <u>Thick</u> and <u>Black</u> it does cover the entire earth.

We know all <u>Smoke</u> is <u>Absorbed</u> by the <u>Earth's Atmosphere.</u> This smoke will be also when it has fulfilled it's purpose. A Great Book could be written on this Subject.

3. And there came out of the smoke locusts upon the earth: and unto them was given power, as the scorpions of the earth have power.

Let's interpret, There came out of the smoke locusts, Notice! upon the earth. This lets us know the entire earth is covered with smoke and now locusts, <u>Locusts</u> are <u>Plural.</u>

We know what these <u>Locusts</u> are (S/L) of these <u>Angels</u> see [2nd. Peter, 2: 4]. The angels of the Dragon that was cast out of heaven [Rev. 12: 9].

Unto them was given <u>Power</u> as the <u>Scorpions</u> of the earth have power. We know who gave this power to the locusts as the scorpions of the earth have power <u>Jesus,</u>

[Mat. 28; 18] he has all power. Notice!! This power was given to the <u>Locusts,</u> and nothing else. The <u>Power</u> of a <u>Scorpion</u> is the <u>Stinger</u> in his <u>Tail</u> very <u>Painful</u> and <u>Poison.</u> The scorpion of the earth that we know will sting, In the night as well as day, so will these <u>Locusts.</u> They will get in the churches, businesses, airplanes, cars, anywhere.

4. And it was commanded them that they should not hurt the grass of the earth, neither any green thing, neither any tree; but only those men which have not the seal of God in their foreheads

Let's interpret, And it was commanded them that they should not hurt the grass of the earth, neither any green thing, neither any tree. This is the (First Command)

This is the <u>Fifth Angel,</u> giving this <u>Command.</u> (Command) Is the <u>Ability</u> to <u>Control</u> We find him here [Rev. 5: 6]. He is one of the <u>Seven Spirits,</u> of <u>God,</u> given to <u>Jesus,</u> (Sent Forth into the all earth) see this also [Zech. 4: 6].

Let's take a look at the (Second Command). But only those men which have not the seal of God in their foreheads. This shows us something this Locusts, is not an insect as we know them. They are angels of the dragon, evil spirits.

The (<u>Seal</u> of <u>God)</u>, see [Eph. 1: 13] [Eph. 4: 30] and [2nd. Cor. 1: 22]. Those that are Born Again have the <u>Seal</u> of <u>God,</u> while living on earth until the day of redemption. We need to understand this covers the entire earth.

5.   And to them it was given that they should not kill them, but that they should be tormented five months: and their torment was as the torment of a scorpion, when he striketh a man.

Let's interpret, This is a <u>Command,</u> and the <u>Third One,</u> of the <u>Fifth Angel.</u> And to them, the pronoun (Them) are the Locusts. It was given that they should not kill them, The pronoun (Them) are the men, and women on earth that have not the <u>Seal</u> of <u>God.</u> in their forehead. The <u>Fifth Angel,</u> knew these locust, have the <u>Sting,</u> as a <u>Scorpion,</u> and they could <u>Sting</u> men, and women, to <u>Death.</u> The command is, don't kill but <u>Torment</u>. We see they have a Time Limit Five Months. We also know this The Locust does not <u>Stop Stinging</u> when the sun goes down, they are busy (Day, and Night).

6.   And in those days shall men seek death, and shall not find it; and shall desire to die, and death shall flee from them.

Let's interpret, In those days shall men seek death. This is a perfect picture of <u>Suicide</u> or suicidal. And shall not find it, this is why in verse (5) They shall be tormented, <u>Five Months</u>. This command cannot be changed.

And shall desire to die, this is Suicide. And <u>Death,</u> shall flee from them. We find death in [Rev. 6: 8] where Death is riding a <u>Pale Horse</u> and <u>Hell</u> followed with him. This is not the time for death it is a time for torment. Death and Hell heard the cries of these people, and saw it. Then turned and fled away. We can see this <u>Torment</u> is so <u>Severe</u> that men, and women had rather die than suffer this torment, This is day, and night.

7. And the shapes of the locusts were like unto horses prepared unto battle; and on their heads were as it were crowns like gold, and their faces were as the faces of men.

Let's interpret, The description of the locusts we have to look at are three. Like unto horses, prepared unto battle. This represents <u>Armor</u> for protection.

On their heads were as it were crowns like gold. This represents a helmet with the color of gold.

And their faces were as the faces of men. The <u>Face</u> of <u>Men,</u> is <u>Forehead, Nose, Eyes, Mouth,</u> and <u>Chin.</u> This is a <u>Mimic</u> to <u>Imitate,</u> The Image of God. This is the Evil Kingdom of the Great Red Dragon [Rev. 12: 3, 9]. Proof see verse(11) Don't let this angel fool you. He is the (Great Red Dragon) he was in heaven an archangel, until the Archangel Michael, and his angels cast him out of heaven into the earth. These Locusts, are (Evil Spirits Angels of the Dragon) [Rev. 12: 9] see [Rev. 16: 13, 14] The bible proves its self.

8. And they had hair as the hair of women, and their teeth were as the teeth of lions.

Let's interpret, They had hair as women; This Suggest the Locusts, is covered with long hair. The pronoun They strongly suggest this. The Locusts, have part of both man, and woman. The face of man, and the hair of a woman. This is a mimic to imitate the image of God. Satan got this image from the Garden of Eden, he saw Adam, and Eve.

Their teeth were as the teeth of lions. This is in the Mouth the face part of the Locusts. These teeth are put there for a purpose the locusts can bite, as well as sting. As we look at this Locusts, no (Legs) were mentioned.

9. And they had breastplates, as it were breastplates of iron; and the sound of their wings was as the sound of chariots of many horses running to battle.

Let's interpret, The breast plates as it were breastplates of iron. These plates over lap each other as Scales of a fish. The scripture doesn't say these breastplates, were iron we are looking back in time.

The sound of their wings, was as the sound of chariots of many horses running to battle. Now we know their mode of travel, their wings. With the sound of many Chariots of many Horses running to battle. This is a sure thing mankind can hear these locusts as they travel world wide all over the face of the earth, day, and night. We know the Locusts, is an Evil Spirit by their (Configuration).

10. And they had tails like unto scorpions, and there were stings in their tails: and their power was to hurt men five months.

Let's interpret, They had tails like scorpions, This tail is Visible as well as the Locusts, People can see, and hear these Locusts. We have a good Description of these Locusts in verses (8-9-10).

And there were stings in their tails; this is specific, and their power was to hurt men five months. Verse (6) shows us how Severe this <u>Hurt</u> is. This will be a terrible time on earth for men, and women who don't have the <u>Seal</u> of <u>God</u>, in their forehead.

11. And they had a king over them, which is the angel of the bottomless pit, whose name in the Hebrew tongue is Abaddon, but in the Greek tongue hath his name Apollyon.

Let's interpret, They had a king over them, which is the angel of the bottomless pit. His name in the Hebrew tongue, is Abaddon; in the Greek tongue, his name is Apollyon. This king is (Lucifer) the Dragon, The old Serpent, Devil, and Satan. This king is the old dragon; over the his angels which were in heaven, till they got cast out. He is still king over the Locusts which are his angels (Evil Spirits) here on earth.

See [2nd. Peter, 2: 4] This is a perfect picture of the <u>Angel</u> of the <u>Bottomless Pit.</u>

(Lucifer) and his angels, which are the locusts which we have followed from [Rev. 9: 1 -thru-11]. [2nd. Peter, 2: 4] Reads like this. For if God, spared not the angels that sinned, but cast them down to hell, and delivered them into chains of darkness, to be reserved unto judgment. A great big book could be written on this subject.

12. One woe is past; and, behold, there come two woes more hereafter.

Let's interpret, One woe is past, This woe is from verses (1-to-11) This is the woe of the locusts.

13. And the sixth angel sounded, and I heard a voice from the four horns of the golden altar which is before God,

Let's interpret, This is the <u>Second Woe</u>, and the <u>Sixth Angel</u> is ready to put in action the plan that was given him to do.

The <u>Sixth Angel,</u> Sounded notice where the voice of the trumpet went to first. <u>The Four Horns</u> of the <u>Golden Altar</u>, which is before

God. This is the Center of Power. The Horns are (S/L) Angels; We know when <u>Horn</u>, is spoken of or used in the Bible it is a <u>Symbol</u> of <u>Power.</u> The voice from the <u>Four Horns</u> of the Golden Altar. Suggest Four Angels of Power <u>Talking</u> to the Sixth Angel, and John, heard them. We know what they said to the Sixth Angel, verse (14) tells us.

14. Saying to the sixth angel which had the trumpet, Loose the four angels which are bound in the great river Euphrates.

Let's interpret, <u>The Four Horns</u> of the <u>Golden Altar</u>, which is before <u>God,</u> said to the Sixth Angel, Loose The four angels which are bound in the great river Euphrates.

This is a <u>Command</u> a Plan of Action for the <u>Sixth Angel,</u> to put in Action. We can strongly see; The Four Horns, of the Golden Altar, Suggest <u>Four Angels,</u> which have power to carry out God's, plan. When they gave the command to loose the four angels which are bound in the great river Euphrates. <u>Command</u> is the <u>Ability</u> to <u>Control.</u>

Let's take a close look at what we are studying. The Four Horns of the Golden Altar are <u>Power</u>. The Horn Symbol proves that. These <u>Four</u> Angels in <u>Heaven</u> said to the Sixth Angel, loose the four angels (Devils) [Rev. 12: 9] which are bound in the great river Euphrates. This suggest one thing from the Four Horns of the Golden Altar. Here it is <u>We</u> have <u>Power</u> to control <u>Them</u>. The angels bound in the great River Euphrates, are <u>Evil Spirits</u> of the Great Red Dragon [Rev. 12: 3, 9].

15. And the four angels were loosed, which were prepared for an hour, and a day, and a month, and a year, for to slay the third part of men.

Let's interpret, The Four Angels, are loose. Now they are on the surface of the earth where men, women, and children live. These angels are of the dragon, the devil.

Which were prepared, this is they are ready for action, and totally equipped to do the job according to God's, plan.

Notice! <u>Prepared</u> for an <u>Hour,</u> and a <u>Day,</u> and a <u>Month</u>, and a <u>Year</u>. (<u>This Is An Example</u>). An Hour, <u>12:00</u> noon. and a day <u>Monday</u>, and a month <u>May,</u> and a year <u>0000.</u> The year can not be documented, only Jesus, knows this. All of these are time, and dates, the place is earth.

The Purpose, to <u>Slay</u> the third part of <u>Men.</u> This covers the entire earth world wide. As we look at this it is going to be <u>(ONE HOUR).</u> When this time comes it will be very quick, and there are no sound. For to slay the third part of men. This is speaking of both Gender Male, and Female. As well as the (Locusts) in chapter (9). They will Torment both Gender. That have not the <u>Seal</u> of <u>God,</u> in their <u>Foreheads</u>.

16. And the number of the army of the horsemen were two hundred thousand thousand: and I heard the number of them.

Let's interpret, We understand now these four angels bound in the great river Euphrates, were of a high rank with the <u>Great Dragon</u> the old <u>Serpent </u>called the <u>Devil</u>, and <u>Satan.</u> when the war was fought in heaven see [Rev. 12: 7 8, 9].

We know this by the <u>Number </u>of the <u>Army.</u> When the four angels were loose from the river Euphrates, their armies were released with them, and they were <u>Prepared</u>.

The number of the army of the <u>Horsemen</u> were (200,000) + (1000). If we break this down equally to the four angels each one would have, (50, 250) horsemen in their army to kill the third part of men on the earth. These men, and women are unrighteous.

Let's take a look at this suggestion. The four Horns of the Golden Altar, are (S/L) Angels, four represent the (Four Corners) of he earth. The four angels loose in the great river Euphrates River, suggest the same thing. Four corners of the earth, East, West, North, South, this covers the entire earth.

17. And thus I saw the horses in the vision, and them that sat on them, having breastplates of fire, and of jacinth, and brimstone: and the heads of the horses were as the heads of lions; and out of their mouths issued fire and smoke and brimstone

Let's interpret, And thus I saw the horses in the vision, And them that sat upon them. We need to understand we are looking at Evil Spirits. The angels that were cast out of heaven when the (Dragon) was cast out [Rev. 12: 7, 8, 9].

All of these are to Mimic (Imitate) These Breastplates, (Fire) Indicates God's Power [Ex. 9: 24].(Jacinth) Is in the Breastplate of the high priest [Ex. 28: 18] see also [Rev. 21: 20]. (Brimstone) Is Sulfur, State of the Wicked [Ps. 11: 6]. Sent as Judgment [Deut. 29: 23]. Condition of Hell [Rev. 14: 10].

Let's look at the horses. Their heads were as the heads of lions, this shows power. And out of their mouth issued Fire, Smoke, and Brimstone. This is very destructive, when these three are mixed together by the Fire they become Sulfur, no one can breath, it is a suffocating death. Brimstone is used in many places in the Bible.

18. By these three were the third part of men killed, by the fire, and by the smoke, and by the brimstone, which issued out of their mouths.

Let's interpret, Notice by these three; (Fire Smoke, and Brimstone) That issued Out of the Mouth of the Horses. The third part of men were killed. This is a Suffocating Death (Can't Breath).

19. For their power is in their mouth, and in their tails: for their tails were like unto serpents, and had heads, and with them they do hurt.

Let's interpret, For their power is in their mouth, and in their tails. We see in this verse the Horse is Death, and Torment. The

Power of their Mouth is Death. The Power of his Tail like Serpents, and had Heads, and with them they do hurt is Torment.

Let's look at the description of the Horse. The heads were as the heads of Lions, and their Tails like Serpents, and had Heads, and with them they do hurt. This is not a real Horse that God, made. What we are looking at is, an Evil Spirit, of the Great Red Dragon his angels. And we have no description of (Them) that sat on the (Horse). We must accept this.

20. And the rest of the men which were not killed by these plagues yet repented not of the works of their hands, that they should not worship devils, and idols of gold, and silver, and brass, and stone, and of wood: which neither can see, nor hear, nor walk:

Let's interpret, All of verse (20) is Pagan Worship, of Idols, sinner people.

21. Neither repented they of their murders, nor of their sorceries, nor of their fornication, nor of their thefts.

Let's interpret, All of verse (21) is Failure to Repent. they were given a chance; but repented not.

SUMMARY

<hr />

The Locusts, from verse (1-to-11) Came out of the Smoke of the Bottomless Pit are the angels of the Great Red Dragon, that was cast out of Heaven [Rev. 12: 7, 8, 9] Evil Spirits. They are Mimics-Imitators of the image of God.

The Locusts, will Sting, anywhere they find men, and women without the Seal of God, in their foreheads see verse (4).

In Church, Cars, Airplanes, Submarines, Ships on the Job, Dining, in the Bed. there are no hiding place. The Stinging Locusts knows no Safety, he will sting anywhere, and any time (Day and Night) .

From verses (13-to-19) The Horses, with heads like a Lion, and Tails like unto Serpents, with Heads. And them that sat on them; with Breastplates, of Fire, Jacinth, and Brimstone. These also are Evil Spirits, of the (Dragon) These angels came out of the Great River Euphrates. They are Mimics-Imitators. Of the things of God.

What we are looking at is a Kingdom Divided against it's self; cannot stand.

A House Divided against it's self; cannot stand. And if Satan rise up against Himself, and be divided he cannot stand. But Hast an End see [Mark, 3: 23, 24, 25, 26].

Here is what we are looking at is The Evil Spirits of Satan, Against these [John, 8: 44] [Rev. 17: 8] sinner people Satan, Has an End [Rev. 20: 9, 10].

God, put an end to this, and fulfilled this scripture [Ps. 110: 1] [Mat. 22: 44].

AMEN!!

CHAPTER 10

1. And I saw another mighty angel come down from heaven, clothed with a cloud: and a rainbow was upon his head, and his face was as it were the sun, and his feet as pillars of fire:

Let's interpret, John, saw another mighty angel come down from heaven. We know John, is on earth at this time. This angel Clothed with a <u>Cloud</u>. is the <u>Glory</u>, of <u>God.</u> We find this same Cloud of Glory here [Acts, 1: 9]. The <u>Rainbow</u> upon his head, is the <u>Glory</u> of <u>God,</u> [Rev. 4: 3] [Ezek. 1: 28] [Gen. 9: 13, 14, 16].

His face was as it were the sun. This is the <u>Glory</u> of <u>God,</u> see [Mat. 17: 2] we find the Glory of God, <u>Shining</u> through the face of Jesus. The Glory of God, shown through the face of <u>Moses,</u> That the children of Israel, couldn't look at Moses, face.

His feet as pillars of fire. This also is the Glory of God. We find this <u>Fire</u> is God, see [Ezek. 1: 27] Jesus, has this Glory here [Rev. 1: 15].

This mighty angel, John, saw come down from heaven, is clothed with the Glory of God, <u>From</u> the top of his <u>Head</u> to his Feet.

2. And he had in his hand a little book open: and he set his right foot upon the sea, and his left foot on the earth,

Let's interpret, The <u>Little Book,</u> is the book of <u>Revelation.</u> This is the <u>Angel</u> of [Rev. 1: 1] Jesus, gave it to his <u>Angel</u>. The <u>Little Book</u> in the <u>Angel's</u> <u>Hand</u> is <u>Open</u>. It was opened here [Rev. 5: 5, 7] by <u>Jesus.</u>

Open means, in action now, The time is at hand. Had not Jesus, opened the book of Revelation, it would still be <u>Sealed</u> see [Rev. 5: 3, 4] see also [Dan. 12: 4, 13] Simple.

This Angel, [Rev. 5: 2] is the same Angel in verse (1). He is still in charge of all things in Revelation. We find the angel of Jesus, here [Luke, 2: 8, 9, 10,11, 12] also here [Mat. 2; 2, 9]. [Rev. 1: 1] Rev. 22: 16].

The Angel, set his Right Foot upon the Sea, and his Left Foot on the Earth. By this we know the Angel, is in Position, for something to happen. The Little Book is still open in his hand.

3. And cried with a loud voice, as when a lion roareth: and when he had cried, seven thunders uttered their voices.

Let's interpret, And cried with a loud voice, as when a lion roareth. We don't know what the angel said. But we know he is talking to someone in heaven. Proof, and when he cried, Seven Thunders uttered their voices.

The Seven Thunders are the Seven Spirits before the throne of God. [Rev. 4: 5].

Jesus, has them now [Rev. 5: 6,]. (The Seven Horns, and Seven Eyes) are the Seven Spirits of God, (POWER) [Mat 28: 18].

4. And when the seven thunders had uttered their voices, I was about to write: and I heard a voice form heaven saying unto me, Seal up those things which the seven thunders uttered, and write them not.

Let' interpret, This is John, doing the talking. And when the Seven Thunders, had uttered their voices; John, said "I was about to write".

This shows us John, understood what the Seven Thunders, said. The Seven Thunders, and the Seven Spirits, before the throne of God, are One. And I heard a voice from heaven saying unto me, seal up those things the seven thunders uttered, and write them not. This voice is Jesus, He has the Seven Spirits now.

The Seven Thunders voices sound like the voice of God, because they are God's, Spirit. God, is a Spirit. [John, 4: 24]. People misunderstood God's, voice and said it Thundered. [John, 12: 28,

29, 30]. [Mark, 3: 17] The sons of Zebedee, James, and John. Jesus, surnamed them, (Boanerges) which are the sons of <u>thunder,</u> (God). [Rom. 8: 14] Simple. Don't be confused when, God, and Jesus Are mentioned they are one see [John, 10: 30].

5. And the angel which I saw stand upon the sea and upon the earth lifted up his hand to heaven,

Let's interpret, This is the same angel, in [Rev. 1: 1] Because he has the book of Revelation, that Jesus, gave to him in his hand.

Lifted up his hand to heaven, We see now this Mighty Angel, is in <u>Position.</u> And ready to do something. This verse (5) is parallel, to verse (2).

In verse (3) This Mighty Angel, cried with a loud voice as when a Lion roareth. Nothing mention of what he said; verse (6) tells us. He is in the same position.

6. And sware by him that liveth for ever and ever, who created heaven, and the things that therein are, and the earth, and the things that therein are, and the sea, and the things which are therein, that there should be time no longer:

Let's interpret. This is a continuation of Verse Five. The angel lifted up his hand to heaven, and sware by him that liveth for ever and ever. The pronoun <u>Him,</u> is <u>Jesus,</u> see [Rev. 4: 8- thru-11] <u>Jesus,</u> is not a <u>Spirit,</u> [Luke, 24: 39] therefore he liveth. <u>God,</u> is a <u>Spirit.</u> [John, 4: 24] God, has forever been, he is all <u>Power.</u>

Who created Heaven, Earth, Sea, and the things therein. This is <u>Jesus,</u> see [John, 1: 1, 2, 3, 4, 5]. (That there should be <u>Time</u> no longer). This is the voice of the <u>Angel,</u> standing on the sea, earth, and his hand in the air toward heaven with the little book open [Revelation] talking to Jesus.

Notice! <u>Earth,</u> has run out of <u>Time</u> It has finished it's purpose for what it was made for. God, and Jesus, has got them self a

Kingdom from it. Made in their own <u>Image</u> and <u>Likeness</u>. A Man, called <u>Adam</u>, God, breathed into his nostrils the breath of life, and man became a <u>Living Soul</u>, see [Gen. 1: 26] [Gen. 2: 7]. We see the book of <u>Revelation</u>, started in the book of <u>Genesis,</u> and ended in the book of <u>Revelation.</u>

With these words from the Mighty Angel, There Should Be Time No Longer.

We know the Seven Thunders Uttered Their Voices. Then John, heard a voice from heaven saying Seal Up Those Things Which The Seven Thunders Uttered, And Write Them Not.

This leads us to look at these scriptures. [Rev. Chapter-8] [Rev. Chapter-9] [Rev. 15: 4-thru-8] [Rev. Chapter 16].

From [Chapter-8] thru [Chapter-20] Is the (Destruction of Mankind), and the (Earth). This makes us think about some things that are silent in the Bible. Verse (6) show us this Mighty Angel, saw something, here on earth that time should be no longer. He reported to Jesus, in heaven. We are looking at the near future; things are changing fast.

7. But in the days of the voice of the seventh angel, when he shall begin to sound, the mystery of God should be finished, as he has declared to his servants the prophets.

Let's interpret, In the days of the voice of the seventh angel, when he shall begin to sound. This is in [Rev. 11: 15] this is the third <u>Woe</u> from the <u>Three Woes</u> in [Rev. 8: 13]. I will list the <u>Three Woes</u>, for a better understanding. First Woe, [Rev. 9: 3, 4, 5, 6, 10] The Locusts, with stings in their tails like unto <u>Scorpions.</u>

Second Woe, [Rev. 9: 14-thru-19], The four angels loose from the great River Euphrates, with their army, of horsemen. With heads like Lions, Tails like Serpents. Fire, Smoke, and Brimstone came out of the mouth of the horses, by these three were the third part of men killed. God, and Jesus, are destroying the Evil Kingdoms of this earth.

We find the <u>Mystery</u> of <u>God,</u> in [Dan. 7: 12, and 22-thru-28]. These are long spans of time in the days of the Prophets. But it is very close now because we are living in the <u>Last Days</u> on <u>Earth</u> see verse (6). God, and Jesus, will keep their promise.

8. And the voice which I heard from heaven spake unto me again, and said, Go and take the little book which is open in the hand of the angel which standeth upon the sea and upon the earth.

Let's interpret, The voice from heaven is Jesus, he spoke to John, the first time in verse (4). This is Jesus, talking to John, the second time. The reason Jesus, is talking to John, is his angle is occupied with the assignment given to him.

Here is the first assignment. The <u>Right Foot</u> upon the <u>Sea</u>, and the <u>Left Foot</u> on the <u>Earth.</u> The Angel, lifted up his hand and sware by him, <u>Jesus,</u> that liveth for ever and ever. <u>That Time</u> should be <u>No Longer</u>!

Here is the second assignment of the angel of Jesus. He has the book of Revelation with him in his hand, standing upon the sea and upon the earth.

There is going to be a <u>Transfer</u> of the book of <u>Revelation</u> from the angel of Jesus, to John. This is why Jesus, is instructing John,

Notice Jesus, said to John, go and <u>Take</u> the <u>Little Book</u> which is open in the hand of the angel.

We need to understand something here. Jesus, took the same book Revelation out of the right hand of him that sat upon the throne. <u>GOD.</u> [Rev. 5: 7]. When Jesus, took the book It was sealed with <u>Seven Seals</u>. Jesus, opened the book and gave it to his <u>Angel</u>, [Rev. 1:1]. Now the <u>Little Book</u>, open is being transferred from the angel to John. John, had to stretch forth his hand and take the Little Book. The angel didn't give it to him.

9. And I went unto the angel, and said unto him, Give me the little book. And he said unto me, Take it, and eat it up; and it shall make thy belly bitter, but it shall be in thy mouth sweet as honey.

Let's interpret, John, went unto the angel, Notice! John, didn't do what Jesus, told him to do, he ask the angel for the Little Book. The angel knew Jesus, told John, <u>To Take</u> the Little Book. The angel said the same thing to John, as Jesus, did, <u>Take It</u> eat it up this is, <u>Read It</u> believe every word of it, for all of it is the truth, and every thing written in it shall be fulfilled.

It shall make thy <u>Belly Bitter</u>. This means it will <u>Grieve</u> you in your mind of what you see and understand of the things to come (The Future) that is written in the Little Book Revelation.

It shall be in thy <u>Mouth Sweet</u> as <u>Honey.</u> This means when you open your mouth to <u>Preach</u> the <u>Words</u> of this <u>Little Book</u> Revelation. They are the words of Jesus, with Power of the <u>Holy Spirit</u> in your mouth. John, knows what it is to <u>Preach</u> the gospel, of Jesus, and to work miracles by the Holy Spirit.

Look at these two <u>Prophets</u> with the same situation <u>John,</u> is <u>Confronted</u> with. [Jer. 15:16] and [Ezek. 2: 8, 9, 10] [Ezek. 3: 1, 2, 3, 4,5]. Many have fought a good fight, and run the race with patience, and kept the <u>Faith</u> see [2nd Tim. 4: 7].

10. And I took the little book out of the angel's hand, and ate it up; and it was in my mouth sweet as honey: and as soon as I had eaten it, my belly was bitter.

Let's interpret, I took the little book out of the angel's hand, and ate it up. This is the same book that John, wept much because no man was found worthy to open and read the book in Heaven see [Rev. 5: 4].

Now we see John, himself is <u>Found Worth,</u> to take the book, and eat it up. This is <u>Faith,</u> and obedient to the words of Jesus, and the Angel. Without faith it is impossible to please God, [Heb. 11: 6].

In my mouth it was sweet as honey. This is the <u>Words</u> of <u>God,</u> in the mouth of the <u>Prophet Ezekiel</u>, and the <u>Words</u> of <u>Jesus,</u> in the mouth of the <u>Apostle John.</u> This is the power of the <u>Holy Spirit</u> in their mouth as they <u>Preach,</u> and <u>Speak.</u> The Prophet, Ezekiel, experienced the same thing as John, see [Ezek. 3: 3] so did [Jer. 15: 16].

Every man that has been called to preach the Gospel of Jesus, Knows what joy it is to <u>Preach</u> the <u>Gospel</u> under the power and demonstration of the Holy Ghost. Oh-yes we have our <u>Bitter Moments Also,</u> criticize, threaten. When a man of God, see the crowd he has to <u>Preach,</u> and <u>Prophesy</u> to; it troubles his mind it is not easy. It will make your belly bitter. "Thoughts of your mind".

11. And he said unto me, Thou must prophesy again before many peoples, and nations, and tongues, and kings.

Let's interpret, The angel in [Rev. 1: 1] is instructing John, Notice both are on earth, the <u>Isle</u> of <u>Patmos,</u> [Rev. 1: 9]. Here are the instructions. Thou Must <u>Prophesy</u> (Preach) <u>(AGAIN)</u> before many <u>Peoples,</u> and <u>Nations,</u> and <u>Tongues,</u> and <u>Kings.</u> This is where John's, Belly was made Bitter. John, has the <u>Little</u> Book now, inside of his mind.

We have two words that we need to <u>Consider. The First, is (AGAIN).</u> this means something has been <u>Said,</u> or a recorded <u>Document</u> in the past. We have a record of John, <u>Preaching</u> with the <u>Twelve Apostles.</u> We also know John, saw all the <u>Miracles</u> Jesus, did.

Saw Jesus, <u>Crucified,</u> Saw the <u>Nail Prints</u> in his <u>Hands,</u> and <u>Feet,</u> and where he was <u>Pierced</u> in <u>His Side.</u> Ate with <u>Jesus,</u> and <u>Talked</u> with him after he <u>Arose From The Tomb.</u> Saw <u>Jesus,</u> Ascend up into <u>Heaven.</u>

John, wrote these books in the <u>Bible. Saint John,</u> (<u>First, Second, and Third John</u>) and the book of <u>Revelation.</u> Five Books.

Now John, has to start <u>Preaching Again.</u> He has the Revelation, of Jesus Christ, to Preach this time. It won't be <u>Repentance.</u> If you will have it John, is Preaching to us now as we <u>Read This Great Book Revelation of Jesus Christ,</u> see [Rev. 1: 3], SIMPLE.

<u>The Second Word is (MANY).</u> This is an <u>Un-told Number.</u> It applies to a number which no man could number see [Rev. 7: 9]. To make it simple this covers the entire <u>World.</u>

Let's prove it, The Angel's, instructions are! Thou must prophesy (Again) Notice before (Many Peoples) and (Nations) and (Tongues), and (Kings).

This is where the Little Book made John's, <u>Belly Bitter,</u> seeing and understanding what he must do. He already did it once, that is what got him exiled to the Isle of Patmos,

[Rev. 1: 9] It is not easy.

Now we see John, was instructed to <u>Preach</u> the <u>Book of Revelation,</u>

CHAPTER 11

1. And There was given me a reed like unto a rod: and the angel stood, saying, Rise, and measure the temple of God, and the altar, and them that worship therein.

Let's interpret, The reed, is in the bamboo family a plant that grows in marsh wet land. They are straight and light. This is why the reed is like unto a rod, straight. They are used as a measuring tool. Graduated Increments of <u>Cubits,</u> which is <u>Eighteen Inches.</u>

The length of the Reed is (11) feet, the length of a Rod is (16.5) feet <u>Jewish Measure.</u>

The <u>Angel,</u> stood, is the same <u>Angel,</u> that had the little book open in his hand in [Rev. 10: 2]

Saying <u>Rise,</u> And measure the <u>Temple</u> of <u>God,</u> and the <u>Altar,</u> and them that worship, therein. This is in the <u>Heavenly Kingdom</u> of <u>God,</u> The Third Heaven.

We find the temple of God, here [Rev. 15: 5, 6, 8] [Rev. 16: 1] no dimension given. We find the altar, here [Rev. 8: 3, 5] no dimension given, or how to measure.

And them that worship therein. There are several places in Revelation, we find where the Four and Twenty Elders, and the Four Beast, which are the Hundred Forty Four Thousand, worship God. [Rev. 4: 8, 10] [Rev. 7: 11] [Rev. 15: 4]. Measure some times is a Term used to count I have no Spiritual understanding as how to measure them that worship therein. Here is all anyone knows [Rev. 7: 9] A great multitude which no man could number.

2. But the court which is without the temple leave out, and measure it not; for it is given to the Gentiles: and the holy city shall they tread under foot forty and two months.

Let's interpret, As we look at what the Angel, is telling John, we can see he is talking about Heaven, and this Earth,

The court which is without the temple. Leave out. This is the earth. (This is Proof) it is given to the Gentiles, and the Holy City, you can find it here also [Rev. 20: 9] is Jerusalem in the land of Israel. they shall tread it under foot forty and two months see [Rev. 13: 5] [Dan. 7: 19. 23] We know now why the angel, said the court which is without the temple leave out, the Earth is being Destroyed.

3. And I will give power unto my two witnesses, and they shall prophesy a thousand two hundred and three score days, clothed in sackcloth.

Let's interpret, I will give Power, unto my two witnesses. Jesus, is the only one in Heaven, and on Earth, that has Power, to give anyone power see [Mat, 28: 18] He has All Power.

The two witnesses are Moses, and Elijah see [Mat. 20; 21, 22, 23,] [Mat. 17: 1, 2, 3, 13]. We know God, gave these two witnesses Moses. and Elijah, to Jesus, see [Mat. 20: 23] proves this.

They shall prophesy, a Thousand two Hundred, and Three Score Days. This is (1260-days) (42-Months) (3 ½- Years).

They are prophesying to the church, and telling the church; What to look for, Where to go, and When, and How to get there see [Rev. 12: 6, 14]. This Time, and Times, and a Half Time is (3 ½- Years). Clothed in sackcloth. Sackcloth is a coarse fabric made of goats hair. Symbol of God's, Severe Judgment [Rev. 6: 12].

4. These are the two olive trees and the two candlesticks standing before the God of the earth.

Let's interpret, This is (S/L) two <u>Olive Trees</u>, are <u>Moses,</u> and <u>Elijah,</u> and the two <u>Candlesticks, </u>are <u>Moses,</u> and <u>Elijah.</u> standing before the God, of the <u>Earth</u> this is Jesus.

Remember God, and Jesus, are one [John, 10: 30] see verse (3) the two witnesses belong to Jesus.

Now we understand why the sons of Zebedee, James, and John, couldn't have the position they ask for; one to sit on the right hand, and one on the left hand of Jesus, in his Kingdom [Mat. 20: 21, 22, 23]. It was given to Moses, and Elijah, by God.

5.   And if any man will hurt them, Fire proceedeth out of their mouth, and devoured their enemies: and if any man will hurt them, he must in this manner be killed.

Let's interpret, If any man will hurt them. This is interfere in any way, the work these two witnesses have to do, to <u>Finish</u> the plan of God, and Jesus.

Fire proceedeth out of their mouth. This is not natural fire as we know it. See [Heb. 12: 29] [Acts, 5: 3, 4, 5] Peter, and Ananias, [Acts, 5: 9, 10] Peter, and Sapphira. Elijah, The captain, and his fifty see [2nd. Kings, 1: 10-thru-13] We understand this <u>Fire</u>, came out of the mouth of <u>Peter,</u> and <u>Elijah</u> is Spiritual Power of God. Both of these men are the <u>Sons</u> of <u>God,</u> [Rom. 8: 14].

He must in this manner be killed. Notice! There is no blood shed to pollute the earth, neither any sound that we have record of. This is the power of Jesus, spoken from the mouth of the two witnesses <u>Moses,</u> and <u>Elijah.</u> (Elijah, used this fire power before).

On Mount Carmel, see [1st. Kings 18: 19, 38].

6.   These have power to shut heaven, that it rain not in the days of their prophecy: and have power over waters to turn them to blood, and to smite the earth with all plagues, as often as they will.

Let's interpret, These two witnesses (<u>Moses</u> and <u>Elijah)</u>, have

Power, to shut Heaven that it rain not in the days of their Prophecy. The days of their prophecy are the Thousand Two Hundred and Threescore days (1,260) this is (3 ½-Years.

And have Power, over Waters to turn them to Blood. And to smite the earth with all Plagues, as often as they will. We don't know what these plagues will be this is (Future) we are looking at.

If Heaven, is shut, and it doesn't Rain we will know why. And if the Waters are turned to Blood we will know why. Moses, and Elijah, are doing their job, that Jesus, told them to do.

These two Prophets, have done this before Elijah, shut up heaven that it rain not; but according to his word see [1st. Kings, 1: 17] also [James, 5: 17] Elijah, prayed and shut up heaven that it rain not for (3 ½- Year). This is while Elijah, was on earth, working for God, in the days of his prophecy many years ago.

Elijah, Fought a good Fight with Faith in God. In one country, Israel. He defeated King Ahab, Jezebel, and the prophets of Baal; and turned the children of Israel back to God, [1st. Kings, 18: 38, 39, 40]

Moses, in the land of Egypt, did what God, told him to do and all the Waters, of Egypt, became Blood see [Ex. 7: 17-thru-21].

Moses, obeyed God, and destroyed Egypt with these plagues. (Waters to Blood) (Frogs) (Lice) (Flies) (Cattle) (Boils) (Hail) (Locusts) (Darkness).

Moses, Fought a good Fight with Faith in God. In one country, Egypt. He defeated

Pharaoh, with all the plagues, and delivered the children of Israel back too their own land.

Here in the Book of Revelation; Moses, and Elijah, will use the Power Jesus, gave them, to do the work Jesus has for them to do. This time against the Entire World.

Their Mode of Travel from country to country around the entire world will be see [1st. Kings, 18: 12] also [Acts, 8: 39, 40]. Amazing Isn't It?

7. And when they shall have finished their testimony, the beast that ascendeth out of the bottomless pit shall make war against them, and shall overcome them and kill them.

Let's interpret, When they have finished their Testimony. This is the last (Sermon) (Preached) on earth. Testimony is a witness borne in behalf of something, this is The Gospel of Jesus.

The Beast that ascendeth out of the Bottomless Pit, Is this beast [Rev. 13: 11] (S/L) (Judas Iscariot) see [John, 6: 70, 71] the devil. [2nd. Thes. 2: 3, 4].

The Bottomless Pit, is the Earth. [Rev. 9: 1, 2] shows us that. Shall make war against them, and shall overcome them and kill them see [Dan. 7: 21].

See also [John, 13: 21, 26, 27] [Luke, 22: 2, 3, 4] [Rev. 13: 18]. He is the False Prophet see [Rev. 19: 20]. A Book Could Be Written On This Subject. All of this is prophecy yet to come.

8. And their dead bodies shall lie in the street of the great city which spiritually is called Sodom and Egypt, where also our Lord was crucified.

Let's interpret, Their dead bodies; we understand is Incarnation, given a body in Earthly Form. They could have not been Killed otherwise. (I will show you) Elijah, was Incarnate of John the Baptist, [Mat. 17: 12, 13] beheaded [Mat. 14: 10].

Moses and Elijah, has Glorified Bodies. (But Incarnate, They have Flesh Bodies). This is so they can be seen, and be Killed, as John The Baptist, was. This is the Power of Jesus.

Shall lie in the street of the great city which Spiritually is called Sodom, and Egypt. The great city is Jerusalem see [Ps. 46: 4, 5] Where also our Lord, was crucified, this also is Jerusalem [Luke 9: 30, 31]. Sodom, is Burnt Egypt is Black both are Sin.

9. And they of the people and kindreds and tongues and nations shall see their dead bodies three days and a half, and shall not suffer their dead bodies to be put in graves.

Let's interpret, We understand; People, Kindreds, tongues, and nations, are the whole world, they covers the entire earth. The world is (S/L) people, not the earth.

Shall see their dead bodies, three days and a half. With Technology, today of Television, and Computers. we can understand this.

The Three, and a Half Days, is this (One Day For Each Year They Prophesied). And a Half Day, for the half year (Six Months). (1260-Days= 3 ½-Years).

And shall not suffer their dead bodies to be put in graves. This is Hateful full of Hate see [John, 8: 44] Verse Seven tells us who put this Hate in the minds of the people of earth. The Beast that ascendeth out of the Bottomless Pit see [John, 6: 70, 71]

We are looking at the prophesy of Jesus, [Mat. 24: 7] Kingdom against Kingdom.

The Saints will possess the Kingdoms of this world see verse (15) also [Dan. 7: 22, 27].

10. And they that dwell upon the earth shall rejoice over them, and make merry, and shall send gifts one to another; because these two prophets tormented them that dwell on the earth.

Let's interpret, This (Verse-10) is the Evil Kingdom of this world. We find the Evil of mankind from here [Gen. 6: 3, 5, 6, 7] to [Rev. 20: 9, 10, 15].

The people of the earth knew these two prophets were of God, see verse (11). These words tells us that, (Rejoice, Make Merry, Send Gifts one to another) Because these two prophets, tormented them. This Torment is in verse (6), and is severe, Shut Heaven, "No Rain"

"Turn Waters to Blood" "Smite The Earth With <u>All Plagues</u>" This is all over the earth.

11. And after three days and an half the Spirit of life from God entered into them, and they stood upon their feet; and great fear fell upon them which saw them.

Let's interpret, This <u>Half Day</u>, depicts Mid-day, Noon Twelve O' Clock. The <u>Spirit</u> of <u>Life</u> from God, entered into them, and they stood upon their feet. Notice! They came alive for the whole world to see. <u>Great Fear</u> fell upon them which saw them. These people knew only God, and Jesus, could raise the dead.

They also knew these two Prophets, Prophesied (Preached) the Gospel of Jesus, to them, and they rejected it. This is why <u>Great Fear</u> fell upon them. "This is the last <u>Sermon Preached,</u> on the earth, no more. This is <u>Prophecy</u> the future and SOON to Come!

12. And they heard a great voice from heaven saying unto them, Come up hither. and they ascended up to heaven in a cloud; and their enemies beheld them.

Let's interpret, Notice! They (Moses, and Elijah) are standing upon their <u>Feet</u> with the <u>Spirit</u> of <u>Life</u> in them. They heard a <u>Great Voice,</u> from heaven (<u>Jesus</u>). Saying unto them (Moses, and Elijah) come up hither. They ascended up to heaven in a cloud which is the <u>Glory</u> of <u>God</u>. Their enemies beheld them. (Saw them).

We need to keep in mind these two <u>Prophets, Moses,</u> and <u>Elijah,</u> Stood on the street in a city that is called <u>Jerusalem</u>, in the land of <u>Israel,</u> and they left this earth from the beloved city <u>Jerusalem</u> in a cloud of glory when the <u>Great Voice From Heaven Jesus,</u> said come up <u>Hither</u>. What a beautiful picture the power of our God, and our Lord, and savior Jesus Christ, showing the whole world they are the Resurrection Amen.

13. And the same hour was there a great earthquake, and the tenth part of the city fell, and in the earthquake were slain of men seven thousand: and the remnant were affrighted, and gave glory to the God of heaven.

Let's interpret, There are some great things happening in one hour in Jerusalem.

Notice! The bodies of two dead prophets, lay in the street of Jerusalem for (3 ½-Days). Then the Spirit of Life from God, entered into them, and they stood upon their feet. A great voice said come up hither, and they ascended up to heaven in a cloud, of glory, and their enemies saw them. The enemies are from here [John, 8: 44], and sinner people.

In the same hour a <u>Great Earthquake</u>, The tenth part of the city fell, and Seven Thousand men were slain. The remnant were affrighted (Frighten) and gave glory to the God of heaven, The remnant of people are these [Is. 1: 9] spoke of. They are righteous this is why they gave glory to the God, of heaven. This took place in Jerusalem, In the land of <u>Israel.</u>

14. The second woe is past; and, behold, the third woe cometh quickly.

Let's interpret, Let us put the <u>Three Woes</u> in sequence so we can better understand the purpose of the woe. We see in [Rev. 8: 13] there are Three Woes. The first Woe, is the (Plague of the Locusts) [Rev. 9: 1-thru-12].The second Woe directs us to verse (10) this preposition <u>Because</u>. These <u>Two Prophets Tormented</u> them that dwell on the earth.

In verse (13) we see more great suffering. (Earthquake) (Tenth Part of The City Fell) (Seven Thousand Men Slain).

The second woe is past, and, behold the third woe cometh quickly. This is in succession.

15. And the seventh angel sounded; and there were great voices in heaven, saying, The kingdoms of this world are become the kingdoms of our Lord, and of his Christ; and he shall reign for ever and ever.

Let's interpret. The <u>Seventh Angel,</u> sounded, and immediately there were <u>Great Voices,</u> heard in <u>Heaven</u>. These great voices heard in heaven knew what the sound of the <u>Seventh Trumpet</u> meant. Here it is [Rev. 10: 7] But in the days of the voice of the seventh angel, when he shall begin to sound, the mystery of God should be finished, as he hath declared to his servants the prophets.

We know what the voices said. The <u>Kingdoms</u> of this world are become the <u>Kingdoms</u> of our <u>Lord</u>, and his <u>Christ.</u> And he shall <u>Reign</u> for <u>Ever</u> and <u>Ever.</u>

You can find the prophesy of (V-15) here [Dan. 7: 13, 14] [Dan. 7: 22, 27].

The Kingdoms of this world are the Saints of God, and Jesus. Scattered all over the whole earth, through the <u>Generations</u> of <u>Time.</u> [Dan. 7: 22, 27] Plainly shows us that.

And he (<u>Jesus),</u> Shall reign for ever, and ever. [Dan, 7: 13, 14], These Kingdoms were bought here, [John, 3: 16] He shall reign is here [Mat. 28: 18]. He is all POWER.

16. And the four and twenty elders, which sat before God on their seats, fell upon their faces, and worshipped God,

Let's interpret, The Four, and Twenty Elders, fell upon their faces and worshipped God. We need to understand <u>God,</u> and <u>Jesus,</u> are one [John, 10: 30]. <u>God,</u> is a <u>Spirit</u> [John, 4: 24] <u>God,</u> is <u>Invisible</u> see [Col. 1: 15]. Jesus, is the <u>Brightness</u> of is <u>Glory</u> And the <u>Express Image</u> of his <u>Person</u> [Heb. 1: 3] Jesus, looks exactly like God, But he is not a Spirit See [Luke 24: 39] Jesus, has a Glorified Flesh Body; in which God, lives in

This is why Jesus, said My Father and I are one.

Look what God, done for, Jesus, see [Heb. 1: 8] Unto the son he saith, Thy throne O God, is for ever, and ever a scepter of righteousness, is the scepter of thy kingdom. This Kingdom is here [Luke, 22: 30]. The title God, is referring to Jesus. and God.

17. Saying, We give thee thanks, O Lord God Almighty, which art, and wast, and art to come; because thou hast taken to thee thy great power, and hast reigned.

Let's interpret, This verse are the words of Worship of the four and twenty elders.

In verse (16) (We give thee thanks) this is one-ness. O Lord God Almighty, this is another one-ness, God, and Jesus, are one. [John, 10: 30]. Which Art, and Wast, and Art to come. See [Rev. 1: 8] we have a Parallel Scripture, here. All these verbs are Jesus, in different places and different times. Notice! (Which Art) In heaven, and (Wast) On Earth, and (Art) To come, from, Heaven and get his children in the Resurrection.

Because thou hast taken to thee thy Great Power. [Mat. 28: 18] and hast reigned.

Jesus, took the Kingdoms of this world; see verses (11, 12, 13, 14, 15].

See these scriptures for a good understanding of JESUS, and Destroying, the Kingdoms of this World. [Dan. 3: 12, 25, 26, 28] [Dan. 6: 16-thru-23] [Dan. 7: 22, 27]

These four children of God, and Jesus, withstood the Mighty Power of Force, against the Kingdom of God, and Jesus. [Daniel, Shadrach, Meshach, Abednego].

18. And the nations were angry, and thy wrath is come, and the time of the dead, that they should be judged, and that thou shouldest give reward unto thy servants the prophets, and to the saints, and them that fear thy name, small and great; and shouldest destroy them which destroy the earth.

Let's interpret, And the nations were angry, this is the whole world is <u>Angry</u>. This is why the two Prophets Tormented them that dwelled on the earth. Thy wrath is come, this is Jesus, we see some of his wrath in verse (13).

And the time of the dead that they should be judged, this is time on earth has run out. God's, plan is finished see [Rev. 10: 6, 7] The mystery of God, should be finished, Verse (15) we see it is finished (The Seventh Angel sounded) This is the end of the three woes.

And that thou should give reward unto thy servants the prophets, and to the saints, And them that fear thy name, <u>Small</u> and <u>Great.</u> These Rewards have names, they are <u>Crown</u> of <u>Righteousness,</u> [2nd. Tim. 4:8] <u>Crown</u> of <u>Life</u> [Rev. 2: 10].

And should destroy them which destroy the earth. We find this here, [Dan. 7: 23] The <u>Fourth Beast,</u> shall be the <u>Fourth Kingdom</u> upon the earth, and shall <u>Devour</u> the <u>Whole Earth</u>, and <u>Tread</u> it down and <u>Break</u> it in <u>Pieces.</u> Jesus, will destroy this Kingdom.

This is the <u>New Babylon Empire,</u> in chapters (13,17, 18) destroyed by <u>Jesus,</u> here [Rev. 19: 20].

19. And the temple of God was open in heaven, and there was seen in his temple the ark of his testament: and there were lightnings, and voices, and thundering, and an earthquake, and great hail.

Let's interpret, The <u>Temple</u> of <u>God,</u> was open in <u>Heaven.</u> This is the third heaven see [2nd. Cor. 12: 2, 3, 4]. A temple is a place of worship, and a center for Church Business Transactions. The <u>Ark</u> is a small box wherein records are stored, or filed. These records were kept in the Ark called the <u>Ark</u> of <u>Testimony;</u> [Ex. 30: 6] also the <u>Ark of Covenant,</u> [Num. 10: 33]. Today we use The Last Will and Testament. This also is a covenant.

There was seen in his temple, the ark of his Testament. Here is what is seen in the Ark of his Testament. Lightnings, Voices, Thundering, and an Earthquake, and great Hail. The ark of his testament is here [Rev. 16: 18, 21]. What ever is written will be fulfilled.

These voices are people on earth. There is a terrible storm of Lightning, Thundering, and great Hail falling from the sky, and a great earthquake of the earth. Mankind has never seen this before, see [Luke, 21: 26] [Rev. 16: 21.

CHAPTER 12

1. And There appeared a great wonder in heaven; a woman clothed with the sun, and the moon under her feet, and upon her head a crown of twelve stars:

Let's interpret, These words are (S/L) Woman, Clothed, Sun, Moon, Crown of Twelve Stars.

There appeared a <u>Great Wonder</u> in <u>Heaven.</u> John, is in heaven seeing this. <u>A Woman,</u> is (S/L) This is the real church. Clothed with the <u>Sun,</u> is (S/L) the <u>Glory</u> of <u>God,</u> and the <u>Moon,</u> (S/L) this shows us the woman is totally covered with <u>Light, Not Made With Hands</u> and walks in Light not made with Hands. (The Glory of God).

Upon her <u>Head</u> a <u>Crown,</u> of <u>Twelve Stars,</u> These <u>Stars</u> are S/L the <u>Twelve Tribes</u> of <u>Israel</u>, the sons of <u>Jacob</u>. See [John, 4: 22] Salvation is of the <u>Jews.</u> It's plain to see the <u>Real Church</u>, was founded in <u>Heaven.</u> This is God's, plan from the beginning of Adam.

We also find the Real Church being founded on <u>Earth</u> by <u>Jesus,</u> and the <u>Twelve</u> <u>Apostles</u> see [Mat. 16: 17. 18]. Upon this rock I will build my church This <u>Rock</u> is <u>God.</u>

John, is looking at the Real Church, he helped <u>Establish</u> here on <u>Earth</u> the <u>Faith Covenant</u>. We now understand God's, plan in heaven before he, and Jesus, made <u>Adam.</u>

Jesus, established God's, plan on earth, with the <u>Twelve Apostles</u> proof [Mat. 16: 17,18].

John, saw Jesus, clothed with the same <u>Glory,</u> the <u>Woman,</u> was clothed with the <u>Glory</u> of <u>God</u> see [Mat. 17: 2]. His face <u>Shine</u> as the <u>Sun,</u> His raiment <u>White</u> as <u>Light.</u>

We can see the woman clothed with the sun, and the moon

under her feet. The woman is between the sun and the moon; this is the <u>Earth</u> with people on it. The <u>Crown of Twelve Stars</u> is (S/L) the <u>Twelve Tribes,</u> of <u>Israel.</u> Where the Real Church came from here on earth.

Look at this, [Rev. 21: 10, 11, 12, 14] This <u>Woman the Real Church</u> is the <u>HOLY CITY NEW JERUSALEM.</u> The <u>Twelve Gates</u> of <u>Pearls,</u> are the <u>Twelve Tribes of</u> Israel.

There are twelve angels at the gates and names written thereon which are the names of the <u>Twelve Tribes</u> of the <u>Children</u> of <u>Israel.</u> [Ezek. 48: 31 thru-34] shows this also on earth.

The <u>Twelve Foundations,</u> of <u>Precious Stones,</u> And in them the names of the <u>Twelve Apostles,</u> of the <u>Lamb. (Jesus)</u>

All the apostles, and the Lamb (Jesus) came from the Crown of Twelve Stars on the head of the woman; the twelve tribes of Israel, The Real Church [John, 4: 22].

Jesus, is the <u>Head</u> of the Church, and the Church is his <u>Body</u> [Eph. 1: 22, 23].

2. And she being with child cried, Travailing in birth, and pained to be delivered.

Let's interpret, This is the <u>Real Flesh Church.</u> of verse (1). And she being <u>With Child Cried</u> "Prayed" <u>Travailing</u> in <u>Birth,</u> is work especially of a painful nature, and pained, this is mental distress.

This took place in the land of <u>Egypt.</u> By this family, Amram, and Jochebed, the parents of Moses, of the tribe of Levi. [Ex. 2: 1-thru-10]. They were in bondage, slavery.

To be <u>Delivered,</u> God, chose this man <u>Moses.</u> A man well Educated in the household of Pharaoh King of Egypt. See [Ex. 3: 7, 8, 9, 10, 23, 24].

The entire nation of <u>Israel</u> brought forth <u>Jesus,</u> out of the land of Egypt. And <u>Moses,</u> prophesied of Jesus, see [Deut. 18: 15, 18], and God, answered see [Gal. 4: 4].

We have proof how God's, son came into this world made of a

woman. [Mat. 2: 1-thru-15] In <u>Bethlehem</u> of <u>Judaea;</u> thus it is written by the Prophet. Please read carefully. [Luke, 1: 26-thru-56], and [Luke 2: 1-thru-21]. These scriptures tell in detail how God, sent his Son, <u>Jesus,</u> to the children of <u>Israel</u> they had been praying for so long.

Here is what they were praying for. Will thou at this time restore the <u>Kingdom of Israel.</u> Verse (2) is, the nation Israel, verse (5) is the virgin Mary, and Jesus.

3. And there appeared another wonder in heaven; and behold a great red dragon, having seven heads and ten horns, and seven crowns upon his heads.

Let's interpret, There appeared another <u>Wonder</u> in <u>Heaven,</u> John, is in heaven seeing this. Behold a <u>Great Red Dragon</u> this is (S/L). This is the Archangel, <u>Lucifer,</u> see [Is. 14: 10-thru-19]. The <u>Angel</u> [Rev. 1: 1] is showing John, the evil kingdom that will take place on earth, in the future.

The <u>Seven Heads,</u> are (S/L). They are the <u>Seven Wealthiest Nations</u> on <u>Earth</u> see [Mat. 4: 8,9] [Luke, 4: 5, 6, 7]. Today they are called <u>Group Seven.</u> this is present time.

The <u>Ten Horns</u> are (S/L) <u>Ten Kings</u> see [Rev. 17: 12]. They are <u>Allies</u> to the <u>Seven Heads</u> see [Rev. 17: 13]. <u>Horn,</u> is a <u>Symbol</u> of <u>Power,</u> by <u>Force.</u> The Seven Crowns upon his Heads. <u>Crown</u> represents <u>Power,</u> and <u>Authority</u> of these Seven Wealthy Nations. We will see more of this evil kingdom [Rev. 13: 1-thru-8] [Rev. 13: 16, 17, 18].

This will take place on earth. In the <u>Near Future,</u> very near.

4. And his tail drew the third part of the stars of heaven, and did cast them to the earth: and the dragon stood before the woman which was ready to be delivered, for to devour her child as soon as it was born.

Let's interpret, And his tail, (S/L) Tale a Lie, [Gen. 3: 1,4, 13, 15] Here is the second lie. [Gen. 4: 9] <u>Cain.</u> Satan, is a Liar, and the

Father of it [John, 8: 44] There has to be an offspring before the title (Father) is given here is the offspring of Satan, Cain.

[1st. John, 3: 12] Satan was a Murderer from the beginning see [Gen. 4: 8, 9] Cain.

Drew the third part of the stars of heaven, is (S/L) the Father, Word, Holy Ghost The third part of the stars of heaven is (Jesus), see [1st John, 5: 7] Father, Word, Holy Ghost; This can be expressed also this way Father, Son, Holy Ghost. [Mat. 28: 19].

What brought Jesus, to this earth is the (Tale) (S/L) Lie the Serpent, the old Devil, told Eve, in the Garden of Eden. [Gen. 3: 1, 4, 5 13] Jesus, came to this world to Destroy, the Works of the Devil [1st John, 3:8] [Mat. 11; 12] And from the days of John the Baptist until now the kingdom of heaven suffered violence, and the violent take it by force. Jesus, destroyed the works of the Devil.

The dragon stood before the woman which was ready to be delivered, to devour her child as soon as it was born. Here is the dragon, in this man Herod, the King, see [Mat. 2: 3,5, 8,13, 16]. To devour her child as soon as it was born. [Mat. 2: 8, 13].

This is the Virgin Mary, with Jesus, the Son, of God, see [Mat. 1: 20-thru-25].

[Luke, 2; 6, 7]. [Rev. 5: 5] Jesus, is the Lion, of the Tribe, of Judah one of the Stars in the Crown of Twelve Stars upon the Head of the Woman. Twelve Stars, Twelve Tribes.

Jesus, was born of the real Church into the Church, proof [John, 10: 1, 2, 3, 4] [Gal, 4: 4].

5. And she brought forth a man child, who was to rule all nations with a rod of iron: and her child was caught up unto God, and to is throne.

Let's interpret, And she brought forth a man child. She, is the Virgin Mary, see [Luke, 1: 26, 27, 30, 31] The man child, is Jesus, [Luke, 1: 31]. Who is to rule all nations with a rod of iron. This is on "Earth" there are no rule of nations in Heaven. Jesus. Is Ruling today from Heaven all nations on earth. Because he has all Power in Heaven, and in Earth see [Mat. 28: 18].

The Rod of Iron, is (S/L) POWER straight, and strong it doesn't change, Jesus Christ, doesn't change either. The same yesterday, and to day, and for ever more, [Heb. 13: 8].

And her child was caught up unto God, and to his throne. This took place here

[Acts, 1: 9, 10, 11] Jesus, was Thirty Three Years, and Six Months Old at this time. The age of Jesus, come from these Scriptures, [Luke, 3: 23] and Jesus, himself began to be about Thirty Years of Age. [Mat. 4: 17] Jesus, begin to Preach.

[Dan. 9: 27] This is Prophesy of Jesus. And he shall confirm the covenant with many for one Week. A Prophetic Week, is (Seven Years) In the Midst of the week; This is Three and a Half Years. We put these Three and a Half Years, with the Thirty Years in [Luke, 3: 23]. We come up with this; Thirty Three, and a Half Years, of Age. At the time he Finished the Work God, gave him to do [John, 17: 4] And was taken up into Heaven.

[Acts, 1: 9, 10, 11]. Heaven is God's, Throne [Is. 66: 1].

6. And the woman fled into the wilderness, where she had a place prepared of God, that they should feed her there a thousand two hundred and threescore days.

Let's interpret. The woman is (S/L) the church Jesus, and his apostles, built while Jesus, was on earth the Faith Covenant [Mat. 16; 18] also [Heb. 10: 7, 8, 9, 10].

And the woman fled into the wilderness, this is the world of sin. Jesus, spoke of this flight while he was on earth, The Abomination of Desolation, spoken of by Daniel, the prophet see [Mat. 24: 15-thru-25].

Where she had a place prepared of God. This information came from here [Rev. 11: 3]. These two witnesses preached this world wide to the church the (Woman)

Interpretation of The Book of Revelation

We can see the woman (Church), was told where to go and how to get there, and what to expect when she got there.

Here is the expectation; that they should feed her there; The pronoun they, is <u>Moses,</u> and <u>Elijah,</u> two witnesses. The Adverb there, is the <u>Place.</u> prepared of God, see [Rev. 20: 9] the camp of the saints. That they should feed her there a thousand, two hundred, and three score days. This is the same span of time as [Rev. 11: 3] the two witnesses prophesy (1,260) this is the future.

God, and Moses, fed the children of Israel, in the <u>Wilderness</u> for <u>Forty Years.</u>

Now Jesus, <u>Moses,</u> and <u>Elijah,</u> are going to feed the (Woman) the Church in the <u>Wilderness</u> for <u>Three,</u> and a <u>Half Year.</u> He that hath an ear let him hear what the Spirit, saith to the churches. We must pay attention to what we hear.

7. And there was war in heaven: Michael and his angels fought against the dragon; and the dragon fought and his angels,

Let's interpret, there was war in heaven. What caused this war, in heaven?

It started in the garden of <u>Eden,</u> <u>With</u> a <u>Lie.</u> [Gen. 3: 1-thru-15] Lucifer, an archangel of heaven, got in the mind of the (Serpent), which was (Subtil-Sly, and Crafty) and beguild, (Deceived) <u>Eve,</u> he told <u>Eve,</u> a lie and she believed it this is the (Fruit) <u>Eve Ate.</u> When Lucifer, saw he accomplished what he came to the Garden of Eden for. He went back to heaven. To establish his kingdom, see [Is. 14: 12, 13, 14, 15]. This caused the <u>War</u> in heaven.

Lucifer, [Rev. 20: 2] The (Dragon) (Old Serpent) (The Devil) and (Satan). Knew <u>Eve,</u> could reproduce the Image of God, (MAN), From the (Serpent) to <u>Eve,</u> came forth (Cain) see [Gen. 4: 1, 2] Cain, is of the (Serpent), the devil see [1st. John, 3: 12] [Gen. 4: 8, 9] Abel. Is of Adam, proof see [Gen. 4: 4] [Mat. 23: 35].

Cain is the first man to lie to God, because there is no truth in him. [Gen. 4: 9] Judas Iscariot, [John 6: 70, 71] is of the <u>Lineage</u> of <u>Cain,</u> so are these people [John, 8: 44].

Michael, and his <u>Angels</u> fought against the dragon, and the dragon fought and his angels. These are two <u>Arch Angels,</u> and their <u>Armies </u>of <u>Angels,</u> at <u>War, </u>in <u>Heaven.</u>

If you will have it this is the <u>Good, </u>and <u>Evil</u> Spirits at war in heaven. Dragon is (S/L) Lucifer. A perfect understanding of this is here [Is. 14: 12-thru-15].

Without the Holy Spirit, guiding us no one would know what started this war in Heaven. Which happen thousands, of years ago. (VERSE SEVEN IS FULFILLED).

8. And prevailed not; neither was their place found any more in heaven.

Let's interpret, And prevailed not. This means the Great Red Dragon, and his angels <u>Lost</u> the <u>War</u> In <u>Heaven.</u> (Defeated). Neither was their place, found any more in heaven. The word <u>Place</u> is a <u>Position.</u>

9. And the great dragon was cast out, that old serpent, called the Devil, and Satan, which deceiveth the whole world: he was cast out into the earth, and his angels were cast out with him.

Let's interpret, The Great Dragon, <u>O Lucifer</u> was cast out see [Is. 14: 12] also [Rev. 20: 1, 2, 3]. Deceiveth the whole world, see [Rev. 20: 7, 8, 9, 10] also [Job, 1: 6, 7]. This <u>Deception</u> started in the <u>Garden </u>of <u>Eden,</u> with <u>Eve.</u> [Gen. 3: 4, 13].

Cast out into the earth, and his angels cast out with him. The first thing Satan, did when he saw he was cast down to the earth. He found <u>Cain,</u> Look what he did, <u>Slew Abel</u>

[Gen. 4: 8] [1st. John, 3: 12]. Satan, knew <u>Abel,</u> was the kingdom of God. "Righteous"

His angels cast out with him, these angels are <u>Demonic Spirits.</u>

They will get into any living thing (Man, or Beast) see [Mark, 5: 11, 12, 13] proof.

The place for The Devil, and his angels, are here. [Mat. 25: 41] [2d. Peter, 2: 4] [Rev. 20: 10] [Is. 14: 15] The pits of (Hell).

10. And I heard a loud voice saying in heaven, Now is come salvation, and strength, and the kingdom of our God, and the power of his Christ: for the accuser of our brethren is cast down, which accused them before our God day and night.

Let's interpret, And I heard a loud voice in heaven, this indicates John, is in heaven, and the voice is of many people. These words Salvation, and Brethren shows us that.

Nothing needs salvation, or have a brother, but man (The Image of God). From these words; Now is come salvation, strength, and the kingdom our God, and the power of his Christ. We can see a Stress Factor, and Relief after the War in Heaven. The word Come, is the Key, to understand this verse see [Rev. 11: 17] plain isn't it?

For the accuser of our brethren is cast down, which accused them before our God, (Day and Night) this is continual there are no day or night in heaven. We see relief, and safety after the war in heaven.

The Arch Angel Michael, and His Angels, saved the Kingdom, of God, by The Great Power of Jesus, given to them.

11. And they overcame him by the blood of the Lamb, and by the word of their testimony; and they loved not their lives unto the death.

Let's interpret, And they overcame (Him) is the dragon. By the blood of the Lamb. (S/L) Jesus. The blood of Jesus, flowed all the way back to (Adam), and all the way to the end of time here on earth. This is the Water of Life, and it is free; see [Rev. 22: 17].

And by the word of their testimony. This is Faith [1st. John, 5: 4, 5] also [Mat. 10: 32, 33] Whosoever therefore shall confess me before men, him will I confess also before my <u>Father</u> which is in <u>Heaven</u>.

And loved not their lives unto death. Here are a few we know of. Deacon Stephen, [Acts, 6:5] [Acts, 7: 58, 59, 60] Apostle James, [Acts, 12:2] John the Baptist, [Mat. 14: 3, 10]. There are many all through the Bible.

See [Dan. 3: 15, 16, 17, 18, 25, 26] <u>Shadrach, Meshach, Abednego.</u> We know where these <u>Souls,</u> are see [Rev. 6: 9, 10, 11.

12. Therefore rejoice, ye heavens, and ye that dwell in them. Woe to the inhabiters of the earth and of the sea! For the devil is come down unto you, having great wrath, because he hath but a short time.

Let's interpret, Rejoice ye heavens, is plural. This is the <u>Third Heaven,</u> where God's, Throne is [2nd Cor. 12: 2, 4] <u>Second Heaven</u> is <u>Paradise</u>. <u>First Heaven</u> is us.

And ye that dwell in them. Look at this man <u>Enoch</u> [Gen. 5: 24] [Heb. 11: 5] This was a long time ago. Righteous <u>Abel</u> was before, Enoch, [Gen, 4: 4] [Heb. 11: 4]. There are people Redeemed, from the earth in their <u>Glorified Flesh Body</u> in heaven. Elijah, Moses, the Hundred Forty Four Thousand, See [Rev. 7: 4] and [Rev. 14: 1]

We are looking at <u>Generations,</u> and <u>Generations</u> of long spans of time. All the way back to <u>Righteous Abel</u>. [Gen. 4: 4] [Heb. 11: 4].

Woe to the inhabiters of the earth, and of the sea. These are people that have not the Seal of God, in their foreheads, [Rev. 9: 4, 11]. [Rev. 13: 8] Woe is great suffering, and trouble.

For the Devil is come down unto you having great wrath; (Wrath) is <u>Violent Anger.</u> The first record we have of Satan, being cast out of heaven is in <u>Cain,</u> [Gen. 4: 8]

Cain, slew Abel, the devil knew Abel was the kingdom of God. Here is Cain, also [1st. John, 3: 12]. Satan, accused Job, before God see [Job. 1: 6, 7, 8, 9, 10, 11]. Consider how Job, suffered because of Satan see [Job, 2: 7, 8, 13].

Because he knoweth that he hath but a short time. This time span is a Time, and Times, and Half a Time (3 ½ years) see verse (14).

13. And when the dragon saw that he was cast unto the earth, he persecuted the woman which brought forth the man child.

Let's interpret, When the dragon saw he was cast unto the earth; he Persecuted the Woman. This woman is (S/L) the real Church, Jesus, built [Mat. 16: 18]. We are looking at a World Wide Persecution. It started here. Peter, and John, [Acts, 4: 1, 2, 3, 18] James, and Peter, [Acts, 12: 1-thru-11] Paul, and Silas, [Acts, 16: 23, 24]. The devil Tempted, Jesus, also [Luke, 4: 1, 2, 3]. Jesus, is the man child the woman, Virgin Mary brought forth Jesus was Born into the Church by the Virgin Mary. Proof [John, 10: 1, 2, 3, 4, 5]

Satan, knew if he destroyed the Leaders of the Church, the church would have no guidance. Satan, is doing the same thing today with the Church world wide. It will get worse see [Rev. 2: 10]. We are looking at the future but Jesus, has a plan [Rev. 20: 9, 10]

Plain, and simple isn't it?

14. And to the woman were given two wings of a great eagle, that she might fly into the wilderness, into her place, where she is nourished for a time, and times, and half a time, from the face of the serpent.

Let's interpret, And to the woman were given two wings of a great eagle. This is (S/L) The Woman is the Real Church. The Two Wings are (S/L) Moses, and Elijah. The Great Eagle is (S/L) Jesus see [Rev. 11: 3].

That she might fly this word (Fly) is (Fled) verse (6) show us that. Jesus, used the word (Flee) [Mat. 24: 15, 16] into the wilderness, this is a world of sin into her place. This is the Camp of the Saints [Rev. 20: 9] guided by the, Prophesy, or (Preaching) of the two witnesses Moses, and Elijah, [Rev. 11: 3]. Where she is nourished for a Time, and Times, and half a Time this is (3 ½ years) From the face of the (Serpent). The Serpent, Devil, Satan, and the Dragon, the deceiver are all one see verse (9) plain isn't it?

Notice this! God, and Moses, Fed the children of Israel, for Forty Years in the Wilderness. Now Jesus, and the two witnesses, Moses, and Elijah, will feed the Church for (3 ½. Years). The Church is Safe, Thank God, and Jesus.

15. And the serpent cast out of his mouth water as a flood after the woman, that he might cause her to be carried away of the flood.

Let's interpret, The serpent cast out of his mouth water as a flood this is (S/L) Words, of false doctrine spoken through his followers. This is called a flood because it covers the entire earth.

The serpent does not know where the Woman, the real Church is. Remember Her Place in the Wilderness Hid from the face of the (Serpent).

That he might cause her to be carried away of the flood. This is impossible see [John, 10: 1, 2, 3, 4, 5] [Mat. 24: 24] very plain. This is coming to us in the near future.

The (Serpent), (Devil) (Dragon) (Satan). All four of these names are used in this (Chapter Twelve) Don't get confused they are all one an Evil Spirit.

16. And the earth helped the woman, and the earth open her mouth, and swallowed up the flood the dragon cast out of his mouth.

Let's interpret, And the earth, helped the woman, and open her mouth, and swallowed up the flood the dragon cast out of his mouth. Let's Analyze this.

The earth is (S/L) people, helped the Woman, the real Church, and the earth open her mouth is (S/L) people, and swallowed up the flood. This is people that worship the dragon see [Rev. 13: 4].

Satan, can not tell the truth, all of his words are false there is no truth in him see [John, 8: 44] very plain isn't it?

17. And the dragon was wroth with the woman, and went to make war with the remnant of her seed, which keep the commandments of God, and have the testimony of Jesus Christ.

Let's interpret, And the dragon was wroth "Angry" with the woman, the (Church). And went to make war with the remnant of her seed. This is the future, and it is coming to us the children of God, and Jesus, today.

Which keep the commandments of God, and have the testimony of Jesus Christ. [Rev. 13: 7, 10, 15] Here is the patience and the faith of the saints.

We have covered Thousands, and Thousands, of Years of (Time), and Generation, after Generation, of people from Adam.

WE MUST BE PREPARED FOR WHAT
WE WILL FACE IN THE FUTURE
THIS IS WHY WE STUDY.

CHAPTER 13

WE NEED TO SORT OUT THESE BEAST.
THERE ARE ONLY TWO (S/L) OF MAN.
AND ONE EVIL SPIRIT THE DRAGON.

The beast in verse one, is not a <u>Man,</u> (S/L) the <u>Great Red Dragon,</u> Having Seven Heads, and Ten Horns, and Ten Crowns on his Horns, upon his Heads the name of Blasphemy (SIN) this is on earth. Because (SIN) cannot be in <u>Heaven.</u> The great red dragon was cast out of heaven [Rev. 12: 9].

This is the same great red dragon John, saw in heaven, without blasphemy on his heads. They had crowns see [Rev. 12: 3, 7, 8, 9]. He is an Evil Spirit, mankind can't see the dragon.

The old dragon, the serpent, and the devil, and Satan. Can get in the mind of man see [John, 13: 26, 27] also [Luke, 22: 3] [1st. Peter, 5: 8] Your adversary the <u>Devil,</u> as a roaring lion walks about <u>Seeking</u> whom he may <u>Devour.</u> Satan, works through mankind to get his <u>Evil Work Done.</u>

We find this beast here also [Rev. 17: 3] The Seven Heads, and Ten Horns, shows us the dragon, and the beast are one. Verse (2), we find the (Dragon) verse (3), is the Dragon, Verse four we see people worshipped the dragon, Satan.. The Sea, in verse one, is (S/L) people [Rev. 17: 15] shows us that. See [Is. 14: 12-thru-15] his name is <u>Lucifer!!</u>

The Beast in verse One, and Two, seem
to have Appeared Simultaneous.

"First Man Beast"

In verse Two this beast is (S/L) a man. He is a descendant, of the Kings, of the old <u>Babylon Empire,</u> of <u>King Nebuchadnezzar.</u> See [Dan. 8: 23, 24, (25), 26] notice verse (25) He shall stand up against the Prince of princes. But he shall be broken without hand, we find this here [Rev. 19: 19, 20]. Now we know we have the <u>Right Beast</u> at the <u>Right time,</u> and the <u>Right Place</u>. From [Dan. 8: 25] to [Rev. 19: 19, 20]. This is the battle of Armageddon. See [Rev. 16: 12-thru-16] The Prophecy of Daniel, is fulfilled here.

This beast is a (Man King) of <u>Fierce Countenance.</u> Understanding Dark Sentence this is Evil dealing in Government Business. See [Dan. 8: 23] this man has a flesh body, but no blood in it. It has the <u>Evil Spirit,</u> of the <u>Dragon in it.</u> Proof see verse (2) The Dragon Gave Him His Power, Seat, and Great Authority. The People of the earth can see this <u>Man Beast King.</u> He can travel over the entire earth at <u>Lightning Speed.</u> This is his <u>Ensign</u> or <u>Flag,</u> a <u>Leopard,</u> <u>Feet</u> of a <u>Bear, Mouth</u> of a <u>Lion.</u>

Let's analyze these The <u>Leopard</u> With his spots, Indicate the earth with all the nations upon it. <u>Feet</u> of a <u>Bear,</u> Indicate Power over the four corners of the earth . <u>East, West, North, South.</u> <u>Mouth</u> of a <u>Lion.</u> Depicts a One World Ruler.

This Beast King will rule the world from his <u>Headquarters</u> in <u>New Babylon</u> from the same location the Ancient Babylon Empire was located. Of South Western Asia. In the Lower Valley of the Tigris, and the Euphrates Rivers. Which are now (Iraq, and Iran). We see the Dragon, gave him his Power, Seat, and Great Authority. This is a one world ruler.

"Second Man Beast"

Verse Eleven, This beast coming up out of the earth, he had <u>Two Horns</u> like a <u>Lamb,</u> This is his Ensign, or Flag, and spake as a Dragon. This is (S/L) of a Man called Judas Iscariot he is a devil see [John, 6: 70, 71] he is also this beast [Rev. 11: 7]

He is the False Prophet [Rev. 19: 20]. He served in both Dimensions of Power. Being of the number of the twelve [Luke, 22: 3] and [John, 13: 26, 27].

The Two Horns like a Lamb, depicts the False Christ, also the False Prophet. [Mat. 24: 24]. Jesus, told us this while he was on earth with us.

Spake as a Dragon, This is each time he speaks it is A Lie. There is no truth in him see [John, 8: 44] betrayal see [Luke, 22: 3] [John, 13: 26, 27] This is the other side of power.

Judas Iscariot, is of the lineage of Cain, who was of that wicked one see [1st. John, 3:12]. He had a flesh body as man, and blood kept him alive. When he came up out of the earth in verse (11). His body is kept alive by the Evil Spirit of the Dragon. He also has the power to travel at the Speed of Lightning, across the earth. Anytime he wants to, he is a Deceiver. Now We Know

1. And I stood upon the sand of the sea, and saw a beast rise up out of the sea, having seven heads and ten horns, and upon his horns ten crowns, and upon his heads the name of blasphemy.

Let's interpret, There are a lot of (S/L) Symbolic Language, In this Chapter. The sea is (S/L) people, see [Rev. 17: 1, 15] The Beast, is (S/L) the Great Red Dragon, That John, saw in Heaven, having Seven Heads, and Ten Horns. [Rev. 12: 3, 7, 8, 9]. The Seven Heads, (S/L) are the Seven Wealthiest Nations on earth. When the devil tempted Jesus, see [Luke, [4: 5, 6] He had these seven kingdoms then.

The ten horns (S/L) are Ten Kings these are allied nations to the Seven Heads. [Rev. 17: 12, 13] This is a One World Army; and a One World Trade Center, with Headquarters in the city of New Babylon. Where the Ancient Babylon Empire used to be.

The Great Red Dragon, with Seven Heads, and Ten Horns, are rebuilding the Old Ancient Babylon Empire. Famous for Great

Wealth, and Luxury, and Wickedness. Located in South Western Asia, in the lower valley of the Tigris, and Euphrates Rivers.

Today this country is called Iraq, and Iran. The Tigris, and Euphrates rivers are there.

The Crowns that were on the Heads, [Rev. 12: 3] are now on the Horns.

Upon his heads the name of Blasphemy; To get a perfect picture of this Beast The (Dragon) see [Rev. 17: 2, 3, 4, 5, 6] Blasphemy is Cursing God, also Great Disrespect Shown to God.

Verse One is all about the Great Red Dragon. Which can't be seen, because he is a evil Spirit, and has no flesh body. Therefore an Image has to be made of him.

The dragon is building the New Babylon Empire, from the seven heads the "Wealthiest Nations" on earth, and the ten horns, which are ten kings [Rev. 17: 12].

2. And the beast which I saw was like unto a leopard, and his feet were as the feet of a bear, and his mouth as the mouth of a lion: and the dragon gave him his power, and his seat, and great authority.

Let's interpret, We need to understand something here. The Beast in verse (1) is (S/L) the Dragon, In Verse Two, the Beast is (S/L) a man King, like a Leopard, Feet of a Bear, Mouth of a Lion. This is his Ensign, or Flag. This Beast is a Man King, and the last of the Old Babylon Empire see [Dan. 7: 23,28]. His Body movement is by the Evil Spirit of the Dragon, as Judas Iscariot (Second Beast). This is why Jesus, cast both the Beast, and the False Prophet, alive into a Lake of Fire burning with Brimstone [Rev. 19: 20]

The old Babylon Empire was Destroyed by a Stone cut out without hands. The Stone that smote the image became a Great Mountain, and filled the whole earth. This is Jesus, [Acts, 4: 11, 12]. See [Dan. 2: 31-thru-45] see also [Dan. 8: 23, 24, 25,26,]

Daniel, prophesied of this King in his day. That will rule the whole earth from the new restored Babylon Empire see [Rev. 17: 18] [Rev. 18: 1, 2, 3].

This indicating the Dragon, in verse (1), and the Beast, in verse (2), appeared Simultaneous.

And the dragon gave him his power, and his seat, and great authority. Let's analyze, the Dragon, gave him his power. This is an (Evil Spirit) and very powerful. Now in the mind of this Beast King. This is why his Fierce Countenance, and understanding of Dark Sentences, Evil Thoughts; are in him see [Dan. 8: 23, 24, 25].

His Seat, this is a city where Rules, and Laws are made this is (Babylon) the Capitol of the, World, and Great Authority, this is the power to command and by force. A one World Army. (With the Seven Heads, and Ten Horns)

We see the Dragon, has got his Kingdom set up, with a Beast King to Rule it. This King comes from here [Dan. 8: 23, 24, 25, 26]. Notice verse (23) and verse (25).   This is the Fourth Beast, and the Fourth Kingdom [Dan. 7: 23, 25] and the last. [Dan. Ch. 7, and 8] are the same, Beast, and King, as [Rev. 13: 2-thru-8]. [Dan. 8: 25] This beast king, is here [Rev. 13: 7]. He will stand up against the Prince of princes, but shall be broken without hand by Jesus, [Rev. 19: 19, 20] cast alive in to a lake of fire.

[Dan. 8: 15, 16, 17] this is Gabriel, the angel that stands before God, doing the talking. Verse (17), are the words of Gabriel, Understand O, son of man: for at the time of the End shall be the Vision. We can see we are looking at the future, and the end.

3.   And I saw one of his heads as it were wounded to death; and his deadly wound was healed: and all the world wondered after the beast.

Lets interpret, This is a continuation; of verse one the Dragon. One of his heads as it were wounded to death. This is the Roman Empire, Which ruled the world when Jesus, was on earth, Setting up his Kingdom see [Luke, 22: 29, 30, 31] also [Dan. 2: 44].

Here is where the head got it's wound from, <u>GOD.</u> [Gen. 12: 3] I will bless them that bless thee, and curse them that curseth thee. Every Empire on earth <u>Got Cursed</u> by [Gen. 12: 3]. Consider <u>Egypt,</u> and <u>Babylon,</u> Ancient Kingdoms God, destroyed them.

The Roman Empire was never conquered. It just got wounded for a span of time. There are many people in Italy today that are the <u>Children</u> of <u>God,</u> and <u>Jesus.</u>

And his deadly wound was healed. It got healed from here The Babylon Empire.

[Rev. 17: 18] [18: 3, 9] The Babylon Empire, has Luxury, and Wealth, World Wide. This head was healed by <u>Financial Assistance.</u> (From the Beast King) He is in Charge now.

All the world wondered after the beast, they have never seen all these riches, and good life before. [Dan. 8: 25] Prophesied of this. The people of the world Wondered after the beast. (Not The Christian People) they know the voice of the good Shepherd.

Here is the beast they wondered after. [Dan. 8: 23, 24, 25, 26]. He is a <u>KING</u> a (Man) from the Old Babylon Empire. He made the world (Rich) through his policy, and caused craft to prosper. <u>Remember we are looking back across Several Thousand Years of Time</u> and <u>Prophecy,</u> Revelation, is prophecy [Rev. 1: 3]. We are looking at the future.

4. And they worshipped the dragon which gave power unto the beast: and they worshipped the beast, saying, Who is like unto the beast? who is able to make war with him?

Let's interpret, And they worshipped the Dragon which is (Invisible) he is an <u>Evil Spirit.</u> The Old Serpent, the Devil. These people of the earth that worship the dragon are these [John, 8: 44] also [Rev. 12: 15, 16, 17]. (They open their mouth and swallowed up the flood). This is the same as worship. They are the Lineage of Cain, [1st. John, 3: 12]

The people knew about the dragon from the mouth of the <u>Beast</u>

King, from his seat (Throne) They can see The Beast King, and hear him. And they worshipped the beast saying, Who is like unto the beast? Who is able to make war with him? Notice the words of worship from the people of the earth. <u>Who is like unto the beast?</u> The people are looking at the Wealth, Luxury, and Riches, of this Beast King he controls all of it.

All this Wealth came from the <u>Seven Heads,</u> which are the Seven Wealthiest Nations on Earth. Consider the (G-Seven).

<u>Who is able to make war with him?</u> He has control of all the armies of the entire earth through his <u>Wealth.</u> From his Headquarters in <u>Babylon</u> that <u>Great City.</u> Notice the Seven Heads are Kings, of these wealthy Nations. The Ten Horns are King also. This makes a mighty army that rules the earth by Force.

These Kings of the earth and their armies come to an end it starts here [Rev. 16: 12-thru-16] The Battle of Armageddon, and ended here [Rev. 19: 19, 20]. This is who can make war with him <u>(JESUS).</u>

5. And there was given unto him a mouth speaking great things and blasphemies and power was given unto him to continue forty and two months.

Let's interpret, And there was given unto him a <u>Mouth, Speaking Great Things,</u> and <u>Blasphemies.</u> The word (Given) is permission to <u>Speak.</u> The beast already has the mouth, of a Lion To speak great things this is boasting, bragging, and pride. This mouth given to him also is the beast in verse (11). He is the false Prophet (Judas Iscariot).

<u>Blasphemies</u> is sin which show <u>Great Disrespect</u> to <u>God.</u> His Mouth of a Lion, is Loud, and Strong. Daniel, prophesied of this <u>Beast King</u> see [Dan. 7: 25]. The span of time is written, A Time, and Times, and the Dividing of Time (3 ½ years) all of this fits.

And power was given unto him to continue forty and two months. This is

(3 ½ years) To speak great things, and blaspheme, which is <u>Sin</u>. This is the same span of time in [Rev. 12: 14] Time, and Times, and a Half Time, (3 ½ years)

Only <u>Jesus,</u> has <u>Power</u>, to grant this span of time. [Mat. 28: 18] Jesus, did this to fulfill God's, plan of time. (Remember Time is Limited) It will end.

6. And he open his mouth in blasphemy against God, to blaspheme his name, and his tabernacle, and them that dwell in heaven.

Let's interpret, And he open his mouth in <u>Blasphemy</u> against <u>God.</u> This is Satan, The Old Devil. Speaking through this Beast King. Blasphemy is <u>Sin,</u> cursing God, and shows great disrespect unto God.

To blaspheme his Name, and his Tabernacle. God's, name is <u>JEHOVAH</u>, [Ex. 6: 3] [Ps. 83: 18]. His Tabernacle is (S/L) the Glorified Flesh Body of Jesus, God, and Jesus, are one see [John, 10: 30]. Notice!! Every child of God, and Jesus, our flesh body is a <u>Tabernacle</u>, for God, and Jesus, to live in [2nd. Peter, 1: 13] [2nd. Cor. 5: 1]. Our flesh bodies are also called a <u>Temple</u> see [John, 2: 19, 21] [1st. Cor. 6: 19], Simple.

Blaspheme, them that dwell in heaven. The dragon, that old Serpent, the Devil. Knew there were people that (Dwell in Heaven) proof [Rev. 12: 12].

This Beast King, didn't know anything about heaven, but the Evil Spirit, of the Dragon (Satan) did. Because he got <u>Cast</u> out of <u>Heaven.</u> The Evil Spirit of the dragon got in the mind of this Beast King, and caused him to do this Blasphemy where the people of the earth could see him. This will be a <u>Terrible Time</u> for the children of <u>God.</u>

We know our self there are people in Heaven. Proof see [Rev. 4: 4] [Rev. 7: 4] [Rev. 5: 3, 4, 5, 6] [Gen. 5: 24] A Great Book could be Written Here.

Notice!! God, is the good Spirit, in the flesh body of Jesus,

[John, 14: 11] The Dragon, is the evil spirit, in the Beast King, Notice the mouth of "Blasphemy" Sin.

7. And it was given unto him to make war with the saints, and to overcome them: and power was given him over all kindreds, and tongues, and nations.

Let's interpret, And it was given unto him to make war with the saints and to overcome them. To <u>Overcome,</u> is to <u>Conquer by Force.</u> Only <u>Jesus,</u> has the <u>Power</u> to grant this <u>War.</u> Jesus, told the <u>Smyrna Church</u> this would happen to them [Rev. 2: 10].

Daniel, saw in a (Dream, and Visions) the same thing in his day while captive in the land of Babylon see [Dan. 7: 21] also [Dan. 12: 8, 9, 10] [Rom. 12: 1] Present your bodies a living sacrifice Holy acceptable unto God. (Here is the <u>Patience</u> and the <u>Faith</u> of the <u>Saints)</u> verse (10).

This is the <u>Fourth Beast,</u> and the <u>Fourth Kingdom</u> see [Dan. 7: 23] and the last see [Dan. 7: 22, 25,26]. "Many shall be purified, and made <u>White,</u> and <u>Tried"</u> [Dan 12: 10].

And power was given him over all kindred, and tongues and nations. This is a <u>One World Power (Government).</u> <u>God,</u> gave King Nebuchadnezzar, this same power over all the earth see [Dan. 2: 37, 38]. We can see (EARTH) has run out of (TIME) [Rev. 10: 6].

8. And all that dwell upon the earth shall worship him, whose names are not written in the book of life of the Lamb slain from the foundation of the world.

Let's interpret, We know this is the Beast in verse two. Like a <u>Leopard,</u> <u>Feet</u> As a <u>Bear,</u> <u>Mouth</u> of a <u>Lion.</u> This is a man (Without Blood in his Body) the evil spirit of the dragon keeps him alive.

This is very plain. If anyone have not their name written in the book of <u>Life</u> of the <u>Lamb (Shall Worship)</u> this (Man Beast King).

By this we shall know the (Righteous) from the (Unrighteous). The Book of Life Is <u>Jesus,</u> [Rev. 20: 12].

The <u>Foundation </u>of the <u>World</u> is <u>Adam.</u> Jesus, was slain from this earthly flesh body of blood, and <u>God,</u> raised him from the dead, and gave him a <u>Glorified Flesh Body.</u> Filled with his Holy Spirit Pure and Clean. He is alive forever more [Rev. 1: 18].

There are many Christian People on earth at this time. Yes, some in prison, some will be killed, see [Rev. 6: 11] some of us will be in the <u>Camp</u> of the <u>Saints</u> [Rev. 20: 9].

9. If any man have an ear, let him hear.

Let's interpret, If any man have and ear, let him hear. <u>Hear</u> is to <u>Understand.</u> This <u>Ear,</u> is a <u>Spiritual Ear,</u> see [Mat. 13: 13, 16] also [Rom. 8: 14].

Verse (9), is directed at verse (10) of the two class of people (Unrighteous), and(Righteous).

10. He that leadeth into captivity shall go into captivity: he that killeth with the sword must be killed with the sword. Here is the patience and the faith of the saints.

Let's interpret, He that leadeth into captivity see [Rev. 2: 10], shall go into captivity. This is the <u>First Beast</u> verse (7) shows that. Shall go into captivity. Here is where he goes into captivity see [Rev. 19: 20]. Jesus, cast him alive into a lake of fire burning with brimstone. <u>Vengeance</u> is <u>Mine</u> I will repay saith the <u>Lord</u> [Rom. 12: 19]

He that killeth with the sword, this is the <u>Second Beast</u> verse (11) see also (15). Must be killed with the sword.

This is the <u>Sword</u> he must be killed with see [Is. 49: 2] [Rev. 1: 16], and [Rev. 19: 15, 21] Jesus, cast him alive into a lake of fire burning with brimstone. <u>Vengeance</u> is <u>Mine</u> I will repay saith the <u>Lord.</u>

Here is the Patience and the Faith of the saints see [1st. Peter, 3: 4] [Rom. 12: 1]. This is coming to us the children of God, and Jesus, in the near future.

11. And I beheld another beast coming up out of the earth; and he had two horns like a lamb, and he spake as a dragon.

Let's interpret, This is the Second Beast (S/L) a man. This is the same man that was numbered of the (Twelve) [Luke, 22: 3] [Acts, 1: 16, 17] Judas Iscariot.

John, saw. This one Coming up out of the earth. had two Horns like a Lamb. The horns like a Lamb, is his (Ensign, or Flag) this is Identification for power and authority.

This is the False Christ, and the False Prophet, Jesus, told us this while he was on earth [Mat. 24: 24].

He knew who Judas Iscariot, was, and John wrote about him in his book see [John, 6: 70, 71] a "Devil" [John, 13: 26, 27] "Satan". WE can find Judas Iscariot, several places in the Bible. His body is not flesh, and blood, his body is active by the Evil Spirit, of the Dragon. He looks like a man, see [Mat. 7: 15] plain isn't it?

And he spake as Dragon; Here is why this (Man) beast, spake as a dragon. Our record is here [John, 6: 70, 71]. Jesus, said have I not chosen you twelve, and one of you is a Devil he spake of Judas Iscariot, that betrayed him. Spake as a dragon, is a (LIE) Satan, is a liar the father of it [John, 8: 44]. Judas Iscariot, is of the Lineage of Cain, [1st. John, 3: 12]. Who was of that wicked one, that old Serpent, and the Devil, Satan. These Scriptures are Proof of verse Eleven. [John, 8: 44] [John, 17: 12] [2nd Thes. 2: 3]. Perdition is Eternal Damnation, (Hell). Hell was made for the Devil, and his Angels [Mat. 25: 41]. Now we know who this beast is.

[Rev. 11: 7] The Beast, that ascendeth out of the Bottomless Pit is (S/L) a man named Judas Iscariot. (It is the same beast John, saw coming up out of the earth).

These two beast are (S/L) a man, (The Image of God). Beware

of False Prophets, which come to you in Sheep's clothing, But inwardly they are Ravening Wolves. [Mat. 7: 15]. Do not be confused there are only two man beast The First, in verse (2), and the Second in verse (11) are people, that look like you, and I But Are Not.

Their bodies are kept alive by the Evil Spirit of the Dragon. This is why Jesus, cast both of them Alive into a Lake of Fire Burning with Brimstone see [Rev. 19: 20].

12. And he exerciseth all the power of the first beast before him, and causeth the earth and them which dwell therein to worship the first beast, whose deadly wound was healed.

Let's interpret, (We are looking at Judas Iscariot) And he exerciseth all the power of the first beast before him. Here is the power of the First Beast. The dragon gave him his Power, Seat, and Great Authority this is over all the earth see verse (7).

And he causeth the earth and them which dwell therein to worship the first beast.

This is an Image of the (Old Dragon Satan) because he is (Invisible). Worship his image here is the results see [Rev. 14: 9, 10] Very Plain Isn't It?

This first Beast is (S/L) the Dragon in verse (1) having seven heads, and ten horns.

Whose deadly wound was healed. This is speaking of the First Beast in verse (1) having seven Heads, and ten Horns, is (S/L) the Dragon, the Old Serpent, Satan, and the Devil. Proof of the dragon called the beast see [Rev. 12: 3] [Rev. 17: 3].

Whose deadly wound was healed, this is one of his heads, the Roman Empire.

13. And he doeth great wonders, so that he maketh fire come down from heaven on earth in the sight of men.

Let's interpret, This whole verse is the works of (Satan) through Judas Iscariot, which is a Devil, the son of perdition (SATAN) see [2nd. Thes. 2: 3, 4, 8, 9]. He does great wonders, and makes fire come down from heaven on earth in the sight of men, this is Deception, by Judas Iscariot.

JESUS, told us False Christs, and False Prophets would arise, and shew Great Signs, and Wonders; in so much that if it were possible, they would deceive the Very Elect [Mat. 24: 24]. Jesus, gave us this also; take heed that no man deceive you [Mat. 24: 4] [Mat. 7: 15]. We are looking at the future. When it comes to us we will know how to defeat (The Beast) Judas Iscariot.

14. And deceiveth them that dwell on the earth by the means of those miracles which he had power to do in the sight of the beast; saying to them that dwell on the earth, that they should make an image to the beast, which had the wound by a sword, and did live

Let's interpret, This verse is continual of verse (13). And deceived them that dwell on the earth by those miracles which he had power to do in the sight of the beast.

This beast is (S/L)the Dragon, with seven heads, and ten horns An Evil Spirit.

Saying to them that dwell on the earth, they should make an image to the beast which had the wound by a sword and did live.

The Key to understand this Deception is make an Image to the Beast. The image is here [Rev. 17: 3, 4, 5] This is the New Babylon Empire; full of names of Blasphemy SIN.

This is the only place in the Bible where we find any thing of an image of the old dragon with seven heads, and ten horns. With a woman sitting upon him arrayed in the wealth of the world. This woman is (S/L) that great city (Babylon) which reigneth over the kings of the earth verse (18). This is why it is stated a One World Government.

15. And he had power to give life unto the image of the beast, that the image of the beast should both speak, and cause that as many as would not worship the image of the beast should be killed.

Let's interpret, He (Judas Iscariot), The Beast, had power to give life unto the image of the beast. This <u>Power,</u> and <u>Life</u> is an <u>Army.</u> Of the seven heads, and then horns, that cover the earth. Proof of this <u>Army</u> is here see [Rev. 19: 19] This Image would be (Similar) to the <u>Shoulder Patch,</u> of the armed Forces, or Police officers, of today.

The Image of the <u>Law Enforcement</u> (Police Officer) Can both speak and he does have <u>LIFE,</u> and <u>Authority,</u> to enforce the laws of the land. The <u>Image Patch</u> on his <u>Shoulder</u> says so. When he speaks he has <u>The Authority</u> to enforce his <u>Words The Law.</u>

This is the same thing as, give life unto the (Image), and speak. This is a world wide army controlled by the, First Man Beast, verse (2) and the Second Man Beast Judas Iscariot, verse (11)

And cause that as many as would not worship the image of the beast should be killed.

This is the <u>Saints</u> of <u>God,</u> They won't worship that image. Judgment has already been passed on those that, Lead the Saints, into Captivity (Prison) and Kill them with the sword, see Verse ten.

This is the same thing that took place in the days of King Nebuchadnezzar. Anyone that didn't worship the image, were cast into a burning fiery furnace (Killed). (Shadrach). (Meshack), (Abednego), and <u>Jesus,</u> Proved King Nebuchadnezzar wrong.

This war the Battle of Armageddon, the beast, and the kings of the earth will be totally destroyed. By Jesus, and his <u>Army</u> [Rev. 19: 14]] see also [Rev. 19: 19,20].

16. And he causeth all, both small and great, rich and poor, free and bond, to receive a mark in their right hand, or in their foreheads:

Let's interpret, And he causeth all, this is classes of people of social rank. Both (Small and Great), (Rich and Poor), (Free and

Bond). To receive a mark in their right hand, or in their foreheads; The word (All) shows us this covers the entire earth

The pronoun He, Is Judas Iscariot, Remember he is a Devil. As we look at this verse, we understand this is by <u>Force</u> all over the entire earth. This force is the army in verse fifteen. We see the people of the earth are being forced into <u>Starvation</u>, or take <u>The Mark</u> of the <u>Beast</u>. The <u>Saints</u> of <u>God,</u> won't starve or go hungry see [Rev. 12: 14] [Rev. 20: 9] Plain Isn't it?

17. And that no man might buy or sell, save he that had the mark, or the name of the beast, or the number of his name.

Let's interpret, The Mark, of the beast is (Sin) the color is <u>Scarlet</u> a <u>Bright Red. Red</u> like <u>Crimson</u> see [Is. 1: 18]. It will be in their right hand or in their foreheads of mankind. The name of the beast is, (Mystery Babylon The Great), The number of his name is (666) The number of a man (Judas Iscariot) <u>The Devil</u> [John 6: 70, 71].

No man can buy of sell without any one of these three. <u>WARNING!!</u> This will last for <u>Forty, Two Months</u> (3 ½ year) see verse (5) then the <u>End of Time</u> [Rev.10:6]. If any man, woman, boy, or girl, receive any one of these three; <u>It Is A Point of No Return.</u> Here is what will happen to you [Rev. 14: 9, 10, 11] [Rev. 19: 20, 21].

The Beast is the Great Red Dragon in [Rev. 12:3]. If you want to know what color the mark is see [Is. 1: 18] see also [Rev. 17: 3]. The <u>Scarlet Coloured Beast,</u> full of names of <u>Blasphemy</u> this is (Sin) the beast is (S/L) of the <u>Great Red Dragon</u> he is Sin Scarlet Coloured is a Bright Red (I can't Stress this Enough).

(I Ask The People of The Entire Earth <u>P-L-E-A-S-E</u>) Do Not Take Either One of These Three or Worship the Beast or his image see [Rev. 14: 9, 10, 11] [Rev. 19: 20, 21].

Here <u>Are The Three</u> (<u>The Mark</u>) (<u>The Name</u>) (<u>The Number</u> of his <u>Name</u>) (<u>666</u>).

18. Here is wisdom. Let him that hath understanding count the number of the beast; for it is the number of a man; and his number is Six hundred three score and six.

Let's interpret, Here is Wisdom, This <u>Wisdom</u>, is given only by God, see [James, 1: 5] Let him that hath Understanding, <u>Count the Number</u> of the beast. This is to Sum up, or Add up all of them. His number is (600) three score (60) and six (6)=666.

Number of a Man, Our record show this man started here. [John, 6: 70, 71] [Luke, 22: 3,4], [John, 13: 26, 27] [Rev. 11: 7] [Rev. 13: 11] Ended here [Rev. 19: 20].

Judas Iscariot.

AND WHOSOEVER LIVETH AND
BELIEVETH IN ME SHALL NEVER DIE
BELIEVETH THOU THIS?
JOHN, 11: 26

ALL OF CHAPTER 13, IS FUTURE.

CHAPTER 14

1. And I looked, and, lo, a Lamb stood on the mount Zion, and with him an hundred forty and four thousand, having his Father's name written in their foreheads.

Let's interpret, John, is looking into heaven, from the Isle of Patmos verse (2) shows us that. The Lamb, (S/L) which is Jesus. Standing on the <u>Mount Zion</u>. This is the real <u>Church Eternal</u> in <u>Heaven,</u> which cannot be removed; abideth forever [Ps. 125: 1]. Which <u>Jesus,</u> is the head of the church see [Eph. 1: 22, 23].

And with him an hundred forty and four thousand. Having his Father's name written in their foreheads. This is the <u>Seal</u> of the <u>Living God,</u> this took place on earth see [Rev. 7: 1, 2, 3, 4]. The hundred forty and four thousand, came from here,

[Mat. 27: 52, 53] after the resurrection of Jesus. This is the <u>First Resurrection</u> [Rev. 20: 5]. Jesus, is the first to be <u>Resurrected</u> from the <u>Dead</u> [Rev. 1: 5] proves this.

2. And I heard a voice from heaven, as the voice of many waters, and as the voice of a great thunder: and I heard the voice of harpers harping with their harps:

Let's interpret, And I heard a voice from heaven, as the voice of many waters. The voice of many <u>Waters</u> is (S/L) <u>People</u> see [Rev. 17: 15] (This is The <u>Sound</u> of <u>Rejoicing).</u> The voice of <u>Jesus,</u> is also referred to as many waters [Rev. 1: 15] [Ezek. 43: 2].

The voice of a great thunder, is the voice of <u>God,</u> [John, 12: 28, 29, 30]. The voice of Harpers, Harping with their Harps. This is the Hundred Forty and Four Thousand playing on their harps. (The word voice is used here instead sound).

All of this verse is <u>Rejoicing</u> over <u>Victory.</u> That God, and Jesus, made (Man) in their own image, and likeness [Gen. 1: 26] lived on earth, died on earth, <u>Resurrected</u> by the <u>Power</u> of <u>God,</u> in a <u>Glorified Flesh Body</u> <u>Undefiled Pure, and Clean;</u> to live forever.

3. And they sung as it were a new song before the throne, and before the four beast, and the elders: and no man could learn that song but the hundred and forty and four thousand, which were redeemed from the earth.

Let's interpret, Let's open this up a little and look at it. In verse (2) the hundred forty and four thousand, are playing on their <u>Harps</u>. Here in verse (3) they are singing. This indicates they are playing and singing with their harps.

Look at the <u>Magnificent Audience</u>, they are playing for. Before the <u>Throne, God,</u> and <u>Jesus,</u> are sitting there, The Four Beast, which are the four sons of <u>Jacob,</u> The <u>Elders,</u> which are the <u>Four,</u> and <u>Twenty Elders,</u> With Crowns of <u>Gold</u> on their <u>Heads.</u>

No man could learn that song but the hundred forty and four thousand. These are the first redeemed from the earth. this is the <u>First Resurrection.</u> This is why no man could learn that song, this shows rejoicing, and victory.

Notice! The harps the hundred forty, and four thousand, are playing. They didn't have them when they were redeemed form the earth. These Harps were already in heaven, they belong to God, and Jesus, see [Rev. 15: 2]. Remember God, and Jesus, are one. [John, 10: 30] see also [Heb. 1: 8] [John, 14: 7-thru-11].

4. These are they which were not defiled with women; for they are virgins. These are they which follow the Lamb whithersoever he goeth. These were redeemed from among men, being the first fruits unto God and the Lamb.

Let's interpret, These are they that were not defiled with women; for they are virgins. We are looking at a <u>Perfect</u> Hundred Forty, and Four Thousand Men, over a <u>Long Span</u> of <u>Time</u> These are the children of Israel.

These are they which follow the Lamb whithersoever he goeth. We are acquainted with a few of them see [Dan. 3: 16, 17, 18, 21, 14, 15, 16] <u>(Shadrach), (Meshach),</u> and <u>(Abednego)</u> Fiery Furnace, Jesus, delivered. [Dan. 6: 16, 20, 21, 22] Den of Lions, Jesus, delivered. These had the faith this scripture comes in view [Rom. 12: 1,2].

These were redeemed from among men. This tells us some of the Hundred Forty Four Thousand were alive, and walking among men that were alive on earth in the Holy City which is <u>Jerusalem,</u> in the land of <u>Israel.</u>

This scripture <u>Proves</u> this see [Mat. 27: 52, 53] This is why the Phrase, <u>Redeemed From Among Men.</u> was used. <u>Marvelous.</u> isn't it? <u>Jesus,</u> also walked, and talked to the living here on earth after he had risen from the dead [John, 20: 15, 17, 21, 23]

At this time Jesus, knew the Hundred Forty Four Thousand, were being Sealed with the Seal of the Living God, in their Foreheads. From every nation on earth see [Rev. 5: 9] this is why he told <u>Mary Magdalene,</u> "Touch Me Not" For I am not yet ascended to my father. When the Hundred forty Four Thousand, were sealed, Jesus, took them to the Heavenly Father <u>God.</u> This explains why the <u>Victorious Celebration</u> that John, heard from heaven verses (2, 3).

Being the first fruits unto God, and the Lamb. This is the First Resurrection [Rev. 20: 5].

5. And in their mouth was found no guile: for they are without fault before the throne of God.

Let's interpret, In their mouth was found no guile "Deceit" perfect men. For they are without fault before the throne of God. This is a continual of verse four the presentation of the Hundred Forty, and Four Thousand.

VERSES ONE THROUGH FIVE ARE FULFILLED.

6. And I saw another angel fly in the midst of heaven, having the everlasting gospel to preach unto them that dwell on the earth, and to every nation, and kindred, and tongue, and people,

Let's interpret, Look close here, Jesus, is gone back to heaven [Acts, 1: 9]. The Everlasting Gospel the Angel has, now goes to the Twelve Apostles [Acts, 1: 8] also [Acts 2: 1-thru-12]. This covered the entire (Earth) it is preached today also.

The (Everlasting Gospel) will guide us on earth, and we will have a home in Heaven by it. Proof see [Eph. 1: 13] [Eph. 4: 30] very plain isn't it?

7. Saying with a loud voice, Fear God, and give glory to him; for the hour of his judgment is come: and worship him that made heaven, and earth, and the sea, and the fountains of waters.

Let's interpret, This is a continual of verse (6) which is the everlasting gospel to be preached on earth. Saying Fear God, this is to show Respect to him. Give glory to him, this is Praise, and Honor. For the hour of his judgment is come. Judgment, is a Decision has been made.

Worship him that made; Look at all the things he made, and gave them to mankind. Heaven, Earth, Sea, Fountains of waters, and all the things that are in them. We still have them today, and enjoy all (Their Wealth, Service, and Beauty) God's, creation is wonderful. He is worthy to be Worshipped, and Praised. He is full of love, and mercy. There is a Powerful Sermon in this verse.

8. And there followed another angel, saying, Babylon is fallen, is fallen, that great city, because she made all nations drink of the wine of the wrath of her fornication.

Let's interpret, This Angel, saying Babylon is fallen, is fallen that great city. This is <u>Degraded</u> from a <u>High Respectable Position,</u> to a <u>Low Disgrace.</u> We have a <u>Parallel Scripture</u> here [Rev. 18: 1, 2, 3] will give us the full view of Babylon, and the End.

Because she made all nations drink of the wine of the wrath of her <u>Fornication,</u> Let's Analyze this; <u>(Because she made)</u> the word made shows (Force) all nations drink; The word (drink) tells us these nations accepted. The (Wine) is <u>False Doctrine</u> Rules, and Regulations. The <u>Wrath</u> of her <u>Fornication,</u> is <u>Utterly Burned With Fire.</u> Follow this close!! Anyone that has anything to do with this <u>Evil Babylon,</u> will be cast into the <u>Lake</u> of <u>Fire Burning</u> with <u>Brimstone;</u> this is the wrath of her fornication, this is all nations.`

Fornication is turning from God, and worshipping (Idols, Devils) The Image of the beast [Rev. 18: 2. 3, 5, 8].

9. And the third angel followed them, saying with a loud voice, if any man worship the beast and his image, and receive his mark in his forehead, or in his hand,

Let's interpret, We can see this is the gospel being preached of verse (6, & 7) to all the world of mankind today this is <u>Great.</u> Notice the direct instructions.

If any man worship the beast, and his image, and receive his mark in his forehead, or his hand. "This Is good Preaching".

10. The same shall drink of the wine of the wrath of God, which is poured out without mixture into the cup of his indignation; and he shall be tormented with fire and brimstone in the presence of the holy angels, and in the presence of the Lamb.

Let's interpret, The same shall drink of the wine of the wrath of God. Let's Analyze, (Shall Drink) is <u>Definite Unquestionable</u> you will suffer the consequence. The (Wine) is (S/L) <u>God's plan,</u> of the (Wrath) of God, wrath is <u>Violent Anger.</u>

Which is poured out without mixture; this is without (Mercy) into his (Cup) of (Indignation).This is <u>Anger</u>, caused by something <u>Unjust</u> or <u>Unworthy</u> we know what is unjust, and unworthy. People that worship the beast and his image, or receive his mark in their forehead or hand.

The Cup is (S/L) God's, plan see [Rev. 19: 20, 21] [Rev. 20: 10] this is the wrath of God. And shall be tormented with fire and brimstone in the presence of the holy angels, and in the presence of the Lamb.(This is self explanatory).

All of verse (10) is for the people that <u>Rejected</u> the <u>Everlasting Gospel</u>. The three Angels, had to Preach unto them that dwell on the earth. The preachers that Jesus, called and sent are <u>Preaching the Everlasting Gospel (Today)</u> [Rom. 10: 14, 15].

We are looking at the <u>Future</u> which is just ahead of the world of mankind; according to the signs of the times, and the things happening every day according to the <u>Fulfilling</u> of the <u>Bible, God's, Word.</u>

11. And the smoke of their torment ascendeth up for ever and ever: and they have no rest day nor night, who worship the beast and his image, and whosoever receiveth the mark of his name.

Let's interpret, This is an extension of the <u>Wrath</u>, of God, from verse (10). The last part of this verse (11) Is some of the preaching in verse (9), word for word. The everlasting <u>Gospel.</u>

12. Here is the patience of the saints: here are they that keep the commandments of God, and the faith of Jesus.

Let's interpret, Here is the <u>Patience</u> of the <u>Saints,</u> Patience is the key see [James, 1: 3,4] Let patience have her <u>Perfect Work,</u> that ye may be perfect, and entire, wanting nothing consider Job. Here are they that keep the commandments of God. It starts here [Gen. 6: 14, 22] (Noah) (Abraham) (Moses) (Joshua) (Elijah) (John, the

Baptist) the Bible is full of them that keep the commandments of God, this is Pure Faith.

And the faith of Jesus, Starts here [Mat. 10: 1] [Luke, 22: 28, 29, 30]. The Bible is full of People that have (Faith) in Jesus, see [Acts, 2: 38-thru- 47]. Faith in Jesus, is strong today. (Faith is believing in something that you have never seen) see [John, 20: 29]

To get a perfect understanding of verse (12) please read [1st. Peter, 1: 1-thru-11]. These are our <u>Divine Guide Lines</u>, Given to Apostle Peter, to write them in a book for us. [2nd. Peter, 1: 5, 6,] is our strength, and power to our <u>Eternal Home</u>, [2nd. Tim. 4: 6, 7, 8] we have <u>Perfect Divine Guidance</u> through out the entire Bible, read it.

This is why it is <u>Written</u>, These are they that keep the <u>Commandments</u> of God, and the <u>Faith</u> of Jesus.

13. And I heard a voice from heaven saying unto me, Write, Blessed are the dead which die in the Lord from henceforth: Yea, saith the Spirit, that they may rest from their labours; and their works do follow them.

Let's interpret, This voice from heaven, is the angel in [Rev. 1: 1] He is still in charge of the book of Revelation.

Blessed are the dead, which die in the Lord, this is; our answer to verse (12).

<u>Patience, Faith</u> [James, 1: 3. 4] also [Mat. 24: 13] [Rev. 2: 10] this is die in the Lord, faith believing. See this scripture also [John, 11: 26] very plain isn't it?

Yea, saith the <u>Spirit,</u> This Spirit, is the <u>Holy Ghost;</u> He that hath an ear let him hear what the Spirit, saith to the Churches. As many as led by the Spirit of God, they are the Sons, of God. [Rom. 8: 14]. The Holy Spirit, guides us in the path of righteous.

That they may rest from their labours; and their works do follow them. The word <u>Labours,</u> is the <u>Physical Action</u> of the word <u>Works,</u> which is the choice of mind of mankind. There are two works <u>Good,</u> and <u>Evil.</u>

If we die in the Lord, (Faith Believing) [John, 20: 29] we will rest in peace, and our Good, Works, will follow us. It is the record of our life on earth. The dead in <u>Christ,</u> shall rise first [1st. Thes. 4: 16].

14. And I looked, and behold a white cloud, and upon the cloud one sat like unto the son of man, having on his head a golden crown, and in is hand a sharp sickle.

Let's interpret, the white cloud is the power and the <u>Glory</u> of <u>God,</u> [Mark, 13: 26].

Upon the cloud one sat like unto the son of man, this is <u>Jesus,</u> On his head a <u>Golden Crown</u> This is <u>Power</u> and <u>Authority.</u> [Mat. 28: 18] In his hand a sharp sickle. This is a reaping tool (S/L) of his voice [John, 5: 28, 29] the Resurrection very plain isn't it?

15. And another angel came out of the temple, crying with a loud voice to him that sat on the cloud, Thrust in thy sickle, and reap: for the time is come for thee to reap; for the harvest of the earth is ripe.

Let's interpret, The angel that came out of the temple, crying with a loud voice to him that sat on the cloud. Is this <u>Arch Angel,</u> [1st. Thes. 4: 16].

Thrust in thy sickle, and reap; for the time is come for thee to reap. This <u>Sickle</u> is (S/L) The voice of Jesus, [John, 5: 28, 29] he is the only one that can do this. Proof see [John, 11: 25, 26]. I am the <u>Resurrection,</u> and the <u>Life.</u>

For the harvest of the earth is ripe. This is the last Soul's name is written in the Lamb's, Book of Life. The end of time for mankind on earth [Rev. 10: 6].

16. And he that sat on the cloud thrust in his sickle on the earth; and the earth was reaped.

Let's interpret, This is Jesus, the Cloud is the Glory of God [Mat. 24: 30] the Sickle (S/L) the voice of Jesus. This is the Second Resurrection, and the Last of the flesh bodies of those that die in the Lord, and we which are alive, on earth shall be changed in a moment in the Twinkling of an Eye see [1st. Cor. 15: 51, 52, 53] and [1st. Thes. 4: 16, 17].

The same Cloud, and the same Jesus, was seen by natural men on earth, proof see [Acts, 1: 9, 10, 11]. Jesus, will come again, and get us, with the same cloud of Glory.

17. And another angel came out of the temple which is in heaven, he also having a sharp sickle.

Let's interpret, Yes there is a Temple in Heaven. This is the Third Heaven where the Throne of God, is see [Rev. 15: 5, 6, 8]. In the Holy City New Jerusalem, there are no Temple see [Rev. 21: 22].

We see this angel, has a tool to reap with; a sharp sickle. this sickle is (S/L) an un-seen power, which is the power of Jesus, [Mat. 28: 18] The angel is ready for his instructions which are in verses (18, 19). Let's take a close look.

18. And another angel came out from the altar, which had power over fire; and cried with a loud cry to him that had the sharp sickle, saying, Thrust in thy sharp sickle, and gather the clusters of the vine of the earth; for her grapes are fully ripe.

Let's interpret, Thrust in thy sharp sickle, The sharp sickle is (S/L) the Power of the Angels Word, proof see [Luke 1: 18, 19, 20] and (Gather the Clusters) this is (S/L) of sinner people in every nation on earth. The vine of the earth is (S/L) Old Satan, the Devil. For her grapes are fully ripe this is (S/L) sinner people. These people are the ones in verses (9,10, 11).

19. And the angel thrust in his sickle into the earth, and gathered the vine of the earth, and cast it into the great winepress of the wrath of God.

Let's interpret, And the angel thrust in his sickle into the earth, the sickle is (S/L) power of the Word of the Angel. And gather the vine of the earth, this is Old Satan, the Devil. And cast it into the great winepress see [Rev. 19: 13, 15, 19, 20, 21] of the wrath of God. The wrath of God, is (Violent Anger Severe).

We understand the Angel, thrust into the earth his <u>Sharp Sickle,</u> and gathered the Vine, Clusters, and the Grapes of the earth. This is Satan, and his followers unrighteous people.

Jesus, reaped all the righteous people of the earth first verse (16) This scripture is here see [1st. Thes. 4: 16] the dead in Christ, shall rise first their (Faith, and Belief).

20. And the winepress was trodden without the city, and blood came out of the winepress, even unto the horses bridles, by the space of a thousand and six hundred furlongs.

Let's interpret, The winepress is (S/L) Jesus, (Trodden) is put under the feet of Jesus, see [Rev. 19: 15] trodden without the city, this is Jerusalem in the land of Israel.

Blood came out of the winepress, even unto the horses bridles. This shows us these people were alive, see [Rev. 19: 21]. By the space of a (Thousand, and Six Hundred) furlongs.

We have no way of knowing what the height is from the ground to the horses bridles; where the blood flowed to, because of different breed of horses.

We know a (Furlong is 660-Feet) We calculate (1,600 X 660 =1056000 feet) Divided by (5280 feet-a mile) = (200-Miles).We now understand why the <u>Great River Euphrates </u>was dried up. To prepare the way for the Kings of the East. This is a lot of blood. This is on earth, Located in <u>Mesopotamia</u>, an ancient country in Southwestern Asia. Between the <u>Tigris,</u> and <u>Euphrates Rivers</u>.

This explains the (Wine Press) was <u>Trodden</u> without the city, Jerusalem in the land of Israel. This is the Battle of Amageddon, fought in the <u>Mesopotamia Valley.</u>

CHAPTER 15

1. And I saw another sign in heaven, great and marvelous, seven angels having the seven last plagues; for in them is filled up the wrath of God.

Let's interpret, And I saw another sign in heaven. This is a good indication John, is in heaven. <u>Great,</u> and <u>Marvelous,</u> this is the highest kind of <u>Quality</u>. Seven Angels, having the seven last plagues; there are no more plagues. For in them is filled up the wrath of God, this is (Violent Anger) punishment for sin. This is the plan of God, for the wicked people on earth.

2. And I saw as it were a sea of glass mingled with fire: and them that had gotten the victory over the beast, and over his image, and over his mark, and over the number of his name, stand on the sea of glass, having the harps of God.

Let's interpret, The <u>Sea</u> of <u>Glass,</u> is the <u>Glory</u> of <u>God.</u> mingled with fire, this is God, all through it see [Heb. 12: 29] [Rev. 4: 6].

Notice John, said I saw them! That had gotten the victory over the beast, his image, and his mark, and over the number of his name. These scriptures show us the ones that got victory over the beast, his image, his mark, and the number of his name. See [Rev. 7: 14, 15] [Rev. 12: 11] this is done by keeping the <u>Commandments,</u> of <u>God,</u> and the <u>Faith</u> in <u>Jesus,</u> [Heb. 13: 5] Jesus, said I will never leave thee nor forsake thee.

Stand on the sea of glass, having the harps of God, this is <u>Victory</u>.

3. And they sing the song of Moses the servant of God, and the song of the Lamb, saying, Great and marvelous are thy works, Lord God Almighty; just and true are thy ways, thou King of saints.

Let's interpret, The song of Moses, is <u>Triumphant Gloriously,</u> after being in bondage "Slavery" (430-years) in the land of <u>Egypt</u> [Ex. 15: 1-thru-21]. God, never left the children of Israel he is still with them today.

And the song of the Lamb, is here in verse (3). Saying, <u>Great,</u> and <u>Marvelous</u> are thy works, <u>Lord God Almighty</u>; This is <u>Jesus,</u> [Rev. 1:8]. Just and true are thy ways, [Rev. 19:2] thou <u>King</u> of <u>Saints</u> [Rev. 19: 16] see this also [Mat. 28: 20]. All of this is a song of praise, and victory.

4. Who shall not fear thee, O Lord, and glorify thy name? for thou only are holy: for all nations shall come and worship before thee; for thy judgments are made manifest.

Let's interpret, This is a continual of the song of the Lamb, which is a song of <u>Praise.</u> Who shall not fear thee, this is <u>Show Respect</u>, O Lord, and glorify thy name?

Glorify, is to worship, Adore, and Praise Highly, the name of Jesus. See [Heb. 1:4]

[Phil. 2: 9, 10, 11] For thou only are Holy, <u>Perfect Pure,</u> and <u>Clean</u> see [Jer. 10: 7].

For all nations shall come and worship before thee. These nations realized that without God, and Jesus, they would perish see [Is. 66: 23].

For thy judgments are made manifest; (Known) see [Rev. 14: 9, 10, 11] God, and Jesus, has warned all nations of their wicked ways.

5. And after that I looked, and, behold, the temple of the tabernacle of the testimony in heaven was opened:

Let's interpret, The temple had in it the Tabernacle of the Testimony. The tabernacle of testimony is a locked box fixed to the side of the altar, where important things were kept in see [Num. 1: 50, 53] today we call it a File Cabinet.

Testimony, is a written statement to establish a fact. Example, The Tables of the Law [Ex. 25: 16] the precepts of God.

This Tabernacle of the Testimony in Heaven, was open. We can see what was in it in verses (6, 7, 8), and the entire chapter of Sixteen.

There are two tabernacles, Tabernacle of the Congregation [Num. 1: 1], and the Tabernacle of the Testimony [Num. 1: 50, 53]. The Levite, shall keep charge of the tabernacle of testimony. This is keeping records of things happening. What we are looking at is Future, of things to come; kept in Heaven all these years till this prophecy.

6. And the seven angels came out of the temple, having the seven plagues, clothed in pure and white linen, and having their breast girded with golden girdles.

Let's interpret, The seven angels came out of the temple having the seven plagues.

These are the Seven Lamps of fire Burning before the throne; [Rev. 4: 5] also the Seven Angels which stood before God, [Rev. 8: 2].

This is the first time we have seen these Seven Angels, clothed. Clothed in Pure and White Linen, this represents The Righteousness of the Saints [Rev. 19: 8].

Their breast girded with golden girdles. This depicts Royalty. Today we call the girdle a vest. These are the Seven Spirits of God. We find the Spirit of God, here [Zech. 4: 6] not by might, nor by power, but by my Spirit, saith the Lord, of hosts. Jesus, has the Seven Spirit of God, now see [Rev. 5: 6]. The Bible proves it's self.

7. And one of the four beast gave unto the seven angels seven golden vials full of the wrath of God, who liveth for ever and ever.

Let's interpret, The Four Beast is (S/L) the four sons of Jacob. One of them gave unto the <u>Seven Angels</u>, Seven Golden Vials, full of the <u>Wrath</u> of <u>God.</u> God, here is Jesus, Because God, and Jesus, are one [John, 10: 30].

These angels came out of the temple with the <u>Seven Plagues</u>. But they didn't have the wrath the <u>Severity</u> of God's, power. Now they have both the Plagues, and the Wrath of God, which is (Violent Anger) who liveth for ever and ever, is referring to <u>Jesus</u> [Rev. 1: 18] [Heb. 1: 8].

8. And the temple was filled with smoke from the glory of God, and from his power; and no man was able to enter into the temple, till the seven plagues of the seven angels were fulfilled.

Let's interpret, The temple filled with,"Smoke" is (S/L) used to describe the glory of God, there are no natural smoke in heaven. The Glory of God, is every where And from his power, this is also his Glory.

And no man was able to enter the temple. This shows us there are people in Heaven in their Glorified Flesh Body. The Four Beast, (S/L) Four sons of Jacob, The Hundred Forty Four Thousand, Four and Twenty Elders, Enoch, Moses, Elijah. Just to name a few, these we know.

Till the seven plagues of the seven angels were fulfilled. This is self explanatory.

IN CHAPTER-16-WE WILL FIND THE SEVEN PLAGUES, AND THEIR SEVERITY.

CHAPTER 16

1. And I heard a great voice out of the temple saying to the seven angels, Go your ways, and pour out the vials of the wrath of God upon the earth.

Let's interpret, This great voice is indicating Jesus, this is what we are looking at see [Rev. 5: 6] This <u>Lamb, Jesus,</u> having <u>Seven Horns,</u> and <u>Seven Eyes</u> which are the <u>Seven Spirits</u> of <u>God,</u> sent forth into all the earth. He is in control of all things [Mat. 28: 18]. We know this voice is not of man coming from the temple. We have proof of this see [Rev. 15: 8]. These seven plagues, and the seven vials, full of the wrath of God, cover the entire earth.

2. And the first went, and poured out his vial upon the earth; and there fell a noisome and grievous sore upon the men which had the mark of the beast, and upon them that worshipped his image.

Let's interpret, The first Angel, poured out his Vial upon the earth, this covered the entire earth. And there fell a <u>Noisome,</u> and <u>Grievous Sore</u> upon the men which had the <u>Mark</u> of the <u>Beast.</u> This is one group of people. The other group of people, are them that worshipped his image [Rev. 19: 20]. The Noisome, and Grievous Sore fell on them also.

Noisome, is a <u>(Disgusting Odor).</u> Grievous, is <u>(Pain),</u> and <u>(Suffering).</u> We can't find where this Odorous, and Grievous, Sore, has any time limit, this indicates until death.

We find in [Rev. 14: 6, 7, 8, (9), 10] Angels, having the <u>Everlasting Gospel</u> to <u>PREACH</u> unto them that <u>Dwell</u> on the <u>Earth</u> verse (9) was preached, about the mark of the beast, and worship of his image. There is no <u>Excuse</u> the same preaching is still going on <u>TODAY</u> with the <u>Preachers,</u> Jesus, has called and sent see [Rom. 10: 14, 15].

3. And the second angel poured out his vial upon the sea; and it became as the blood of a dead man: and every living soul died in the sea.

Let's interpret, The second Angel, poured out his Vial upon the sea. This is every Sea on earth; there is no escape.

It became as the blood of a dead man. We know the blood of a dead man, doesn't move, it (Clots-Jells) there is no life in it. And every <u>Living Soul</u> Died in the Sea.

Living Soul is Mankind Both Male, and Female. [Gen. 1: 27] also [Gen. 2: 7]. This also suggest the (Marine Life) in the sea, would have died also.

Consider all the Ships of every country on earth, trade vessels, pleasure boats, Military ships, Submarines, Fishing boats, This is a huge number of souls, in the Sea.

Please see this scripture [Rev. 20: 13]. The sea gave up the dead which were in it.

This is a huge picture we are looking at, and the end of time for mankind.

4. And the third angel poured out his vial upon the rivers and fountains of waters; and they became blood.

Let's interpret, This is for the people that have the mark of the beast, and worship his image verse (6) proves this.

5. And I heard the angel of the waters say, Thou art righteous, O Lord, which art, and wast, and shalt be, because thou hast judged thus.

Let's interpret, Notice the Praise of the Angel, of the "Waters" Thou art righteous, <u>O Lord.</u> These verbs are Jesus, Which art (In Heaven) Was (On Earth) and Shall be (Forever). Because thou hast judged thus. <u>Jesus,</u> is the Righteous Judge, see [Rev. 19: 11] [Rev. 11: 16, 17]. This is all Praise, and worship to Jesus, see [Heb. 1: 6].

6. For they have shed the blood of saints and prophets, and thou hast given them blood to drink; for they are worthy.

Let's interpret, These words are the words of <u>The Angel, in</u> verse (5).

For they have shed the blood of Saints, and Prophets. The pronoun "They" are the people in verse (2).That have the Mark of the Beast, and worship his Image see [Rev. 13: 8] and [John, 8: 44]

Shed the blood of the Saints, and Prophets. See [Rev. 6: 10, 11] [Rev. 13: 15] also [Rev. 18: 24] [Mat. 23: 34, 35, 37]. And thou hast given them blood to drink. This is simple, you reap what you sow [Gal. 6: 7]. For they are worthy. This is they deserve what they got (Blood to (Drink).These are people that are deceived by the <u>Beast,</u> [Rev. 13: 2, 7, 8] and this Beast. [Rev. 13: 11, 13, 14, 15] this is the False Prophet <u>Judas Iscariot.</u>

7. And I heard another out of the altar say, Even so, Lord God Almighty, true and righteous are thy judgments.

Let's interpret, And I heard another out of the altar, this suggest an angel's voice.

Say even so <u>Lord God Almighty,</u> this is <u>Jesus,</u> [Rev. 1: 8] [Mat. 28: 18]. True and Righteous are thy Judgments se [Rev. 19: 2]. In him are hid all treasures of wisdom and knowledge of God, [Col. 2: 2, 3] This verse is <u>Praise</u> to <u>Jesus,</u> for his <u>Excellence</u> high quality of <u>Work.</u>

The first (7) verses we can see Jesus, is using his Great Power see [Rom. 12: 19] Vengeance is mine; I will repay saith the <u>Lord.</u>

8. And the fourth angel poured out his vial upon the sun; and power was given unto him to scorch men with fire.

Let's interpret, The fourth angel poured out is vial upon the sun. This is the Plague. And Power was given unto him this power is (Jesus). To Scorch Men with Fire. This is burnt Skin and very painful, to men. and women that rejected the preaching, of the word of God. This is the Wrath of God, in the Vial. This covers the entire earth; because the (Sun Covers the Earth).

9. And men were scorched with great heat, and blasphemed the name of God, which had power over these plagues: and they repented not to give him glory.

Let's interpret, And men this is both men and women were Scorched with Great Heat. This is to Burn the surface of the Skin of these Men, and women. This type of Burn Is Very Painful.

And they blasphemed the name of God. Blaspheme is (Cursing, and SIN) and shows great disrespect to God, this is Jesus, with all of this power. Jesus, started this Destruction of earth, and man see [Rev. Chapter-6]. Take a look at it and put it together. All this destruction of the earth will end here see [Rev. 20: 15] the end of time for mankind on earth.

Which has power over these plagues. Notice! The word "Plagues" is plural this indicates the men, and women of the earth have suffered through all these plagues, and still alive.

And they repented not to give him glory. Here is why see [Rev. 13: 8]. Their names are not written in the Book of Life of the Lamb, see also [John, 8: 44].

10. And the fifth angel poured out his vial upon the seat of the beast; and his kingdom was full of darkness; and they gnawed their tongues for pain,

Let's interpret, The Fifth Angel, poured out his vial upon the seat of the beast.

The seat of the beast, is the New Babylon Empire. Located in the Mesopotamia Valley between the (Tigris, and Euphrates Rivers) in Southwestern Asia. This is the same location as King Nebuchadnezzar's, Babylon Empire was, today is (Iraq, and Iran).

The seat is a one world Electronic trade center all business transactions are done at the seat of the Beast Babylon by Satellite Computers. We are looking at the future. This beast is a man here is his Ensign or Flag (Leopard, feet as a Bear, Mouth of a Lion) see [Rev. 13: 2]. He came from this Prophecy [Dan. 8: 23, 24, 25, 26]. Here is what happen to him see [Rev. 19: 20].

The dragon with Seven, Heads, and Ten Horns [Rev. 13: 1] gave him, his (Power) (Seat), and Great Authority. This is an Evil Kingdom; that covers the entire earth.

This is why his Kingdom was full of Darkness Sin. And they gnawed their tongue for pain. This show us the (Pain) is (Severe) it get worse see [Mat. 13: 41, 42], and [Rev. 20: 15]. These are the same people that suffered the plagues from verse (2) to verse (10).

11. And blasphemed the God of heaven because of their pains and their sores, and repented not of their deeds.

Let's interpret, Blasphemed the God, of heaven. This is curse God, and show disrespect. Because of their pains and their sores. These people are the ones that Ignored the Everlasting Gospel Preached, to them in [Rev. 14: 5, 6, 7, 8, 9, 10].

And repented not of their deeds. Here are some of their "DEEDS" Shed the blood of Saints, and Prophets.

Repent, shows they had a chance to escape their suffering. But they blamed God, for their suffering they brought upon themselves.

Notice the word (Sores) this is the first Plague, and Vial of the wrath of God. These people still have the (Sores) from verse (2).

Theses people are the ones that worshipped the, (Dragon

"Satan" Devil. Serpent), and the (Beast) see [Rev. 13: 4]. These same people suffered the <u>First Five Plagues,</u> and the <u>Wrath</u> of <u>God</u>. Their end is here [Rev. 14: 9, 10, 11] also [Rev. 19: 19, 20, 21].

12. And the sixth angel poured our his vial upon the great river Euphrates; and the water thereof was dried up, that the way of the kings of the east might be prepared.

Let's interpret, The Sixth Angel, poured out his vial upon the <u>Great River Euphrates,</u> and the water thereof was dried up. When we see the Euphrates river being dried up mankind will know the Battle of Armageddon is neigh

And the water was dried up that the way of the <u>Kings</u> of the <u>East</u> might be prepared.

The <u>Kings</u> of the <u>East</u>, are these. [Rev. 5: 10] [Rev. 14: 1, 4] [Rev. 19: 14] These are they which follow the Lamb whithersoever he goeth the (144,000). These will fight the <u>Battle</u> of <u>Armageddon with Jesus,</u> and win see [Rev. 19: 14] [Rev. 19: 19, 20, 21]

13. And I saw three unclean spirits like frogs come out of the mouth of the dragon, and out of the mouth of the beast, and out of the mouth of the false prophet.

Let's interpret, The Dragon, Beast, and the False Prophet. None of these three have a flesh body with blood in it to keep them alive.

They have an <u>Evil Spirit</u> in them. [Rev. 13: 1, 2] the Dragon, and the Beast, appeared Simultaneous. (S/L) The dragon is Satan [Rev. 20: 2]

The Beast, is a man King, see [Dan. 8: 23, 24, [25] Verse (25) shows us he is the one Jesus, cast into the lake of fire [Rev. 19: 20]. The False Prophet, is Judas Iscariot, he is a Devil see [John, 6: 70, 71].

The three unclean spirits like frogs, came out of the mouth of the Dragon, Beast, and the False Prophet; are all one thing (A Lie) Deception, and they are <u>Very Strong.</u>

Jesus, told us this while he was on earth with us see [Mat. 24: 24].

14. For they are spirits of devils, working miracles, which go forth unto the kings of the earth and of the whole world, to gather them to the battle of that Great day of God Almighty.

Let's interpret, For they are spirits of devils, working miracles. The evil spirit of these devils can work a (Miracle), and make it look so real that it would deceive the very elect if possible [Mat. 24: 24].

Which go forth unto the kings of the earth and the whole world. This is to deceive them. These kings, and the whole world are people that, Received the Mark of the Beast. And Them that Worshipped his Image see [Rev. 19: 20] very plain isn't it?

To gather them to the battle of that Great day of God Almighty, this is (Jesus).

The kings of the earth, and the whole world; were eager to go to Battle against God Almighty Here is the reason, they had Pain, Sores, Skin Scorched, and Blood to Drink.

The Battle of that Great Day of God Almighty, This is Jesus, and his army the Hundred Forty Four Thousand [Rev. 19: 14]. Against the Beast, and the Kings of the earth, and their armies see [Rev. 19: 19].

15. Behold I come as a thief. Blessed is he that watcheth, and keepeth his garments, least he walk naked, and they see his shame.

Let's interpret, This is Jesus, talking, "I come as a thief". This is you will not know when Jesus, will come. Blessed is he that watcheth, and keepeth his garments.

This is the Righteous People on Earth. Blessed is he that Watcheth, this is doing what Jesus, told us to do [Mat. 24: 44, 45, 46] watch and pray see [Mark, 13: 32, 33. 35]. And Keepeth, his Garments, are these (Heart, Soul, Mind) and Body. This is keep the faith, keep his commandments [John, 14: 15], and keep ourselves unspotted from this world of sin [James 1: 25, 27] [Mat. 24: 44, 45, 46, 47].

Least he walk <u>Naked,</u> [Gen. 3: 10] this is <u>Sin</u> the word <u>Walk</u> is the mind of mankind proof see [Mat. 24: 48]. And they see his shame, see his <u>Sin,</u>

The pronoun <u>They</u> are the Hundred, Forty and Four Thousand. The armies which were in heaven [Rev. 19: 14]. This is what will happen to them that keepeth not his garments [Mat. 24: 50, 51].

This scripture comes into view here [Rev. 5: 9, 10] this is the hundred forty four thousand, that shall reign on the earth. See also [Rev. 20: 14] " And they lived and reigned with Christ a Thousand years". Remember One Day is with the Lord, as a thousand Years, and a thousand Years as one day [2nd. Peter, 3: 8] We understand now the <u>Battle</u> of <u>Armageddon</u> is (One Day) verse (14) shows the battle of that great (Day) of God Almighty.

16. And he gathered them together into a place called in the Hebrew tongue Armageddon.

Let's interpret, This is the <u>Sixth Angel,</u> gathered the kings and all the people, of the whole world. These have the Mark of the Beast, and worship his Image. Into a place called in the Hebrew tongue Armageddon. This is in the <u>Mesopotamia Valley</u> where the Tigris and Euphrates Rivers are, but the Euphrates river is dried up for this battle. (The dragon, he didn't gather) here is why see [Rev. 20: 2, 3, 7, 8, 9].

[Rev. 14: 20]. We see from this battle the blood, was <u>Even </u>to the <u>Horses Bridle;</u> a <u>Thousand,</u> and <u>Six Hundred Furlongs,</u> this is (200) miles long.

There are no more on this subject of <u>Armageddon,</u> until [Rev. 19: 11-thru-21].

17. And the seventh angel poured out his vial into the air; and there came a great voice out of the temple of heaven, from the throne, saying, It is done.

Let's interpret, The <u>Seventh Angel</u>, poured out his vial into the air. We see now the <u>Seven Plagues</u> have covered the <u>Air, Land,</u> and <u>Sea</u> where mankind live.

There came a <u>Great Voice</u>, out of the <u>Temple</u> of <u>Heaven,</u> from the <u>Throne.</u> This indicating some one is sitting on the <u>Throne.</u> <u>(Jesus)</u>, saying it is done. These words belong to Jesus, see [Rev. 21: 6] [John, 17: 4] [John, 19: 30]. Jesus, is in control.

18. And there were voices, and thundering, and lightnings; and there was a great earthquake, such as was not since men were upon the earth, so mighty an earthquake, and so great.

Let's interpret, The voices, thundering, and lightnings, all three of these are on earth. The voices are from people with <u>Great Fear</u> see [Rev. 6: 15,16,17] of what is coming upon them see [Luke, 21: 26] [Luke, 23: 30]. There are no thunderings, lightnings, and earthquakes in heaven.

And there was a <u>Great Earthquake,</u> such as was not since men were upon the earth, so <u>Mighty</u> an <u>Earthquake</u>, and so <u>Great</u>, the entire earth is in a <u>Earthquake</u> see [Heb. 12: 26].

This is the <u>Wrath</u> of <u>God,</u> in the <u>Golden Vial</u> of the seventh angel, and the seventh plague. We understand earth, and mankind has run out of time, see [Rev. 10: 6].

19. And the great city was divided into three parts, and the cities of the nations fell: and great Babylon came in remembrance before God, to give unto her the cup of the wine of the fierceness of his wrath.

Let's interpret, The Great City is <u>Babylon</u>, was divided into three parts.

The three parts are <u>The Beast,</u> with <u>Seven Heads,</u> <u>Ten Horns,</u> [Rev. 13: 1] and This <u>Beast</u>, like unto a <u>Leopard</u>, feet as a <u>Bear</u>, mouth of a <u>Lion</u>, [Rev. 13: 2], and this <u>Beast</u>, two horns like a lamb, and spake as a <u>Dragon</u> [Rev. 13: 11] <u>The False Prophet;</u> Judas Iscariot, the devil see [John, 6: 70, 71]. This is the Kingdom of Satan, the old Dragon, divided against it's self, it cannot stand see [Mark, 3: 24, 25, 26]

There is a <u>War</u> going on here; between the Seven Heads, and the Ten Horns, over the Great City Babylon, the great Whore see [Rev. 17: 16].

<u>God,</u> and <u>Jesus,</u> are destroying these Seven wicked nations see [Rev. 13: 1] upon his heads the name of <u>Blasphemy</u> (SIN). Also [Rev. 17: 2, 3, (16), 17, 18] verse (16) shows us the Great City (Babylon) divided.

And the cities of the nations fell. These are the <u>Seven Head</u> the <u>Seven Wealthiest Nations</u>, on earth. The verb Fell Indicates these cities fell by the Great Earthquake, destroyed.

And great Babylon came into remembrance before God, to give unto her the cup of the wine of the fierceness of his wrath.

[Mat. 10: 26] Nothing covered that shall not be revealed; and hid that shall not be known. Vengeance is mine; I will repay saith the <u>Lord,</u> (Jesus) [Rom. 12: 19].

The <u>Cup</u> of <u>Wine</u> is (S/L) God's, plan. The <u>Fierceness</u> of his <u>Wrath.</u> This is total destruction see [Rev. 18: 8, 9]. God, and Jesus, destroyed Babylon, not the earthquake.

20. And every island fled away, and the mountains were not found.

Let's Interpret, Every Island fled away, and the mountains were not found. This is from the <u>Great Earthquake</u>, so Mighty and Earthquake and so Great verse (18). This indicating the earth is <u>Without Form</u>, and <u>Void,</u> as in the beginning [Gen. 1: 2].

The earth was covered with water, this is very plain.

21. And there fell upon men a great hail out of heaven, every stone about the weight of a talent: and men blasphemed God, because of the plague of the hail; for the plague thereof was exceeding great

Let's interpret, And there fell upon men a great hail out of heaven, this is heaven being shaken [Heb. 12: 26]. Every stone about the weight of a talent. According to the Jewish Measure, and weights, a (Talent) is (93-pounds).

And men blasphemed God, because of the plague of the hail Blaspheme is Sin. men cursed God, For the plague there of was exceeding great; This plague of hail was as great as the earthquake. It covered the entire earth.

[Rev. 6: 12-thru-17] Sixth Seal, is explicit; about the above verses (18, 20, 21) we are studying. Please read the Sixth Seal, it is very plain.

CHAPTER 17

WE ARE LOOKING AT THE NEW BABYLON EMPIRE!!
WITH MODERN DAY ELECTRONICS!

1. And There came one of the seven angels which had the seven vials, and talked with me, saying unto me, Come hither; I will show unto thee the judgment of the great whore that sitteth upon many waters:

Let's interpret, This Angel, is one of the Seven Spirits, of God. Talking to John, these words, Come hither indicates John, is in heaven.

I will show unto thee the judgment of the great whore that sitteth upon many waters. This is (S/L) let's analyze it, (Judgment) is a decision has been made. The Entire Chapter of Eighteen is the (Judgment) of the great whore, please read it.

The (Great Whore) is the False Church in the great city of New Babylon. These scriptures shows us there were a Real Church, in Babylon; see [1st. Peter, 5: 13] also [Rev. 18: 4]. The (Great Whore) got it's name when it turned from following Jesus, and went after the Riches of things of this World. Proof see [Rev. 3: 14-thru-19].

The word (Sitteth) is seat, a position where rules, laws, and regulations, are made, and enforced from a city (Babylon). "Example our State Capitols ".

The many (Waters) are (S/L) people in every nation upon the earth see verse (15).

Notice this phrase; "Sitteth upon many Waters". This shows us the Great Whore; the (False Church) is the Controlling (Ruler of Authority) over (Many People) on Earth.

This is why the inhabitants of the earth have been made <u>Drunk</u> with the <u>Wine</u> of her <u>Fornication</u>; which is false Doctrine see verse (2).The word <u>Many</u> is used in this verse, and all through the Bible; because it is an <u>(Un-told Number)</u>.

2. With whom the kings of the earth have committed fornication, and the inhabitants of the earth have been made drunk with the wine of her fornication.

Let's interpret, With whom the Kings of the earth have committed fornication. This is willfully indulging in (False Trade, Rules, Law, and False Doctrine); and turned away from the things that are good. Which are, (Truth, Just, Honest, Righteousness).

These Kings of the earth, today are <u>Presidents, Prime Ministers,</u> or what ever their Title may be.

And the inhabitants of the earth have been made drunk with the wine of her fornication. These rulers of each nations on earth by the <u>Dictatorship of The Great Whore</u> from the Great City Babylon. Have brought this (Wine of her Fornication). To their own nations of people and made drunk. this is not of (Alcohol or Drugs).

This is a disarray of (Mind) From all the false rules, laws, regulations, and false doctrine the wine of her fornication. The people of the earth have been deceived. They don't know that which is <u>Right</u> from that which is <u>Wrong</u> the word (Deceived) is here see [Rev. 19: 20]. We need to use this scripture see [Mat. 24: 4].

3. So he carried me away in the spirit into the wilderness: and I saw a woman sit upon a scarlet colored beast, full of names of blasphemy, having seven heads and ten horns.

Let's interpret, So he carried me away in the Spirit. We know this Angel, is one of the Seven Spirits of God, showing John, these things. John, is also in the Spirit, see [Rev. 4: 2].

The <u>Wilderness</u> is (S/L) a <u>World</u> of <u>Sin</u> that covers the entire earth. And I saw a woman sit upon a scarlet colored beast. This is the (Image) of the (Beast) from [Rev. 13: 14]. Remember this beast is the old Devil, and Satan (The Dragon) an evil spirit (Invisible). This is why the image was made so people could see it.

Full of names of blasphemy; this is sinner people, all over the world blasphemy is (Sin), and sin is (Red) see [Is. 1: 18] this is the mark of the Beast. Consider the <u>Mark</u> God, set upon Cain. It is still with mankind today <u>SIN</u>.

This Scarlet colored beast is (S/L) the dragon having seven heads, and ten horns proof see [Rev. 12: 3] also [Rev. 13: 1]. Don't be confused by all these names. (Dragon, Serpent, Devil, Satan, Beast). These are all (One Evil Spirit) See the <u>Heading</u> of <u>Chapter Thirteen.</u>

Notice this <u>Image</u> shows a woman, sitting upon the <u>Scarlet Colored Beast</u>. The (Dragon, that Old Serpent, the Devil, and Satan). This depicts mockery, from the Garden of Eden. Notice Scarlet Colored Beast, which is (<u>Bright Red)</u> this is the image of the beast.

4. And the woman was arrayed in purple and scarlet color, and decked with gold and precious stones and pearls, having a golden cup in her hand full of abominations and filthiness of her fornication:

Let's interpret, In verse (3) John, showed us a description a woman sit upon a scarlet colored beast, having seven heads, and ten horns. This is part of the image of the beast.

And the woman was arrayed in purple, and scarlet color. (This depicts Royalty), decked with Gold, Precious Stones, and Pearls. This shows Luxury, and Wealth of this world. (Looks Good), but is (Not Good), this is <u>Deceiving</u>

See [Mat. 16: 26] What would it profit a man if he gained the whole world, and lose his own soul? Or what shall a men give in exchange for his soul?

Having a golden cup in her hand full of abominations and filthiness of her fornication.

The Golden Cup in her hand is her way of (Life on Earth). Let's take a look at her life. Full of Abominations, this is things Utterly Repulsive. Filthiness is Moral Impurity, Vulgar Language, Defiled, Pornographic. Of her Fornication, this is turning from God, to worship Idols, and Devils see [Rev. 18: 2, 3].

We are looking at the Great City New Babylon, and the Image of the Beast. We can see what is on the inside of this Great City Babylon. The Angel Showed John, and John, Showed us. This is total Corruption in Babylon.

This New Babylon Kingdom came from this prophecy [Dan. 7: 19, 23, 25] [Dan. 7: 23] The Fourth Beast shall be the Fourth Kingdom. It started here [Rev. 13: 1,2].

We are looking at a Modern Day Babylon. With Computers, Satellites, and Nuclear Weapons. Modern Day Electronics, in every place of business. No one can buy or sell without it. The telephone, Television, computers, and all Vehicles. Everything is controlled by This Electronic System in this new Babylon Empire, The One World Trade Center controlled by One Man see [Dan. 7: 19, 23]. This center can Hear, See and Talk.

Everything (On Earth) is in place (Today) ready for the Beast of Babylon, to take over the entire world. How many time have we talked to a Computer by Phone ?

The Beast is; Leopard, Feet of a Bear, Mouth of a Lion is (S/L) a man see [Rev. 13: 2], and this Beast Two Horns like a Lamb, Spake as a Dragon is (S/L) is Judas Iscariot, [Rev. 13: 11]. This Beast Seven Heads, and Ten Horns, this is the Dragon, the old Devil, an Evil Spirit [Rev. 20: 1, 2, 3]. All three of these are in the New Babylon Empire. (The Beast, False Prophet, and Dragon) an Evil Kingdom, here on earth.

This New Babylon is not, the old King Nebuchadnezzar, Babylon Empire. New Babylon will be built in the same place the

Ancient Empire Babylon of the Chaldean. In South Western Asia; In the lower valley of the Tigris, and Euphrates Rivers.

5. And upon her forehead was a name written, MYSTERY, BABYLON THE GREAT, THE MOTHER OF HARLOTS AND ABOMINATIONS OF THE EARTH.

Let's interpret, Let's follow these steps; verse (3) John, shows us a woman sit upon a scarlet colored beast full of names of blasphemy (Sin),having seven heads and ten horns. Do not be deceived this is the Great Red Dragon see [Rev. 12: 3] [Rev. 13: 1].

In verse (4) we see the same woman arrayed in clothes the finest on earth. Decked with gold, precious stones, and pearls.

Here in verse (5) we have the (Name of the Beast) with seven heads and ten horns. Written upon the forehead of the woman. This woman is still sitting upon the beast. This is the Image of the beast.

This is the Name of the beast (MYSTERY BABYLON THE GREAT). The Mystery here is prophecy fulfilled by Daniel the Prophet see [Dan. 7: 19, 23, 25]. We are looking at the Fourth Beast, and the Fourth Kingdom, of the entire world. A total (Nuclear, and Electronic) Kingdom that will destroy the whole earth this is why the title (Great) is applied see [Dan. 7: 23] Prophesied by Daniel, several thousand years ago.

THE MOTHER OF HARLOTS AND ABOMINATIONS OF THE EARTH.

This shows us what is in the Great City Babylon. The mother of harlots; depicts the center of it, or the location of it. This is where the Kings of the earth Committed Fornication with Her, in the city of Babylon prostitutes, and pornography Filthiness of Her Fornication.

AND ABOMINATIONS OF THE EARTH. These are things (Repulsive), and (Detestable) By this we see the whole earth is (Corrupt) by the Great City Babylon. As it were in the days of <u>Noah</u> before the flood see [Mat. 24: 37]

SUMMARY

Verses (3,4, 5) Is the Great City Babylon. The woman sitting upon the Scarlet Colored Beast, having seven heads, and ten horns is the great Red Dragon. Clothed in (Purple, and Scarlet) decked with Gold, Precious Stones, and Pearls, and a Name written upon her forehead; MYSTERY BABYLON THE GREAT, THE MOTHER OF HARLOTS AND ABOMINATIONS OF THE EARTH. This is the Image of the Beast and the name of the beast see [Rev, 13: 14,15].

6. And I saw the woman drunken with the blood of the saints, and with the blood of the martyrs of Jesus: and when I saw her, I wondered with great admiration.

Let's interpret, And I saw the woman drunken with the blood of the saints, and the martyrs of Jesus. This woman is (S/L) The great city Babylon see verse (18) The Great Whore, is (S/L) the False Church, which is active in Babylon, and world wide.

Notice!! Drunken with the blood of the saints, and the martyrs of Jesus. This shows Opposed, to God, and Jesus.

The word Drunken is (S/L) Power That Destroys the Mind of Mankind. Consider this man, King Nebuchadnezzar; see [Dan. 3: 13, 14, 16, 17, 18] also [Dan. 4: 27-thru-32].

This is where the Blood of the Saints, and the Martyrs of Jesus, came from. They were slain for the word of God, and the Testimony of Jesus. Here is the Patience and the Faith of the Saints [Rev. 13: 10].

Notice we have two Spans of Time. Blood of the Saints These are the Prophets see [Mat. 23: 31, 34, 35, 37]. The Martyrs of Jesus, see there scriptures [Acts, 7: 59, 60] Stephen. [Acts, 12: 2] Apostle James. [Rev. 2: 13]. Antipas.

The Angel, showed John, this Blood in Babylon see [Rev. 18: 24] very plain now we know.

And when I saw her, I wondered with great admiration. Wondered is Curiosity. Admiration is Feeling of Great Delight.

There is no way anyone can describe how John, felt when he saw all this Glory, Wealth, Luxury, Riches, and Power, of this earth. And a Scarlet coloured Beast having Seven Heads, and Ten Horns. This is the Image of the Beast. We are looking at the Future, and all the Blood from Righteous Abel [Gen. 4: 10] also [Mat. 23: 35] from generation to generations is in this Great City Babylon see [Rev. 18: 24] proof very plain.

7. And the angel said unto me, Wherefore didst thou marvel? I will tell thee the mystery of the woman, and of the beast that carrieth her, which hath the seven head and ten horns.

Let's interpret, Wherefore didst thou marvel? The Angel knew what was on John's, mind. Marvel is totally "Surprise" We need to understand we are looking at the future, so was John. We are looking at two things here look close.

(The mystery of the woman is (S/L) Babylon, see verse (18) this is one). The other one is (The beast) (S/L) the great red Dragon see [Rev. 12: 3] [Rev. 13: 1]. The Seven Heads, are the seven wealthiest nations on earth. The Ten Horns, are Ten Kings, which are allies to the Seven Heads, Verse (12, 13) shows that. This is a mighty army, and world wide they rule the earth with the force of power, with the authority of the Beast [Rev. 13: 2].

8. The beast that thou saweth was, and is not; and shall ascend out of the bottomless pit, and go into perdition: and they that dwell on the earth shall wonder, whose names were not written in the book of life from the foundation of the world, when they behold the beast that was, and is not, and yet is.

Let's interpret, The beast that thou saweth is (S/L) the Dragon having seven heads, and ten horns see verse (7). Look at these verbs. Was, (On earth)

And is Not, (Cast Out) of this earth see [John, 12: 31]. The

Prince of the Air is the Dragon Satan. Jesus, cast him out, and here is where he was cast to see [Rev. 20: 1, 2, 3] And shall ascend out of the bottomless pit. This is here [Rev. 20: 7, 8, 9]. And go into perdition. This is here [Rev. 20: 10]. Perdition is Eternal Punishment.

And they that dwell on the earth shall wonder, whose names were not written in the book of life from the foundation of the world, when they behold the that was, and is not, and yet is. These people are here [Rev. 13: 8], and [John, 8: 44] [Rev. 20: 8, 9].

The book of life is Jesus. From the Foundation of the World, this is Adam, He is the foundation of the world. All of mankind are from Adam, this includes Jesus, flesh body. The Book of Life see [Rev. 20: 12, 15] Jesus, keeps a perfect record.

When they behold the beast that was, and is not, and yet is. These sinner people

[Rev. 20: 7, 8, 9] will see the Beast, That old Serpent which is the Devil, and Satan. The one that deceived them, and they worshipped the old Dragon. All were cast into the Lake of Fire, and Brimstone, tormented day, and night for ever, and ever [Rev. 20: 10].

9.   And here is the mind which hath wisdom. The seven heads are seven mountains, on which the woman sitteth.

Let's interpret, The mind of Wisdom, is a Spiritual Gift, see [1st. Cor. 12: 7, 8] also [James, 1: 5].

The Seven Heads, (S/L) are Kings, of the seven wealthiest nations on earth.

The Seven Mountains, (S/L) are these Kings. Mountain is a Symbol of Power, in the Bible. See [Zech. 4: 7] [Jer. 51: 24, 25]. Verse (18) shows us Babylon, rules the world with these Kings. The Seven Heads, and Seven Mountains Notice!! are ONE. And they are on the Beast, on which the woman sitteth verse (3). The word (Sitteth) is control.

10. And there are seven kings: five are fallen, and one is, and the other is not yet come; and when he cometh, he must continue a short space.

Let's interpret, These Seven Kings, are of the Old Babylon Empire of King Nebuchadnezzar. His kingdom was divided, [Dan. 5: 28, 30], and given to the <u>Medes,</u> and the <u>Persians</u>. <u>Darius,</u> is the <u>King. of the Medes, Cyrus,</u> is the <u>King of the Persians.</u>

These two <u>Kings</u> fell to the <u>Grecia,</u> (Greek). From the Greek's, came up Four Kingdoms, <u>Four Kings</u>. Now we have <u>Six Kings.</u> You can find all of this in Daniel, chapters Seven, and Eight; this is a long subject.

The Seventh King, we are looking for is here. [Dan. 8: 23, 24, 25, 26, 27].

This prophecy will be fulfilled we see the signs every day.

The Seventh King, from [Dan, 8: 25], Notice! He shall stand up against the (Prince of Princes) this is <u>Jesus, King of Kings,</u> [Rev. 19: 16].

This same king [Dan. 7: 25] is the beast in [Rev. 13: 2]. The beast I saw was like a <u>Leopard,</u> <u>Feet</u> of a <u>Bear,</u> <u>Mouth</u> of a <u>Lion</u>. This is the Fourth Beast and the fourth kingdom, from [Dan. 7: 23]. This is the last of the Great Kingdoms. He shall destroy the <u>Whole Earth</u> and shall tread it down, and break it to pieces.

This is in the future. It was prophesied thousands of years ago by Daniel.

Jesus, said "Except those days should be shorten, there should no flesh be saved".

[Mat. 24: 22]. We are looking at a <u>Nuclear War,</u> see [Rev. 11: 18] destroy them which destroy the earth also [Dan. 7: 23] Shall devour the whole earth, and shall tread it down, and break it in pieces. This is the world rulers of today; under Babylon see verse (18).

Now let's get back to (Verse-10); "and the other is not yet come". see [Dan. 7: 23] [Rev. 13: 2] prophesy (and when he cometh, he must continue short space).

This show us we are looking at the future we find this here [Rev. 13: 5] Forty and Two Months (3 ½ years) see [Dan. 7: 11] now see [Rev. 19: 20]. Now we know we have the right <u>King,</u> and the right <u>Beast.</u>

We need to understand this is the Angel, of God, that had the seven vials, doing the talking. Notice he uses the word "Space" Jesus, used the word "Space" [Rev. 2: 21].

Time has no place in God's, plan. We are looking at prophecy, and INTERPRETING it.

11. And the beast that was, and is not, even he is the eighth, and is of the seven, and goeth into perdition.

Let's interpret, This beast is (S/L) the Dragon, old Satan, the Devil. The verb <u>Was</u>, on earth, till Jesus, cast him out [John, 12: 31]. and is not, on earth any more. Here is where he is [Rev. 20: 1, 2, 3] Bottomless Pit. And goeth into perdition. Here is where he goes into perdition [Rev. 20: 10] Eternal punishment. God, put him there to fulfill These scriptures, [Ps. 110: 1] [Mat. 22: 44] very plain. This is the last battle fought on earth between God, and the Devil. God, has the last thing to say in anything.

"Even he is the eighth, and is of the seven". This is back in the Babylon Empire of King Nebuchadnezzar. Until [Rev. 13: 1] This beast, came to build the New Babylon Empire with his seven heads, and ten horns, this is future. This is the Great Red Dragon [Rev. 12: 3]. These beast are men see [Rev. 13:2] and [Rev. 13: 11].

12. And the ten horns which thou sawest are ten kings, which have received no kingdom as yet; but received power as kings one hour with the beast.

Let's interpret, Horn in the Bible is a (Symbol) of power. We can see these Ten Kings, which have received no kingdom as yet.

This shows us they have no power, or permission to rule except granted by the beast.

But Received Power One Hour with the Beast. This is Commission Granted Power to perform in action, War.

13. These have one mind, and shall give their power and strength unto the beast.

Let's interpret, These have one mind. This is a conference, and agreed upon by all Ten Kings. This power is their countries these Kings Rule over, To give their Power, and Strength to the Beast. This is their army, Fuel, Food, and finance support.

This Beast is this one, Leopard, Bear, Lion. [Rev. 13: 2], and the dragon gave him his Power, his Seat, and Great Authority. He rules the world from New Babylon.

14. These shall make war with the Lamb, and the Lamb shall overcome them: for he is Lord of lords, and King of kings: and they that are with him are called, and chosen, and faithful.

Let's interpret, These shall make war with the Lamb; You will find these (Kings) Here [Rev. 16: 14]. And the Lamb shall overcome them, for he is Lord of lords, and King of kings [Rev. 19: 16] also [Rev. 19: 19, 20]. Remember these (Ten Kings) are allies to the Seven Heads, which are kings (Upon the Dragon's Head).

And they that are with him are called, and chosen, and faithful. This is the Hundred Forty Four Thousand, the armies in heaven see [Rev. 19: 14]. These are they which followed the Lamb, whithersoever he goeth [Rev. 14: 4].

We see two mighty Powers coming together to war against each other (Good, and Evil). These are the two kingdoms, Jesus, spoke of in [Mat. 24: 7] Kingdom against Kingdom. This is the Battle of Armageddon see [Rev. 16: 14, 16].

15. And he saith unto me, The waters which thou saweth, where the whore sitteth, are peoples, and multitudes, and nations, and tongues.

Let's interpret, Remember this is the <u>Angel</u> that had the seven vials, talking to John. This is (S/L) Waters, is people. The Whore, is (S/L) the <u>False Church</u> in Babylon. [Rev. 18: 2] proves that.

This is <u>Self Explanatory,</u> The waters where the whore sitteth, are People, Multitudes, Nations, and Tongues, this is world wide.

Don't get confused the <u>Whore,</u> false church <u>Rules</u> the <u>World</u> through her <u>Wealth.</u> From Babylon, and the <u>Woman,</u> is that <u>Great City</u>, which reigneth over the <u>Kings</u>, of the Earth see verse (18) very plain isn't it?

16. And the ten horns which thou saweth upon the beast, these shall hate the whore, and shall make her desolate and naked, and shall eat her flesh, and burn her with fire.

Let's interpret, The <u>Ten Horns</u> which thou saweth upon the beast, is (S/L) <u>Ten Kings</u> see verse (12). These shall hate the <u>Whore</u> (S/L) the <u>False Church.</u> And shall make her desolate, and naked, and shall eat her flesh, and burn her with fire.

This attack took place in the city of New Babylon, and the entire earth. Where ever they found the <u>Whore</u>, the <u>False Church</u>, These <u>Ten Kings</u>, attacked, and destroyed.

They didn't <u>Attack</u> the city of Babylon, only the <u>Whore,</u> the <u>False Church,</u> in the city.

17. For God hath put in their hearts to fulfill his will, and to agree, and give their Kingdom unto the beast, until the words of God shall be fulfilled.

Let's interpret. Notice! God, rules over these <u>Ten Kings,</u> and their <u>Kingdoms,</u> God, rules in all kingdoms proof see [Dan. 2: 21] . For God, hath put in their hearts to fulfill his will. "And give their kingdom unto the beast" this is God's, will. Until the words of God, shall be fulfilled. We understand now why these Ten Kings, hated the <u>Whore</u> the <u>False Church,</u> and destroyed it. [Rom. 12: 19] Vengeance Is mine; I will repay saith the Lord.

18. And the woman which thou sawest is that great city, which reigneth over the kings of the earth.

Let's interpret, The woman is (S/L) New Babylon, that great city which reigneth over the kings of the earth this is prophecy.

The rulers of the earth today are, <u>Presidents, Prime Ministers,</u> or what ever their title may be of any country.

We know this New Babylon is a <u>Electronic Powered One World Government.</u>

That will rule the entire world. Even the food we eat, and the water we drink, everything that is bought or sold, comes through this (One World Trade Center) <u>Electronic Computer System,</u> and they know where every one is by their (Zip Code). The <u>Satellite</u> that <u>Orbit's</u> the <u>Earth,</u> knows where every Vehicle, Airplane, Ship, Train, or anything that moves at any given time.

This is the <u>Prophecy</u> of [Dan. 7: 19, 23] Thus he said, the fourth beast shall be the fourth kingdom upon the earth, which shall be <u>Different From All Kingdoms.</u> We see this Electronic System in every Business Transaction today. BUT when the Beast takes over the Entire World; He has all this <u>Electronic System</u> under his control. (The Mark) of the (Beast), The (Name) of the (Beast), or the (Number) of his (Name) <u>(666).</u> No business transaction can be done without one of these three. No one can (BUY) and no one can (SELL). [Rev. 13: 16, 17].

Please Have Nothing To Do With This Beast [Rev. 14: 9, 10]!!
This New Babylon Kingdom; will end here [Rev. 20: 15].

THIS ELECTRONIC SYSTEM THE COMPUTER
IS ALREADY IN PLACE READY
FOR THIS BEAST TO TAKE OVER, THE
NEW BABYLON EMPIRE. HIS POWER
IS HERE [Rev.. 13: 2] THE DRAGON GAVE
HIM HIS POWER, SEAT, AND GREAT
AUTHORITY!!

The Angel, one of the Seven Angels, showed John, all this
future, and John, wrote it down for us to read and be ready
for all that is coming upon the earth, and mankind.

CHAPTER 18

———•◦•———

1. AND AFTER these things I saw another angel come down from heaven, having great power; and the earth was lightened with his glory.

Let's interpret, And after these things, this is referring to Chapter 17. We know The Angel, was showing John, the future in the wilderness all through Chapter 17. Is one of the Seven Angels Before the Throne of God. Which are the (Seven Spirits) of God. Sent forth into all the (Earth) see [Rev. 5: 6].

I saw another angel come down from heaven. This Angel, is one of the (Seven Spirits) of God, also. Having great power; this confirms he is one of the Seven Spirits, of God.

The (Earth) was lightened with his glory, this is the (Entire Earth). This is the Glory of God. We know Jesus, has the Seven Spirits. of God, [Rev. 5: 6] shows that. We also know John, is on the Isle of Patmos. When he saw this Angel, come down from heaven. And the earth was lightened with his Glory. This is Brighter than the Sun, amazing isn't it?

2. And he cried mightily with a strong voice, saying, Babylon the great is fallen, is fallen, and is become the habitation of devils, and the hold of every foul spirit, and a cage of every unclean and hateful bird.

Let's interpret, And he cried mightily with a strong voice, this tells us he is talking to someone in heaven. Saying, Babylon the great is fallen, is fallen, This fall is from a <u>High Degree</u> of <u>Respect,</u> and <u>Favor,</u> to a <u>Low Degree</u> of <u>Dishonor.</u>

Here is what this Angel, found in Babylon which covers the entire earth Verse (3) shows that. (Devils) demon spirits in people. And the hold of every (Foul Spirit), This is sinner people (Possessed) with an evil spirit, (Disgusting Look, and Smell).

The word <u>Hold</u> is <u>Habitation.</u> And a cage of every unclean and hateful bird. The word <u>Cage</u> is also <u>Habitation</u>. The unclean and hateful birds are these, (Vultures, Buzzards, Ravens) they will eat anything (Sick, Dead, or Dying) they are in the (Law Covenant) don't eat.

Everything the Angel, reported to heaven about Babylon is (SIN).

3. For all nations have drunk of the wine of the wrath of her fornication, and the kings of the earth have committed fornication with her, and the merchants of the earth are waxed rich through the abundance of her delicacies.

Let's interpret, For all nations have drunk of the wine of the wrath of her fornication. This is they have participated in all the <u>False Doctrine, Rules, Regulations,</u> and <u>Trade</u> in Babylon. The wrath of her fornication. Wrath is <u>Violent Anger,</u> Punishment for (SIN). The <u>Adjective All,</u> shows us every nation on earth will suffer the wrath of Babylon's sins. Fornication is willful turning from God, to worship devils, and idols which Babylon is full of; the Angel told us that.

And the kings of the earth have committed fornication with her. This shows us the rulers of the world today have willful Participated in all of Babylon's <u>Sinful Ways</u>.

These kings which are rulers of the earth; today they are called <u>Presidents, Prime Ministers,</u> or what ever their title may be remember we are looking at the <u>Future</u>.

And the merchants of the earth are waxed rich through the abundance of her delicacies.

We need to understand this is world wide the (Earth) shows us that. We are looking at the One World Trade Center New Babylon.

The merchants of the earth; let's look at the merchants of the earth. Consider all the <u>Large Chain Store</u>, and the <u>Giants</u> of On Line Electronic Trading. There is one thing for sure. All of these Merchants, will have the (Mark of the Beast), and every one that buy their Merchandise will have to have the (Mark of the Beast) see [Rev. 13: 16, 17] very plain isn't it?

No Money Is Involved. The Mark of the Beast, will have control of your money, and your Bank Account all done by Electronics.

The Righteous people on earth will have nothing to do with any of this see [Rev. 14: 9, 10, 11] very plain isn't it?

Consider this!! The Time will Come and Now is; when people of this earth go to any store to buy anything. They will have to have the (Mark of the Beast) in their (Right Hand) or in their (Foreheads). The Entrance Doors, will be Locked. The Mark in the Right Hand, or in the Foreheads, will unlock the Entrance Doors. When people buy what they want, they check themselves out through the Electronic System. No money involved the Beast has got your Bank Account, in Babylon, a One World Trade Center. A Huge Book could be written on this subject.

4. And I heard another voice from heaven, saying, Come out of her, my people, that ye be not partakers of her sins, and that ye receive not of her plagues.

Let's interpret, This voice belongs to Jesus. Here is why "Come out of her <u>My People</u>". This tells us there was a <u>Real Church</u> in Babylon see [1st. Peter, 5: 13] verse (6) shows us that also.

That ye be not partakers of her sins, and that ye receive not of her plagues. This is the same thing that happen to <u>Gomorrah,</u> and <u>Sodom,</u> as the Angels, led Lot, his wife and two daughters out of Sodom. So is Jesus, leading his people out of Babylon before he destroying it.

5. For her sins have reached unto heaven, and God hath remembered her iniquities.

Let's interpret, For her sins have reached unto heaven. We know how her sins reached unto heaven. Let's look at it, and prove it. See verses (1-2-3) The Angel, came down from heaven with Great Power, and Glory, and reported back to <u>Jesus,</u> How sinful Babylon was very plain isn't it?

And God, hath remembered he iniquities. These two words <u>Remembered,</u> and <u>Iniquities</u> goes back to [Rev. Chapter, 17] read it. Remembered is a past tense verb.

6. Reward her even as she rewarded you, and double unto her double according to her works: in the cup which she hath filled fill to her double.

Let's interpret, Reward her the pronoun (Her) is the <u>False Church</u> in Babylon, as she rewarded you. Jesus, is speaking to his people see [Rev. 17: 6] This is revenge, "Pay back time" see [Rom 12: 19] simple isn't it?

This time the righteous people have permission to "Retaliate" this <u>Order,</u> came from <u>Jesus.</u> [Ps. 137: 8] [Jer. 50: 15] Double unto her double according to her works. We know what her works are evil poof the <u>Golden Cup</u> in her <u>Hand</u> full of Abominations, Filthiness, of her Fornication.

In the cup which she hath filled fill to her double. Here is the cup she hath filled "I saw the woman <u>Drunken</u> with the <u>Blood</u> of the <u>Saints</u> and with the <u>Blood</u> of the <u>Martyrs</u> of <u>Jesus.</u> The <u>False Church</u> (Whore) will be destroyed by the <u>Real Church</u> The <u>People</u> of <u>Jesus,</u> verse (4). The Ten Kings, [Rev. 17: 16] will make her desolate, naked, eat her flesh, and burn her with fire. This is total destruction, see [Rom. 12: 19]. Vengeance is mine, I will repay saith the <u>Lord.</u>

7. How much she hath glorified herself, and lived deliciously, so much torment and sorrow give her: for she saith in her heart, I sit a queen, and am no widow, and shall see no sorrow.

Let's interpret, How much she hath glorified herself. This is boasting, bragging.

This is Exalt Herself she shall be abased see [Luke, 14: 11] Consider the Laodiceans Church [Rev. 3: 17]. And lived Deliciously, this is Great Pleasure.

So much torment and sorrow give her. Torment is extreme pain, and suffering of the body. Sorrow is sadness, and grief of the mind from a loss.

For she saith in her heart, I sit a queen, and am no widow, and shall see no sorrow.

This is she Exalt Herself, She shall be Abased. [Mat. 23: 12] this is the False Church, in Babylon was destroyed, by the Ten Horns (Ten Kings) see [Rev. 17: 16] very Plain. We need to keep in mind this is world wide.

8. Therefore shall her plagues come in one day, death, and mourning, and famine; and she shall be utterly burned with fire: for strong is the Lord God who judgeth her.

Let's interpret, Therefore shall her plagues come in one day. Let's Analyze; [In One Day) The Great City New Babylon, will be totally destroyed.

The plagues are (Death) No place or time to bury the dead, they will be scattered throughout the city of Babylon. (Mourning), Can be heard throughout the city of Babylon. (Famine) No food or drink can be found hunger, and thirst throughout the city of Babylon.

And she shall be utterly burned with fire; the sinner people in Babylon were burned to death with Great Babylon. Jesus, got the righteous people out of it, simple.

For strong is the Lord God, who judgeth her. This is Jesus, see [Rev. 19: 1,2]. (Utterly) is Completely destroyed by (Fire) see [Rom. 12: 19] the Bible proves it's self.

9. And the kings of the earth, who have committed fornication and lived deliciously with her, shall bewail her, and lament for her, when they shall see the smoke of her burning,

Let's interpret, let's break it down. The King of the earth who have Committed Fornication, with her this is <u>Willfully</u> Committed <u>Sin.</u> And <u>Lived Deliciously,</u> with <u>Her.</u> This is <u>Great Pleasure.</u> Notice!! All these <u>Rulers</u> of the <u>Earth Lost It All,</u> (But Their SIN). Look what they are going to loose next see [Rev. 19: 18, 19, 20, 21].

They Bewail her, this is "Expressed" Great Sorrow, and Lament for her, this is Crying out in Grief. When they see the smoke of her burning, this is completely destroyed.

This is the "<u>Love</u> of <u>Money</u>" the "<u>Root</u> of all <u>Evil</u>". [1st. Tim. 6: 10].

The Rulers of the earth today are called Presidents, Prime Ministers, or what ever their title may be. (G-7) comes into focus here we are looking at a "One World Trade Center" Called Babylon. It is swiftly coming upon mankind; with the Mark of the Beast. This is the future we are looking at.

10. Standing afar off for the fear of her torment, saying, Alas, alas, that great city Babylon, that mighty city! for in one hour is thy judgment come.

Let's interpret, We see these Kings, Presidents, Prime Ministers, and rulers of the nations on earth. Standing afar off for fear of her torment. The word <u>Fear</u> shows <u>Guilt.</u> Having done something wrong this is (Committed Fornication).

Saying Alas, alas, that great city Babylon, that mighty city! For in one hour is thy (Judgment come). The rulers of the world knew this <u>Wickedness</u> couldn't last. <u>Alas, alas</u>, is (Unhappiness, Pity) All of this shows these rulers of the earth are Miserable Unhappy, they lost all of their Wealth in one (HOUR).

That great city Babylon, that mighty city! This is words of (Praise) from these rulers. For in one hour is thy judgment come.

This indicates; these Kings, Presidents, Prime Ministers, and rulers of the earth knew <u>Babylon,</u> was a <u>Wealthy, Luxurious, Wicked City.</u> The word <u>Judgment</u> shows that.

11. And the merchants of the earth shall weep and mourn over her; for no man buyeth their merchandise any more:

Let's interpret, And the merchants of the earth shall weep and mourn over her.

(Weep) is to show emotion, and sorrow by shedding tears. (Mourn) To show grief or sorrow. All this weeping and mourning; is for the <u>Love</u> of <u>Money</u> [1st. Tim. 6: 10]. The Verb <u>Shall</u> is future tense; and we are looking at the future of all these things are yet to come. Remember these merchants have the mark of the <u>Best.</u>

For no man buyeth their merchandise any more. We can see why it is all burnt up, destroyed, and the Computers, through which the business transactions took place are gone verse (12) shows us what these merchants are weeping, and mourning over <u>Wealth.</u>

12. The merchandise of gold, and silver, and precious stones, and of pearls, and fine lining, and purple, and silk, and scarlet, and all thymine wood, and all manner vessels of ivory, and all manner vessels of most precious wood, and of brass, and iron, and marble.

Let's interpret, We can see from the City of Babylon, the one world <u>Trade Center.</u> These merchants had the best of merchandise the earth had to offer. God, and Jesus, made all of this precious merchandise.

This merchandise came to this <u>New Babylon,</u> From the <u>Seven</u> Heads. The seven <u>Wealthiest Nations,</u> and every nation on earth. Babylon, is a <u>One World Trade Center.</u>

This is all <u>Electronic Trade.</u> We are looking at the <u>Future</u> The shipping movement of this merchandise is by air <u>Airplanes,</u> on land <u>Trucks,</u> and <u>Trains,</u> water <u>Rivers Oceans,</u> and <u>Seas.</u>

Babylon knows Where every package of merchandise is at all time.

(24-Hours a day) (7-Days a week) (365-Days a year). Babylon, doesn't stop for anything, nor respect anything.

Keep in mind! This is <u>Future,</u> and very near. Today the entire earth can't do any business transactions with out this Electronic System the Computer.

There will be a <u>One World Bank,</u> and a<u> One World Trade Center</u> (BABYLON).

With this comes the <u>Mark </u>of the <u>Beast,</u> or the <u>Name</u> of the <u>Beast,</u> or the <u>Number</u> of his name <u>(666)</u> [Rev. 13: 16, 17]. Even today it takes a Number to transact business.

<u>Please Do Not Take Any of The </u>(Mark, Name, or Number [Rev. 14: 9, 10, 11].

13. And cinnamon, and odours, and ointments, and frankincense, and wine, and oil, and fine flour, and wheat, and beast, and sheep, and horses, and chariots, and slaves, and souls of men.

Let's interpret, The merchandise in verses (12, and 13) are world wide today. It is Ordered with a computer, and shipped all over the entire world, even to our front door.

Two things we don't have today are (Slaves, and Souls of Men). I do not understand the <u>Souls, of Men</u> Being Merchandise. [2nd. Peter, 2: 1, 2, 3] says they will make <u>Merchandise</u> of you. Peter, is speaking of the <u>False Doctrine,</u> from Babylon, and across the entire earth. There are righteous people in Babylon verse (4) show us that.

When Babylon takes over the entire earth. They will have everything in their control. All <u>Freedom</u> of the <u>World,</u> will be gone This is where the <u>Mark </u>of the <u>Beast,</u> comes into action. No one can buy or sell except they have the (Mark, of the Beast) the (Name, of the Beast) or the (Number of his name) (666). No Food No Water Nothing.

The Mark of the Beast will last for (3 ½ years) (42 months) (1,260-days) [Rev. 13: 5] [Rev. 12: 6, 14].

14. And the fruits that thy soul lusted after are departed from thee, and all things which were dainty and goodly are departed from thee, and thou shall find them no more at all.

Let's interpret, The fruits that thy soul lusted after are departed from thee. This is the Great City Babylon, and the Famine spoken of in verse (8).

These are the Dainty a tasty delicious delicacy, food, pleasing in appearance this is luxury. This is the merchandise in verses (12, and 13). Are departed from thee, and thou shall find them no more at all.

This New Babylon is stripped down to nothing, desolate, and naked. No buying and selling going on. There will be a great famine world wide.

(The Real Church) will be here [Rev. 12: 14] [Rev. 20: 9] plain isn't it?

15. The merchants of these things, which were made rich by her, shall stand afar off for the fear of her torment, weeping and wailing,

Let's interpret, These merchants of these things; this is the merchandise mentioned in verses (12,13,14). Were made rich by her, (New Babylon). The one world trade center.

Shall stand afar off for the fear of her torment. The verb Shall is future tense.

For the fear of her torment. The verb Fear, shows guilt of committing fornication sin, with Babylon.

We need to understand also, these merchants had to have the Mark of the Beast. We find them here [Rev. 19: 19, 20, 21] very plain.

Weeping, is show emotion of shedding tears. Wailing, is a long cry, a sound of grief. All of this shows us the merchants world wide Grieve over the loss of Money.

The <u>Love</u> of <u>Money</u> is the <u>Root</u> of all <u>Evil</u> [1ˢᵗ. Tim. 6: 10]. We must understand also no one can <u>Buy</u> nor <u>Sell</u> without the <u>Mark</u> of the <u>Beast</u> !!! [Rev. 13: 17]. Consider these merchants, and people world wide, buying, and selling simple very plain.

16. And saying, Alas, alas, that great city, that was clothed in fine linen, and purple, and scarlet, and decked with gold, and precious stones, and pearls!

Let's interpret, Alas, alas, is unhappiness and pity. That Great City is (S/L) Babylon. All of this verse is a description of Babylon (Wealth) see [Rev. 17: 4]

17. For in one hour so great riches is come to naught, And every shipmaster, and all the company in ships, and sailors, and as many as trade by sea, stood afar off,

Let's interpret, For in one hour so great riches is come to naught. Verses (9, 10, 11) they are all saying the same thing, and the time is "One Hour"

We see a huge business by sea, from around the world ships large, and small coming to the shipping, and receiving ports of Babylon.

Here are a few things verse (12) of natural material, or raw material unfinished they brought to Babylon. Lumber, Brass, Gold, Silver, Iron, Wheat, Spices, Cloth, Silk, and everything on earth. Babylon took this material, and made it into a <u>Fine Beautiful Product</u> to be <u>Sold</u> around the <u>World.</u>

We know where all this <u>Prosperity,</u> came form; this <u>King</u> see [Dan. 8: 25] also [Rev. 13: 2] [Rev. 19: 20] he is the Beast that controls the whole world from Babylon.

And now these merchants see all of their business, and money gone in one hour for ever.

18. And cried when they saw the smoke of her burning, saying, What city is like unto this great city!

Let's interpret, We can see all these merchants are crying, weeping, wailing, for one thing. The love of money the root of all evil [1st. Tim. 6: 10].

Saying, what city is like unto this great city? This is praise for New Babylon. We are looking at the Giants of Businesses around the World. Seven Heads, Ten Horns, and G- Seven, and (CEO) Chief Executive Officers of these Giant Businesses. These are the rulers of the Business World.

These are the ones The Angel, come down from heaven having Great Power, and the earth was (Lightened) with his Glory. Reported back to Jesus, when he saw the (SINS) of Babylon see verses (1,2,3) also [Rev. 17: 18]. The Bible is True!!.

This is in the (Near Future) everything is in place for the building of the Great City Babylon. It will have the glory of King Nebuchadnezzar's Babylon Empire.

19. And they cast dust on their heads, and cried, weeping and wailing, saying, Alas, alas, that great city, wherein were made rich all that had ships in the sea by reason of her costliness! For in one hour is she made desolate.

Let's interpret, And cast dust on their heads. This is an act of cursing, resentment, anger, low in spirit, sad, depressed. We see this by these words. Cried, Weeping, Wailing,

Alas, alas. That Great City, "Babylon" this is praise for Babylon.

Notice! Wherein were made Rich all that had ships in the sea. By her "Babylon" costliness! This is gain at great expense.

For in one hour she is made desolate. These merchants see they lost all their business, and money in one hour. This cried, weeping, wailing, Alas, alas. Is the love for money, it is all gone, and for ever.

See verse (8) this is the answer <u>Jesus,</u> gave to the <u>Angel,</u> having <u>Great Power</u> verses (1,2,3).

We need to understand also when this was prophesied, and written the mode of transportation of this merchandise by land, was a <u>Caravan</u> of <u>Camels,</u> or some other pack animal. <u>Daniel, Shadrach, Meshach, and Abednego.</u> were in this Babylon Empire of King Nebuchadnezzar.

Today New Babylon, have all of the modern day transportation. Babylon, can receive, or ship within hours around the world.

We must not lose the understanding of the <u>Mark</u> of the <u>Beast,</u> with all of this <u>Buying,</u> and <u>Selling.</u> (Do Not Take The Mark, of The Beast)!! [Rev. 14: 9, 10, 11].

20. Rejoice over her, thou heaven, and ye holy apostles and prophets; for God hath avenged you on her.

Let's interpret, Rejoice over her thou <u>Heaven</u> and ye <u>Holy Apostles,</u> and <u>Prophets</u>

These are the ones that are found here verse (24)The Angel, in verses (1, 2, 3) He knows all about heaven, and the Holy Apostles, and Prophets see [Luke, 11: 49, 50] also [Mat. 23: 34]

For God, hath avenged you on her. This scripture comes into view see [Rom. 12: 19] Vengeance is mine, I will repay saith the Lord.

This is Jesus, doing the (Avenged) see [Rev. 19: 2]. Jesus, is the one that utterly burned the Great City Babylon verse (8) shows us that. <u>God,</u> has avenged you on her, God, is <u>Jesus,</u> [Heb. 1: 8] [Rev. 19: 1, 2] [John, 10: 30] proof.

21. And a mighty angel took up a stone like a great mill stone, and cast it into the sea, saying, Thus with violence shall that great city Babylon be thrown down, and shall be found no more at all.

Let's interpret, And a mighty Angel, took up a stone, like a great mill stone, and cast it into the sea. This is (S/L) of Babylon as this

Great Stone, cast into the sea, it will sink to the bottom of the sea out of sight of mankind, and not be found any more.

Notice! Thus with Violence shall that great city Babylon be thrown down, and shall be found no more at all. Thus with Violence, is here Babylon is totally destroyed, and burned up. Jesus, is the one that destroyed Babylon. Here is why [Rev. 17: 6] also [Rom. 12: 19] Vengeance is mine I will Repay saith the Lord (Jesus).

22. And the voice of harpers, and musicians, and of pipers, and trumpeters, shall be heard no more at all in thee; and no craftsmen, of whatsoever craft he be, shall be found any more in thee; and the sound of a millstone shall be heard no more at all in thee;

Let's interpret, These words are the Fulfillment of the mighty Angel, in verse (21).

All the Musicians, are Gone, All the Craftsmen are Gone, All of the Millers, are Gone no more sound of a millstone where wheat used to be ground into fine flour.

We see this scripture is being fulfilled [Rev. 10: 6]. These Angels are working for Jesus, and they are Mighty!!.

We can see how busy the City of Babylon was; plenty of (Jobs) of all Craft, good (Musicians) good (Flour Mills) plenty of everything.

23. And the light of a candle shall shine no more at all in thee; and the voice of the bridegroom and the bride shall be heard no more at all in thee: for thy merchants were the great men of the earth; for by thy sorceries were all nations deceived.

Let's interpret, And the Light of a Candle shall shine no more at all in thee. This is (S/L) of righteous men [Mat. 5: 14, 15, 16] [Prov. 4: 18, 19] see also verse (4) proof.

The voice of the Bridegroom this is (S/L) of Jesus, [John, 3: 29]. And the Bride, this is (S/L) of the Church, [Rev. 21: 2, 9, 10, 11] [Rev. 22: 17] see verse (4) proof.

Shall be heard no more at all in thee. God, said "My Spirit shall not always strive with man" [Gen. 6: 3]. The voice of Jesus, is calling to the sinner man in Babylon, through the <u>Church</u> the <u>Bride.</u> Jesus, is doing the same thing today to the entire world of mankind through the church see [Rev. 22: 17]. Soon his voice will be heard no more on earth, see [Amos, 8: 11, 12] this is very plain, and today people have gotten away from the (Old Path) see [Jer. 6: 16].

For thy merchants were the <u>Great Men</u> of the <u>Earth.</u> These great men are <u>CEO Chief Executive Offers</u> of the <u>Giant Department Stores,</u> <u>Food Stores</u> and the <u>Giant Electronic Trade System</u>, world wide. Ever thing is in place for the Beast of Babylon to take over.

For by thy sorceries were all nations deceived. We find these (Sorceries) here see verse (1, 2, 3) [Rev. 13: 11-thru-18] this is Judas Iscariot, see [John, 6: 70, 71].

The <u>Great Whore</u> the <u>False Church</u> in <u>Babylon</u> will deceive many, see [2nd. Peter. 2: 1, 2, 3] and cause people to receive the mark of the Beast see [Mat. 24: 4, 24] [Col. 2: 8].

"He that hath an ear let him hear what he Spirit, saith unto the <u>Churches</u>".

24. And in her was found the blood of prophets, and of saints, and of all that were slain upon the earth.

Let's interpret, In her (Babylon) was found the <u>Blood</u> of <u>Prophets,</u> and of <u>Saints</u> See [Rev. 17: 6] [Rev. 2: 10, 13] [Rev. 13: 7, 10, 15]. All these scriptures are kill, or killeth with the sword.

And of all that were slain upon the earth. This goes all the way back to <u>Righteous Abel,</u> [Gen. 4: 8] and through the <u>Generations</u> of <u>Time</u> see [Mat. 23: 33, 34, 35] also [Acts, 12: 2] till we get to here [Rev. 18: 24]. These are just a few; there are many.

CHAPTER EIGHTEEN IS THE JUDGMENT
OF THE GREAT WHORE, THAT SITTETH
UPON MANY WATERS; WHICH ARE PEOPLE,
MULTITUDES, NATIONS, AND TONGUES.

BABYLON WILL RULED THE ENTIRE WORLD FOR
FORTY TWO MONTHS. (3 ½ years) A TIME, AND
TIMES, AND A HALF TIME WHICH IS (3 ½ years).

NOW BABYLON IS TOTALLY
DESTROYED DESOLATE, GONE.

We See The Earth Has Run Out of Time; We Find It Here [Rev. 20: 11, 15].

CHAPTER 19

1. And After these things I heard a great voice of much people in heaven, saying, Alleluia; Salvation, and glory, and honour, and power, unto the Lord our God:

Let's interpret, After these things this is referring to chapter Eighteen. Jesus, destroyed the New Babylon Empire. This is John, doing the talking.

I heard a great voice of Much people in Heaven. This great voice is, they are all saying the same thing at the same time.

They are saying this, Alleluia, Salvation, Glory, Honour, and Power. This is all praise, to Jesus, the Lord our God. is Jesus, see [Heb. 1: 8] God, and Jesus, are one [John, 10: 30]. The word "Alleluia" is the Greek form of Hebrew "Hallelujah"

2. For true and righteous are his judgments: for he hath judged the great whore, which did corrupt the earth with her fornication, and hath avenged the blood of his servants at her hand.

Let's interpret, For true and righteous are his judgments: this is Honor. For he hath judged the great whore, this also is Honor, Which did corrupt the earth with her fornication. This fornication is (Sin) we can get a good understanding from [Rev. 17: 4].

The Whore has a Golden Cup in her hand. Look inside of the cup, full of Abominations, an Filthiness, of her fornication a disgusting sight. We see now how True, and Righteous are his Judgments.

And hath avenged the blood of his servants at her hand. See [Rev. 6: 9, 10] [Rev. 17: 6 This comes to view [Rom. 12: 19] Vengeance is mine, I will repay, saith the Lord, this Lord, is Jesus.

3. And again they said, Alleluia, And her smoke rose up for ever and ever.

Let's interpret, Alleluia is a praise, to Jesus. And her smoke rose up for ever and ever. This is eternal no end to it, in the Lake of Fire, and Brimstone.

We can see by the first three verse people in <u>Heaven</u> knew what happened on earth. They have their <u>Glorified Flesh Body.</u>

4. And the four and twenty elders and the four beasts fell down and worshipped God that sat on the throne, saying, Amen Alleluia.

Let's interpret, We know from [Rev. 4: 4, 7] who these <u>Elders</u> are. Twelve of them are the <u>Saints</u> of <u>God</u>, Twelve of them are the <u>Apostles</u> of <u>Jesus,</u> see [Luke, 22: 29, 30].

The <u>Four Beast,</u> are (S/L) the four sons of <u>Jacob.</u> You will find them here see [Num. 2: 3, 10, 18, 25] their names are <u>Judah, Reuben, Ephraim, Dan.</u> (Ephraim) is the son <u>(Joseph)</u>.

These four with their brother tribes, are the (144,000) the army in heaven see verse (14). The word <u>Amen</u> is from the four and twenty elders, and the four beast, they agree with all that was said and done in the first three verses, Alleluia, is a praise to Jesus.

5. And a voice came out of the throne, saying, Praise our God, all ye his servants, and ye that fear him, both small and great.

Let's interpret, And a voice came out of the throne. There is no way this can be identify in <u>Specific</u> who this voice belongs to .Except in verse four, we know it is people.

The Four and Twenty Elders, and the Four Beast fell down, and worshipped God, that sat on the throne.

This voice came out of the throne, This <u>Suggest</u> the voice came from, the Four, and Twenty Elders, or the Four Beast, or both.

Saying <u>Praise</u> our God, ye his servants, the <u>Adverb Our</u>, is relating to us. The Four and Twenty Elders, and the Four Beast. All of them are working for Jesus.

All ye his servants, and ye that fear him, both small, and great. We see now the voice from the throne is (Referring) to us on earth the word "Fear" Is show respect, faith, [Heb. 11: 6], and Love, [1ˢᵗ. John, 4: 18].

We understand all of verse (5) is directed at the <u>Servants</u> of <u>Jesus,</u> both small, and great. The pronoun (All) is Everybody, in Heaven, and on Earth.

6. And I heard as it were the voice of a great multitude, and as the voice of many waters, and as the voice of mighty thundering, saying Alleluia: for the Lord God omnipotent reigneth.

Let's interpret, And I heard as it were the voice of a great multitude, This is of nations, tongues, and people; (One Voice). And as the voice of many waters, this is (S/L) of people; (One Voice). And as the voice of mighty thundering, (One Voice). With all these people saying the same thing at the same time, it suggest the sound like a <u>Mighty Thunder</u>. These are giving praise to Jesus, for the work he did on earth Saying <u>Alleluia</u> for the <u>Lord God, Omnipotent Reigneth.</u>

We see these people are <u>Extremely Happy</u>. Because they know they will have no more trouble, or opposition (Victory). See [Rev. 6: 9, (10) 11] These people knew they were (Slain) on earth!!

The "Word Omnipotent" is having <u>Power,</u> and <u>Authority</u> without limit, <u>The Almighty</u>. See [Rev. 1: 8] and [Mat. 28: 18]. This is Jesus, remember God, and Jesus, are one.

7. Let us be glad and rejoice, and give honour to him: for the marriage of the Lamb is come, and his wife hath made herself ready.

Let's interpret, In the first six verses we see <u>Rejoicing</u> because of <u>Victory.</u> Here we see rejoicing because the <u>Lamb,</u> (S/L) Jesus, is getting married.

Let us be glad and rejoice, and give honor to him, This is the Saints of God, giving praise to Jesus.

And his wife hath made herself ready.(This is The Real Church) Saints of God.

And his wife hath made herself ready. She made herself ready on earth proof see [Mat. 25: 10] [Rev. 7: 9, 13, 14, 15]. This earth is a <u>Dressing Place</u>, for mankind to get ready for the <u>Marriage</u> in <u>Heaven.</u> Verse (9) shows us that; "Blessed are they which are called unto the <u>Marriage Supper </u>of the <u>Lamb".</u> The Saints of God, are all through the Bible, From Genesis, to Revelation. The First is Righteous Abel.

A marriage is <u>Joining</u> together two opposite things that will work perfect; according to God's, plan. Example <u>Adam,</u> and <u>Eve</u> Man, and Woman, the <u>First Marriage,</u> by <u>God.</u>

The marriage we are looking at here is join together of <u>Two Kingdoms</u> opposite of each another. <u>The Heavenly Kingdom,</u> and <u>The Earthly Kingdom.</u> God, and Jesus, made both of them, and <u>Join,</u> them together through <u>Jesus.</u>

Here is how the marriage took place in <u>Heaven.</u> Proof [Rom. 8: 16, 17] We are the children of God, and Joint Heirs With Christ. [Rev. 21: 7] He that overcometh shall Inherit All Things. This is where we are joined together, with Jesus, a Marriage.

8.   And to her was granted that she should be arrayed in fine linen, clean and white: for the fine linen is the righteousness of saints.

Let's interpret, And to her was granted. This is the real church, [Mat. 16: 18]. <u>Granted</u> is <u>Given</u>. We start with [John, 3: 16] [Is. 1: 18] [Ps. 51: 7, 10] [Rev. 6: 11] [Rev. 7: 13, 14] [Rev. 4: 4] The <u>White Robe</u>, is a <u>Heavenly Garment</u> [Acts, 1: 10] also [Mat. 22: 11, 12] see also [Rev. 3: 4, 5]. Fine linen, clean and white; for the fine linen is the righteousness of the saints [Rev. 19: 8] this is self Explanatory.

9. And he saith unto me, Write, Blessed are they which are called unto the marriage supper of the Lamb. And he said unto me, These are the true sayings of God.

Let's interpret, And he saith unto me, Write Blessed are they which are called unto the marriage supper of the Lamb. These are the words of God, brought to John, by the Fellowservant in verse (10).

You can find the calling here, [John, 6: 37, 44] [John,, 4: 23, 24] [Mat. 11: 28, 29] [Rev. 3: 20, 21], and [Rev. 22: 17].

And he said unto me, These are the true sayings of God. This is the Fellowservant in verse (10) talking to John, for God, (Jesus). The Book of Revelation, is Jesus.

10. And I fell at his feet to worship him. And he said unto me, See thou do it not: I am thy fellowservant, and of thy brethren that have the testimony of Jesus: worship God: for the testimony of Jesus is the spirit of prophecy.

Let's interpret, And I fell at his feet to worship him. And he said unto me see thou do it not. This shows us John, didn't know Who, or What, was talking to him. Whether an Angel, or Man. This suggest John, is on the Isle of Patmos. We get a identification here from the one talking to John.

I am thy Fellowservant, this is "I work for God, and Jesus, also". And of thy brethren, that have the testimony of Jesus; worship God: for the testimony of Jesus, is the spirit of prophecy.

And of thy Brethren, This tells us the Fellowsevant is a Jew, for salvation is of the Jews see [John, 4: 22]. That Have The Testimony of Jesus. This is a Spiritual Gift. For the Testimony of Jesus, is the Spirit of Prophecy. This tells us the Fellowservant is a Prophet.

When the Fellowservant, said "Worship God," this was with Authority. We must remember John, is not in his Glorified Flesh Body. Here is where we are, and looking at. See [Rev. 1: 10], and [Rev. 4: 1, 2] very plain. See also [Rev. 10: 11].

11. And I saw heaven opened, and behold a white horse; and he that sat upon him was called Faithful and True, and in righteousness he doth judge and make war.

Let's interpret, And I saw heaven open, this suggest that John, is on earth. The White Horse, is the Power of God. He that sat upon the "White Horse" is Jesus.

Was called Faithful, and True see [John, 16: 33] "I have overcome the world".

In righteousness he doth judge and make war. Righteousness, is that which is (Right).

Judge, is a (Decision has been made). Make war, this is the (Consequence) of the decision. This entire verse is a description of Jesus.

12. His eyes were as a flame of fire and on his head were many crowns; and he had a name written, that no man knew, but he himself

Let's interpret, His eyes were as a flame of fire. This is color, but we don't know of what hue. And on his head were many crowns. This represents the Reward, given to every man according to his work shall be [Rev. 22: 12].

And he had a name written, that no man knew, but he himself. Jesus, knows who he is, The Word of God. [John, 1: 1, 14] [1st. John, 5: 7]. God, is in the Glorified Flesh Body of Jesus, these two are one [John, 10: 30].

13. And he was clothed with a vesture dipped in blood: and his name is called The Word of God.

Let's interpret, And he was clothed with a vesture Dipped in Blood; The verb (Was) is past tense. The vesture dipped in blood is the flesh body of Jesus, while he was on earth establishing his

Kingdom. The same body is alive for evermore, with God, in it [Rev. 1: 18] also [Luke, 24: 39] [John, 14: 10] "I am in the Father, and the Father is in me.

His name is called The Word of God. Now we know what his name is. Jesus, is the word of God. [John, 1: 1, 2] [1st. John, 5: 7, 8].

14. And the armies which were in heaven followed him upon white horses, clothed in fine linen, white and clean.

Let's interpret, And the armies which were in heaven, this is the Hundred Forty Four Thousand, these are they that follow the Lamb whithersoever he goeth. [Rev. 14: 1, 4]. They are going to war against men on earth, the Battle of Armageddon.

The White Horses are the Power of God. clothed in fine linen, white and clean. This is the Righteousness of the Saints see verse (8).

The White Horse Jesus, is on is the same White Horse the Holy Ghost sat on see [Rev. 6: 2] (The Power of God) The Holy Ghost went here see [Acts, 2: 1, 2, 3, 4].

Jesus, is going to war, the Battle of Armageddon with his army verse (14)

15. And out of his mouth goeth a sharp sword, that with it he should smite the nations: and he shall rule them with a rod of iron: and he treadeth the winepress of the fierceness and wrath of Almighty God.

Let's interpret, And out of his mouth goeth a sharp sword. This is the word of God, power see [Heb. 4: 12]. That with it he should smite the nations. We see this in action in verse (21). And shall rule them with a rod of iron. The rule is a law or a commandment, that cannot be changed. The rod of iron, is (S/L) of Jesus, straight, and strong, and all power see [Heb. 13: 8] The same yesterday, and today, and for ever.

And he treadeth the winepress of the fierceness and wrath of Almighty God. This is total destruction of the nations of people on earth that have the Mark of the Beast, and worshipped his Image verse (20).

This is the same winepress, that blood came out of unto the horse bridles, by the space of a thousand and six hundred furlongs (200-miles) [Rev. 14: 20].

Wrath of Almighty God. This is violent anger (Punishment for sin). Jesus, is carrying out God's, plan. This scripture comes into view [Rom. 12: 19].

16. And he had on his vesture and on his thigh a name written, KING OF KINGS, AND LORD OF LORDS.

Let's interpret, And he had on is vesture, and on his thigh a name written. Vesture is a Vest. A short sleeveless piece of clothing The name is written on the vest. And on his thigh the name is written on his garment at the thigh.

There are no Tattoos written on the body of Jesus. Tattoos, are forbidden by God, see [Lev. 19: 28].

The name written KING OF KINGS, AND LORD OF LORDS. Are Titles of the Highest Power Known. There is none Greater or Powerful than Jesus.

The name, (Titles) written are on the garment of his clothes. We have seen the Heavenly Garment; Fine Linen Clean, and White, in verses (8, 14) [Rev. 15: 6] which is the righteousness of the saints. This suggest Jesus, is clothed in the same Heavenly Garment.

17. And I saw an angel standing in the sun; and he cried with a loud voice, saying to all the fowls that fly in the midst of heaven, Come and gather yourselves together unto the supper of the great God;

Let's interpret, The angel standing in the sun, is in a position that covers the entire earth, and above everything on earth.

And cried with a loud voice; saying to all the fowls that fly in the midst of heaven, These fowls hear and understand, the voice of the Angel.

Come and gather yourselves together unto the supper of the Great God. This great God, is Jesus. [Heb. 1: 8]. The Supper is the Battle of Armageddon [Rev. 16: 16] [Rev. 19: 19]. Located in the Mesopotamia Valley. Where the blood flowed even unto the bridles of the horse a thousand six hundred furlongs (200-miles) [Rev. 14: 20].

18. That ye may eat the flesh of kings, and the flesh of captains, and the flesh of mighty men, and the flesh of horses, and of them that sat on them, and the flesh of all men, both free and bond, both small and great.

Let's interpret, This verse shows us Jesus, Had A Plan, to clean up the dead bodies of men, and horses before they were Slain. By using the fowls that fly in the midst of heaven in verse (17) This heaven is the one in [Gen. 1:1]. Some of these people have the Mark of the Beast, and some of them Worshipped his Image verse (20) shows that.

This is the Battle of Armageddon; here on earth.

19. And I saw the beast, and the kings of the earth, and their armies, gather together to make war against him that sat on the horse, and against his army.

Let's interpret, The Beast is this Man [Dan. 8: 23, 24, 25] This Beast, is the same Man [Rev. 13: 2]. See [Dan. 8: 25] This King Beast, shall stand up against the Prince of Princes, this is Jesus, KING OF KINGS, and shall be broken without hand. Now we know we have the right Beast, a Man.

The kings of the earth are the, Seven Heads, and the Ten Horns, that rule the people of the nations of the earth. Their armies are the people that have the Mark of the Beast, and those that worship his Image, of all the nations on earth.

Gathered together, to make war against him (Jesus) that sat on the (White) horse, and his army. The Hundred Forty Four Thousand.

These people are the ones that <u>Suffered</u> in all the <u>Plagues,</u> and <u>Blasphemed God.</u> Jesus, destroyed all of their merchandise, and money, when he <u>Burned Babylon With Fire.</u>

Now they want to go to <u>War With Him, and his Army.</u> The army of Jesus, is only a Hundred Forty Four Thousand see [Rev. 14: 1, 4]. Against the <u>Kings,</u> of the earth and the <u>Whole World</u> [Rev. 16: 14, 16]. This is the <u>Battle</u> of <u>Armageddon.</u>

20. And the beast was taken, and with him the false prophet that wrought miracles before him, with which he deceived them that had received the mark of the beast, and them that worshipped his image. These both were cast alive into a lake of fire burning with brimstone.

Let's interpret, And the beast was taken, and with him the false prophet that wrought miracles before him.

The Beast is (S/L) He is this <u>King</u> here [Dan. 8: 23, 25]. He is the <u>Beast</u> like a Leopard, Feet of a Bear, Mouth of a Lion. He is the King of Babylon. The dragon gave him his Power, Seat, and Great Authority and they Worshipped the <u>Beast</u> see [Rev. 13: 2, 4, 8].

The False Prophet, was taken also. This False Prophet, is (S/L) the Beast here see [Rev. 13: 11], and [Rev. 11: 7]. I saw another beast came up out of the earth. Having two horns like a Lamb, and spake as a dragon. This is the same Beast and false Prophet.

Here is why he spake as a dragon see [John, 6: 70, 71] he is a Devil Judas Iscariot. Jesus, told us there shall arise, false Christs, and false Prophets, and show Great Signs, and wonders see [Mat. 24: 24]. This is it see [Rev. 13: 11-thru-18].

Notice!! The first thing <u>Jesus,</u> did in this war was <u>Capture</u> the <u>Beast,</u> and the <u>False Prophet.</u> These two men, have no blood in their bodies. The Evil Spirit, of Satan kept them alive, and gave them movement, and life.

Jesus, knew this, and these both were Cast Alive into a Lake of Fire Burning with Brimstone.

The false Prophet, is Judas Iscariot, [John, 6: 70, 71]. We find all the miracles, that he deceived the people with here [Rev. 13: 12-thru-18]. This is the False Church in Babylon the great Whore.

21. And the remnant were slain with the sword of him that sat upon the horse, which sword proceeded out of his mouth: and all the fowls were filled with their flesh.

Let's interpret, The remnant that was slain, are the people in verse (18). With the Sword of him that sat upon the (White Horse). Which Sword proceeded out of his Mouth. This is Power of his Word see verse (15) this is Jesus.

This Sword started here see [Is. 49: 2] [Rev. 1: 16] See the power of the Sword, The words of Jesus, in action here [John, 11: 43, 44] [Mark, 4: 37, 38, 39].

And all the fowls were filled with their flesh. This is the clean up detail after the battle of Armageddon. Jesus, did a great job, of destroying the Great City Babylon, and the people that had the Mark, of the Beast, and those that worshipped his Image.

This is the end of the Mark of the Best, His Image, his Name, and Number of his name. In the day of Judgment, these same people will have to stand before Jesus, to be judged.

Notice!! The Beast, and the False Prophet, got their reward. At the beginning of the Battle of Armageddon. The Battle of Armageddon, was fought between these two Kingdoms, Good, and Evil.

Jesus, and the Hundred Forty Four Thousand. Against the Beast, False Prophet, and the Kings of the earth, and their armies. Jesus, won this War, because he is the KING OF KINGS AND THE LORD OF LORDS.

Jesus, spoke of this war <u>Kingdom,</u> against <u>Kingdom,</u> see [Mat. 24: 7] He knew then he was, going to <u>Fight</u> this <u>War</u>. Which is in the future, yet to come shortly. During this War the Battle of Armageddon, The <u>Saints</u> of <u>God,</u> and <u>Jesus,</u> will be here [Rev. 12: 14] and [Rev. 20: 9]. God, and Jesus, take care of their own.

CHAPTER 20

1.　And I saw an angel come down from heaven, having the key of the bottomless pit and a great chain in his hand.

Let's interpret, John, saw this <u>Angel</u> come down from heaven. We know John, is on earth at this time.

Having the key of the <u>Bottomless Pit</u> the key is (S/L) This <u>Key</u> is <u>Power,</u> the Bottomless Pit is (S/L) <u>The Earth</u> And a <u>Great Chain</u> in his <u>Hand,</u> the chain is (S/L) it also is <u>Power</u>. This power is <u>Spiritual Power.</u> A spirit, can not be bound with a natural chain. <u>The old Dragon is an Evil Spirit</u>.

2.　And he laid hold on the dragon, that old serpent, which is the Devil, and Satan, and bound him a thousand years,

Let's interpret, This <u>Angel,</u> of <u>God,</u> and <u>Jesus,</u> Laid hold on the dragon, Notice!!

This <u>Angel,</u> had to come down to earth to lay hold on the dragon, for he was cast out of heaven into the earth [Rev. 12: 9].

Here is where this took place see [John, 12: 31] Now is the judgment of this world: now shall the prince of this world be cast out. This is <u>Jesus,</u> doing the talking. We can see <u>Jesus,</u> cast the Dragon, that old Serpent, which is the Devil, and Satan, out of this world. And laid hold on the Dragon that old Serpent which is the Devil, and Satan.

The <u>Angel,</u> laid hold on him and bound him a <u>Thousand Years.</u> We know that one day is with the <u>Lord,</u> as a <u>Thousand Years,</u> and a <u>Thousand Years,</u> as one day see [2nd. Peter, 3:8].

This tells us <u>Time</u> is not a <u>Governing Factor,</u> in <u>Jesus,</u> and

God's, plan. The old Dragon, Serpent, Devil, and Satan, is still Bound Today. "He has another name Lucifer" see [Is. 14: 12].

Notice!! This took place while Jesus, was still on earth; thousands of years ago.

3. And cast him into the bottomless pit, and shut him up, and set a seal upon him, that he should deceive the nations no more, till the thousand years should be fulfilled; and after that he must be loosed a little season.

Let's interpret, And cast him, into the Bottomless Pit, this is (S/L) the earth. and shut him up. This shows the dragon was buried alive a spirit cannot be killed see [Is. 14: 15] puts some light on this.

And set a seal upon him that he should deceive the nations no more. This Seal is took away the Power of the Dragon, see [Is. 14: 10].

Till the thousand years should be fulfilled. We know that one day is with the Lord, as a thousand year and a thousand years as one day [2nd. Peter, 3: 8] There is no time limit we can put on this. For God, and Jesus, are not governed with (TIME).

And after that he must be loosed for a little season. We can put a time figure on this phrase Loose for a little season. See verse (7) and verse (9), Notice and compassed the camp of the saints, about and the beloved city. The little season is (3 ½ years).

See [Rev. 12: 14] A Time, and Times, and a half a Time. this is (3 ½ years). This is the Camp of the Saints. (The Real Church). She will be Fed there, from the Face of the Serpent, for (3 ½ years) this is the little season.

4. And I saw thrones, and they sat upon them, and judgment was given unto them: and I saw the souls of them that were beheaded for the witness of Jesus, and for the word of God, and which had not worshipped the beast, neither his image, neither had received his mark upon their foreheads, or in their hands; and they lived and reigned with Christ a thousand years.

Let's interpret, And I saw thrones, and they that sat upon them. These thrones are here [Rev. 4: 2, 4] they were called seats. And they that sat upon them, are the <u>Four</u>, and <u>Twenty Elders</u>, Twelve of these Four and Twenty are the twelve Apostles of Jesus. See [Luke, 22: 30] The other Twelve we have no Record of; but they are chosen of God.

And judgment was given unto them. These <u>Four,</u> and <u>Twenty Elders</u>, are given the <u>Spiritual Power,</u> of <u>God,</u> and <u>Jesus,</u> to make <u>Righteous Judgments.</u> [Mat. 19: 28].

And I saw the souls of them that were beheaded for the witness of Jesus, and for the word of God. We know some of these Souls; Abel, [Gen. 4: 8, 9, 10] John the Baptist, [Mat. 14: 3, 10] Apostle James, [Acts, 12: 2] Stephen, [Acts, 7: 59, 60]. All of these Souls are here [Rev. 6: 9, 11] see also [Rev. 12: 11].

And which had not worshipped the beast, neither his image, [Rev. 13: 15] neither had received his mark upon their foreheads, or in their hands. This is another span of time.

We are looking at the future; To worship the Beast, or his Image, or receive his Mark has not come yet. This tells us we must not take the mark of the beast or worship his image see Rev. 12: 11] Faith of the saints.

[Rev. 13: 10, 15] [Rev. 21: 6]. This is the future John, is telling us about, it is yet to come.

And they lived and reigned with Christ a thousand years. This is the Hundred Forty Four Thousand. This is the <u>First Resurrection,</u> verse (5, 6) proves this.

[Rev. 5: 10] is the parallel scripture; it mentions. "Made us unto our God, kings, and priests. Notice!! This is the last verse in the New Song [Rev. 5: 9, 10] And we shall reign on the earth. Here is where they are going to Reign with Christ.

[Rev. 19: 19, 20, 21]. We know that one day with the Lord, as a thousand years, and a thousand years as one day. <u>Jesus,</u> is not governed by time see [2nd. Peter, 3:8].

[Rev. 19: 20, 21] is the end of this Reign on earth, and the end of the Mark of the Beast and those that worship him or his Image. This is the Battle of Armageddon.

5. But the rest of the dead lived not again until the thousand years were finished. This is the first resurrection.

Let's interpret, But the rest of the dead lived not again until the thousand years were finished. Here are the rest of the dead, [Rev. 14: 13] Blessed are the dead which die in the Lord, Yea saith the Spirit, that they may rest from their labours; and their works do follow them. All of these are righteous people. These words prove this, (Lived not again). We know the righteous die from this flesh life on earth; but live again in the resurrection.

This resurrection is of the whole world, both Jew, and Gentile. See [Rev. 7; 9, 13] [1st. Thes. 4: 16, 17] [1st. Cor. 15: 51, 52]

6. Blessed and holy is he that hath part in the first resurrection: on such the second death hath no power, but they shall be priests of God and of Christ, and shall reign with him a thousand years.

Let's interpret, Blessed and holy is he that hath part in the first resurrection: The first resurrection is the Hundred Forty Four Thousand. [Rev. 14: 1-thru-5]. Blessed, is Enjoying Happiness, Holy, is pure and Clean, (Divine), coming direct from God.

On such the second death hath no power. The second death is Judgment Day. This shows us the Hundred Forty Four Thousand, were Dead, and in their Graves, the first Death. Let's prove it see [Mat. 27: 51, 52].

But they shall be priests of God and of Christ, and shall reign with him a thousand years. Priest, has the authority to lead, The word Reign, are the Kings authority to rule. This is the New Song of the Hundred Forty Four Thousand. We find the Kings, and Priests here [Rev. 5: 10] the last verse of the New Song. "We shall Reign on the earth".

Heaven is a Perfect Place, it don't need any adjusting!! The thousand year Reign begin here [Mat. 27: 52, 53] and will end here, verses (11, 12, 13, 14, 15]. Time is not a governing factor with God, and Jesus. One Day is as a (Thousand Years), and a (Thousand Years) as one day [2nd. Peter, 3: 8]. Only the Hundred Forty Four Thousand are going to Reign on Earth. [Rev. 19: 14, 19, 20, 21] and [Rev. 14: 4] shows us that.

7. And when the thousand years are expired, Satan shall be loosed out of his prison,

Let's interpret, And when the thousand years are expired. This is the end of a span of time in God's, plan. Now to put in action another span of time in God's, plan.

Satan shall be loosed out of is prison. This is (S/L) the bottomless pit. We know what the prison of Satan, is see verses (1, 2, 3] Satan, is the Dragon, the Beast, that ascend out of the Bottomless Pit, see [Rev. 17: 8], and go into perdition eternal punishment verse (10).

8. And shall go out to deceive the nations which are in the four quarters of the earth, Gog and Magog, to gather them together to battle: the number of whom is as the sand of the sea.

Let's interpret, And he shall go out to deceive the nations. Which are in the four quarters of the earth, this is East, West, North, South. Notice "Deceive"

Gog, is a descendant of Reuben, [1st. Chr. 5:4] A Leader of the Final Battle. Magog, Meshech, Tubal, are descendant of Japheth, [Gen. 10: 2] associated with Gog. All of these can be found in [Ezek. chapters 38, and 39] also Persia, Ethiopia, Libya.

Gog, is a Warrior a nation of thieves, and the Prince or a leader of all these nations. This is why he is a leader of the final battle.

To gather them together; This is (Satan) gathering them together. To battle, the number of whom is as the sand of the sea.

(The number whom is as the sand of the sea). Are the children of God's, blessing to <u>Abraham.</u> [Gen 22: 17]. We all are the <u>Seed</u> of <u>Abraham</u> by <u>Faith</u>, through Jesus.

This is two <u>Great Powers</u> <u>Good,</u> and <u>Evil,</u> <u>Kingdom</u> against <u>Kingdom.</u> Coming together to <u>Fight The Last War On Earth,</u> this is a <u>World War,</u> the last one. We are covering a <u>Huge Span of Time.,</u> and all of this is in the <u>Future.</u> "Near Future".

9. And they went upon the breadth of the earth, and compassed the camp of the saints about, and the beloved city: and fire came down from God out of heaven, and devoured them.

Let's interpret, And they went upon the breadth of the earth, this is they covered the entire earth. And compassed the camp of the saints about. This shows us that The <u>Camp</u> of the <u>Saints,</u> is world wide. By using this scripture [Rev. 12: 6, 14] there is no place or location where the camps of the Saints are located. As we look at this it is out of our reach of <u>Understanding.</u> The <u>Beloved City</u> is <u>Jerusalem,</u> in the land of <u>Israel.</u> The followers of Satan, compassed the Beloved City also. And fire came down from God, out of heaven, and devoured them. God, destroyed the army of Satan. This took place outside the camp of the Saints, and the Beloved City.

Notice!! There are only two left of this War; <u>God,</u> and the old Devil, Satan. The Devil was cast into the Lake of Fire, and Brimstone where the Beast, and the False Prophet are.

<u>God,</u> kept his promise to his son <u>Jesus.</u> The Lord said unto my Lord, Sit thou on my Right Hand, till I make thine enemies thy footstool see [Mat. 22: 44] [Ps. 110: 1].

NOTICE This!! Who is left standing on the EARTH. Let's find out see [1st. Cor. 15: 51,52,52] and [1st. Thes. 4: 15, 16, 17]. Plain Isn't It? (The Saints).

10. And the devil that deceived them was cast into the lake of fire and brimstone, where the beast and the false prophet are, and shall be tormented day and night for ever and ever.

Let's interpret, We see the (Three) (Deceivers) all in the same place. Tormented Day, and Night for ever, and ever this is continually. There are no day or night in the lake of Fire, and Brimstone, it is called Outer Darkness see [Mat. 22: 13].

Jesus, cast the beast, and the false prophet in the lake of fire, in the Battle of Armageddon. God. Destroyed the army of Satan, verse (9) and cast the Devil into the lake of fire where the beast, and the false prophet are. To fulfilled these scripture, [Ps. 110; 1] [Mat. 22: 44]. The Lord said unto my Lord Sit thou at my right hand until I make thine enemies thy footstool. God, kept his word, to his son Jesus.

We need to consider one thing here!! All the People in the Camp of the Saints, and the Beloved City, are still on earth. The Saints are the last ones to leave this Old Earth. Here is where they leave it see, [1st. Thes. 4: 15, 16, 17] [1st. Cor. 15: 51, 52] this we know.

Saints of God, and Jesus, are in every nation on earth. So the Camp of the Saints are all over the entire earth. Notice this!! Some of the Saints of God, and Jesus, are asleep in their Graves, see [1st. Cor. 15: 51, 52, 52, 54] also [1st Thes. 4: 15, 16, 17]

See [Mal. 3: 16, 17, 18] [Mal. 4: 1, 3, 5] Ye shall tread down the wicked; for they shall be Ashes Under the Soles of your Feet this is plain.

11. And I saw a great white throne, and he that sat on it, from whose face the earth and the heaven fled away; and there was found no place for them.

Let's interpret, And I saw a great white throne. This is the Throne God, gave Jesus, [Heb. 1: 8]. This is the Power God, gave

Jesus, [Mat. 28: 18] this is the <u>Kingdom God,</u> gave Jesus, [Luke, 22: 29] also [Dan. 7: 13, 14]. See [John, 10: 30] [John, 14: 10].

And he that sat on it, from whose face the earth and the heaven fled away. This is <u>Jesus,</u> proof see [Mat. 24: 35] [Like, 21: 33] simple isn't it?

All of this old sinful earth is gone, and with is the Devil, Beast, False Prophet, and sinner people. We understand by these scriptures [Mat. 8: 12] [Mat. 22: 13] cast into <u>Outer Darkness.</u> There shall be weeping and gnashing of teeth. This indicates the earth has become the Lake of Fire. [2nd. Peter, 3: 10, 11] sheds some light on this for us.

And there was found no place for them. This is cast away, no more use for them.

We see a (Void) here it will be filled, when we get to Chapter 21, verses (1 and 2)

12. And I saw the dead, small and great, stand before God; and the books were opened: and another book was opened, which is the book of life: and the dead were judged out of those things which were written in the books, according to their works.

Let's interpret, And I saw the dead small and great, stand before God. This is God, in the Glorified Body of Jesus. God, is <u>Invisible,</u> see [1st. Tim. 1: 17] [Heb. 11: 27] [Col. 1: 15] see [John, 10: 30]. This scripture comes into view also [Mat. 25: 31, 32].

And the books were opened. This is the <u>Sixty Six Books </u>of the <u>Holy Bible.</u> And another book was opened, which is the book of life. This book is <u>Jesus,</u> he is life, see [John, 1: 4] [John, 14: 6] proof.

And the dead were judged out of those things which were written in the books, according to their works. The <u>Dead</u> are <u>Sinner People.</u> According to their works, We know "Works" is a choice of mind. Mankind has a choice to do <u>Good,</u> or <u>Evil.</u> Anyone that reads the <u>Bible,</u> has this choice.

[Mat. 7: 7,8] Ask, and it shall be given, Seek, and ye shall find, Knock, and it shall be open to you. There is no <u>Excuse</u> [John, 3: 16].

13. And the sea gave up the dead which were in it; and death and hell delivered up the dead which were in them: and they were judged every man according to their works.

Let's interpret, And the sea gave up the dead which were in it. These dead are sinner people. See [Rev. 8: 9] and [Rev. 16: 3], consider all the wars storms at sea through the generations of time, and now.

And death and hell delivered up the dead which were in them. Death is Sin, Hell is a place of Confinement. Proof see [Luke, 16: 23, 24], and [Jonah, 2: 1, 2].

And they were judged every man according to their works. We know works is a choice of mind. We must consider all the wars at sea. Both righteous, and unrighteous, could have lost their life, during these wars. When the sea gave up the dead, this is sinner people. The dead which die in the Lord, shall rise first [1st. Thes. 4: 16].

But every man will get a Righteous Judgment, according to their works, Good, or Evil. We are looking at a long span of time, and world wide it covers the entire earth. This is the day of judgment. This is the End, of the way of Life for mankind on earth.

14. And death and hell were cast into the lake of fire. This is the second death.

Let's interpret, Death is Sin, Hell is a place of Confinement. Cast into the Lake of Fire, explains both of these. The First Death; we all die from this earthly flesh body. The Second Death, is judgment cast into the lake of fire. This is always dying and never die. See [Mark. 9: 44] Where their worm dieth not, and the Fire is not Quenched, proof.

15. And whosoever was not found written in the book of life was cast into the lake of fire.

Let's interpret, This <u>Book</u> of <u>Life,</u> is <u>Jesus.</u> [John, 14: 6] [John, 10: 27]. Jesus, keeps a <u>Perfect Record,</u> and it started with <u>ADAM,</u> see [Mal. 3: 16, 17, 18].

And whosoever was not found written in the book of life was cast into the lake of fire. This is self explanatory. All of this is Future; and the <u>Time</u> is <u>Neigh</u>. This is the end of life on earth for mankind.

CHAPTER 21

1. And I saw a new heaven and a new earth: for the first heaven and the first earth were passed away; and there was no more sea.

Let's interpret, And I saw a New Heaven, and a New Earth. This was Prophesied here [Is. 65: 17] [2nd. Peter, 3: 13] this is faith according to his promise, look for a New Heaven, and a New Earth, wherein Dwelleth Righteousness. Now John, saw the real thing of the Prophecy, and the Faith.

For the First Heaven, and the First Earth, were passed away, and there was no more Sea see [Rev. 20: 11]. And there was no more Sea, this suggest the sea went with the earth. Revelation, is the Book of Prophecy.

2. And I John, saw the holy city, new Jerusalem, coming down from God out of heaven, prepared as a bride adorned for her husband.

Let's interpret, John, saw the Holy City, New Jerusalem. The city is called Holy because it is built of Holy People. It started with Abraham, Isaac, and Jacob.

Coming down from God, out of heaven. This shows us The Holy City, was built in Heaven, by God, and Jesus.

With the Holy City coming down from God, out of heaven. It must have a place to stay forever. If we look at verse (1) we found it The New Heaven and the New Earth. Remember the Void we discussed in [Rev. 20: 11]. Now see verse (5), He that sat upon the throne said behold I make all things (New) this is Jesus, see [Ps. 102: 25, 26, 27].

Prepared as a bride adorned for her husband. This is the Most

Beautiful Thing, that the eyes of mankind will ever see. The Old Church!! The Bride is the Church. The Husband is Jesus. This is the Marriage that took place in Heaven see [Rev. 19: 7] we that are saved by his Grace will be see [Rom. 8: 16, 17] the children of God, are Heirs of God, and joint Heirs with Jesus; Glorified Together very plain.

3. And I heard a great voice out of heaven saying, Behold, the tabernacle of God is with men, and he will dwell with them, and they shall be his people, and God himself shall be with them, and be their God.

Let's interpret, And I heard a Great Voice out of Heaven saying, Behold the tabernacle of God, is with men. The tabernacle of God, is the Glorified Flesh Body of Jesus. Verses (4, 5, 6, 7] shows us it is Jesus, doing the talking. In verse (6) I am Alpha, and Omega this is Jesus, see [Rev. 1: 8]. We are looking at Jesus, in his Kingdom that God, appointed unto him [Luke, 22: 29] [Heb. 1: 8].

And he will dwell with them, and they shall be his people. Remember [2nd. Peter, 3: 13] New Heaven, and a New Earth, wherein dwelleth righteousness.

And God, himself shall be with them, and be their God. Verse (7) explains this. Remember [John, 10: 30] Jesus, said "My Father and I are one".

4. And God shall wipe away all tears from their eyes; and there shall be no more death, neither sorrow, nor crying, neither shall there be any more pain: for the former things are passed away.

Let's interpret, and God, shall wipe away all tears from their eyes. This a Glorified Flesh Body. Alive for ever, and ever; By the Holy Spirit of God.

The rest of this verse is self explanatory; For the former things are passed away.

5. And he that sat upon the throne said, Behold I make all things new. And he said unto me, Write: for these words are true and faithful.

Let's interpret, And he that sat upon the throne, This is Jesus, said Behold I make all things new. Notice!! All things new; are these <u>New Heaven, New Earth, Holy City, New Jerusalem.</u> And a <u>New Glorified Flesh Body!!</u> The <u>Image</u> of <u>God.</u> Keep in mind this is the Kingdom, God, Appointed unto Jesus. [Luke, 22: 29, 30] [Dan. 7: 13, 14].

We need to understand the Kingdom of Jesus, is made up of the people of the earth. Made in the Image and likeness of God, and Jesus.

And he said unto me, Write: for these words are true and faithful. These words are <u>True,</u> here are the words that are true. "Behold I make all things new". And <u>Faithful,</u> This is Jesus, The true and Faithful Witness keeping his promise [Rev. 1: 5].

6. And he said unto me, It is done. I am Alpha and Omega, the beginning and the end. I will give unto him that is athirst of the fountain of the water of life freely.

Let's interpret, And he said unto me, it is done, is referring to verse (5). Here it is Behold <u>I Make All Things New.</u> this is the Kingdom of Jesus. He is the one doing the talking. The following words prove it.

I am Alpha, and Omega, the beginning and the end this is (S/L) of Jesus, see [Rev. 1: 8] notice the <u>Almighty.</u> [Mat. 28: 18] all power.

I will give unto him that is athirst of the fountain of the water of life freely.

This is believe in <u>Jesus,</u> see [John, 6: 35]. Notice! this <u>Fountain,</u> is (S/L) <u>Jesus,</u> The water of Life is (S/L) the <u>Holy Ghost,</u> that we are <u>Baptized With</u> see [Mat. 3: 11] see also [John, 7: 37 38], and [John, 4: 10, 14].

7. He that overcometh shall inherit all things and I will be his God, and he shall be my son.

Let's interpret, He that overcometh shall inherit all things. This is the <u>Victory</u> that overcometh the world of (Sin), <u>Our Faith</u> [1ˢᵗ. John, 5: 4] also [Heb. 11: 6].

And I will be his God. This is Jesus, in his <u>Kingdom.</u> And he shall be my <u>Son </u>see [Rom. 8: 14]. <u>Notice!!</u> shall <u>Inherit</u> all things. [John, 3: 16] comes into focus also.

Fear not little flock; for it is your Father's good pleasure to give you the kingdom [Luke, 12: 32]. <u>This is our Inheritance.</u> See [Gal. 5: 22, 23, 24, 25] fruit of the Spirit. This is our part that helps us to overcome.

8. But the fearful, and unbelieving, and the abominable, and murders, and whoremongers, and sorcerers, and idolaters, and all liars, shall have their part in the lake which burneth with fire and brimstone: which is the second death.

Let's interpret, All of this verse is, <u>Works</u> of the <u>Flesh</u> see [Gal. 5: 19, 20, 21].

9. And there came unto me one of the seven angels which had the seven vials full of the seven last plagues, and talked with me, saying, Come hither, I will show thee the bride, the Lamb's wife.

Let's interpret, This <u>Angel,</u> is one of the Seven Spirits of God, which Jesus, has now see [Rev. 5: 6].

This Angel came to John, and talked to him, saying, Come hithere I will show thee the bride the Lamb's wife. The Bride is (S/L) That Great City Holy Jerusalem verse (10). The Lamb, is (S/L) Jesus. The Bride becomes the <u>Lamb's Wife</u> here [Rev. 19: 7].

10. And he carried me away in the spirit to a great and high mountain, and showed me that great city, the holy Jerusalem descending out of heaven from God,

Let's interpret, With John, carried away in the Spirit, "Realm" it would be difficult to place this great and high mountain in a location that we can relate to. We have this verb Descending; which is coming down this would suggest The Great High Mountain is some where in the New Earth which is already in place. For the First Heaven and earth were passed away.

Now the Holy City New Jerusalem, is in it's place, The New Heaven, and The New Earth forever, and ever.

Notice! All things are NEW, NEW, NEW see verse (5). Very Plain, isn't it? In the following verses we will get a more Indepth Description of the Holy City.

11. Having the glory of God: and her light was like unto a stone most precious, even like a jasper stone, clear as crystal;

Let's interpret, Having the Glory of God, which is a Distinguished Quality, of Brilliant, and Splendor. We know the Glory of God, is Jesus, see verse (23).

And her light was like a stone most precious The pronoun Her is the Holy City New Jerusalem. The Light is Jesus, the stone most Precious, is Jesus. The Chief Corner Stone of this Holy City see [Eph. 2: 20, 21].

Even like a jasper stone, clear as crystal, Jesus, is all light, and no darkness in him at all. [1st. John, 1: 3, 5, 7], Jesus, and God, are one, [John, 10: 30].

Jesus, is the door into the Holy city New Jerusalem. Those that are saved by Grace enter in through the door "Jesus", into the Holy City while here on earth [John, 10: 7, 9].

12. And had a wall great and high, and had twelve gates, and at the gates twelve angels, and names written thereon, which are the names of the twelve tribes of the children of Israel:

Let's interpret, And had a wall great and high, this wall is around the Holy City; Symmetrical, and had twelve gates, and at the gates twelve angels, and names written thereon, which are the names of the twelve tribes of the children of Israel. The twelve tribe of the children of Israel, Are the Twelve Sons of Jacob, which is Named Israel.

Here are the names of the, twelve sons of Jacob, in order from the oldest to the youngest. Ruben, Simeon, Levi, Judah, Issachar, Zebulun, Joseph, Benjamin, Dan, Naphtali, Gad, Asher, see [Gen. 35: 23, 24, 25, 26].

Jerusalem, in the land of Israel [Ezek. 48: 31-thru-35] you can find these Twelve Gates, and the Twelve Tribes of Israel. Around Jerusalem; in their order This is on Earth.

Three Gates Northward, Reuben, Judah, Levi. East, Joseph, Benjamin, Dan.

South, Simeon, Issachar, Zebulun, West, Gad, Asher, Naphtali.

13. On the east three gates; on the north three gates; on the south three gates; and on the west three gates.

Let's interpret, This is the position or location, of the gates in the Holy City. The names of the children of the Israel, are not given.

[Ezek. 48: 31-thru-35] the gates in Jerusalem, in the land of Israel, are positioned identical to the ones in New Jerusalem the Holy City. In the Kingdom of Jesus.

14. And the wall of the city had twelve foundations, and in them the names of the twelve apostles of the Lamb.

Let's interpret, The wall of the city had Twelve Foundations. And in them the names of the twelve apostles of the Lamb. This shows us each foundation has a name.

The Holy City, is built upon the Foundation of the Twelve Apostles, and Prophets, Jesus Christ, himself being the Chief Corner Stone. See [Eph. 2: 20, 21, 22].

Here are the names of the Twelve Apostles. Peter, Andrew, James, John, Philip, Bartholomew, Thomas, Matthew, James, Lebbaeus, Simon, Matthias. See [Matt. 10: 2, 3] and [Acts, 1: 23, 24, 25, 26]. This shows us again why the Holy City, New Jerusalem, is called Holy. It was built by Holy People. (Apostles, and Prophets).

15. And he that talked with me had a golden reed to measure the city, and the gates thereof, and the wall thereof.

Let's interpret, And he that talked with me, is the Angel, that had the seven vials of the seven last plagues see verse (9).

Had a Golden Reed, to measure the City, Gates, and the Wall. This is the entire city. The word Measure, is linear measure. A Reed of Jewish Measure. Is (11-feet).

16. And the city lieth foursquare, and the length is as large as the breadth: and he measured the city with the reed, twelve thousand furlongs. The length and the breadth and the height of it are equal.

Let's interpret, This Angel measured the city with the Golden Reed. Twelve Thousand Furlongs in Length. Twelve Thousand Furlongs in Breadth, and Twelve Thousand Furlongs High.

We are looking at a very large city. Let's break it down so we can get a good understanding of just how big it is.

A Furlong is (220- yards) (660-feet) 12,000 furlongs X 220 yards= 2,640,000 yards. 12,000 furlongs X 660 feet=7,924,000 feet.

The height of this city is Twelve Thousand Furlongs. (2,640,000 yards) (7,924,000 feet). This New Jerusalem The Holy City, is a huge city.

The city lieth foursquare, this is Twelve Thousand, Times Twelve Thousand, is a Hundred Forty Four Thousand Furlongs. (12000 X 12000= 144,000) Furlongs.

You can figure out the Square Yards of the first floor, or Foundation of the Holy City, by 144000 furlongs times 220 yards. (144000 X 220=31,680,000) Square yards. The same formula is used for Square Feet. (144000 X 660=95,040,000) Square feet.

The Length, times the Breadth, times the Height, are equal. In out terms today we are looking at a (Cube) Length, times the Width, times the Height, a huge figure.

We are looking at the Kingdom, God, gave Jesus, see [Luke, 22: 29, 30] and [Dan. 7: 13, 14]. All of our calculations are not important; but interesting.

17. And he measured the wall thereof, an hundred and forty and four cubits, according to the measure of man, that is, of the angel.

Let's interpret, All indication of this measure is suggesting the thickness of the wall of the Holy City. The measure is given in (Cubits)

And he measured the wall thereof, an Hundred and Forty Four Cubits. A cubit measure is accepted to be (18-inches). To receive this in our terms today we turn the Hundred Forty Four Cubits into inches by (144 cubits X 18 inches =2592) inches. Divide the Inches by Twelve gives us (216 feet) (2592 inches divided by 12=216) feet.

We can see by the information given us the Wall of the Holy City, is 216 feet thick. The description used in verse (10) showed me that "Great City Holy Jerusalem". We understand now the word "Great". There is no City known to man greater than, The Holy City New Jerusalem.

18. And the building of the wall of it was of Jasper: and the city was pure gold, like unto clear glass

Let's interpret, The wall of the building is <u>Jasper.</u> According to the research <u>Jasper</u> is a <u>Green Precious Stone.</u> This is the Original color of the Stone. Today we have a Variety of color of the Jasper Stone, (Man made)

The jasper Stone is the first Foundation of the wall in the city the City is Pure Gold, like unto clear glass.

19. And the foundations of the wall of the city were garnished with all manner of precious stones. The first foundation was Jasper; the second, sapphire; the third chalcedony; the fourth, emerald;

Let's interpret, These foundations, which rise up are twelve thousand furlongs high verse (16). Today in our terms we call a tall building (Stories, or Floors) Example five stories or the fifth floor. These Precious Stones, are pure. They are not contaminated with the soil of this earth. Nor by any Jeweler, they are perfect.

20. The fifth, sardonyx; the sixth, sardius; the seventh, chrysolite; the eighth, beryl; the ninth, a topaz; the tenth, a chrysoprasus; the eleventh, a jacinth; the twelfth, an amethyst.

These precious Stones are Self Explanatory. They are in the Twelve Foundations of the wall of the Holy City, verse (19) shows us that. This is a <u>Magnificent, Impressive Beauty.</u>

21. And the twelve gates were twelve pearls; every several gate was of one pearl: and the street of the city was pure gold, as it were transparent glass.

Let's interpret, And the <u>Twelve Gates,</u> were <u>Twelve Pearls;</u> every several gate was of one Pearl. These Twelve Gates of Peals, are the (Twelve Sons of Jacob) see verse (12). See also [Ezek. 48: 31-thru-35]. Every <u>Gate </u>was of <u>One Pearl.</u> This one <u>Pearl</u> is (S/L) is <u>Jacob.</u>

"Example" all these sons are of <u>One Man Jacob.</u> The sons of Jacob, see [Gen. 35: 23, 24, 25, 26] proof.

The twelve sons of Jacob, are the "Goodly Pearls" see [Mat. 13: 45]. The "One Pearl" of <u>Great Price</u> is <u>Jacob</u> [Mat. 13: 46]. Jesus, bought these "Pearls" with his <u>Own Blood</u> while he was on earth. See [Acts, 20: 28] [1ˢᵗ. Cor. 6: 20] [2ⁿᵈ. Peter, 2: 1].

All the <u>Preaching,</u> and <u>Teaching,</u> That Jesus, did was in the <u>Land</u> of <u>Israel.</u> He never went any where else, see [Mat. 15: 24]. Plain isn't it? <u>Salvation</u> is of the <u>Jews</u> see [John, 4: 22] this is Jesus, talking. God, made the way for mankind here [John, 3: 16]

And the street of the city was pure gold, as it were transparent glass. This <u>Street</u> of <u>Pure Gold,</u> as it were transparent glass is one street. Where ever it goes in the Holy City, it is the <u>Same</u> it never changes. It is there forever.

Have you notice there are no <u>Roads,</u> mentioned in the <u>New Earth?</u>

22. And I saw no temple therein: for the Lord God Almighty and the Lamb are the temple of it.

Let's interpret, And I saw no temple therein. Temple is a <u>Sanctuary</u> a space marked or a room for <u>Worship.</u> We have the same thing today in our churches. Notice!

We have Class Rooms, Library, Office, Study, Chapel, (Sanctuary for Worship).

For the Lord God Almighty, and the Lamb are the temple of it. These three Titles; <u>Lord God Almighty,</u> and <u>Lamb,</u> are one see [John, 10: 30] This is God, and Jesus, can be worshipped any where in the Holy City. Not in a "Designated Place".

23. And the city had no need of the sun, neither of the moon, to shine in it: for the glory of God did lighten it, and the Lamb is the light there of.

Let's interpret, We can see in this verse the only <u>Light</u> in the Holy city is <u>Jesus.</u> The <u>Glory</u> of <u>God</u> is in Jesus, and shining through the <u>Glorified Flesh Body</u> of <u>Jesus,</u> proof see [Luke, 24: 39] [John, 17: 5] [John, 10: 30] [John, 14: 11] Very plain.

24. And the nations which are saved shall walk in the light of it: and the kings of the earth do bring their glory and honour into it.

Let's interpret, And the nations which are saved shall walk in the light of it. This covers the entire earth all <u>Nationality.</u> This comes into view [John, 3: 16] the gift of God.

And the kings of the earth do bring their glory and honour into it. This tells us some of the <u>Great Kings</u> of the earth were saved. This Great King (David) [Ps. 23: 6] "I will dwell I the house of the Lord, for ever". There are others, Nebuchadnezzar, <u>Extol</u> which is praised God, highly [Dan. 4: 37], and many more.

25. And the gates of it shall not be shut at all by day: for there shall be no night there.

Let's Interpret, The gates of it shall not be shut at all by day. This shows us we are safe for ever more. This scripture shows us that [Mat. 6: 20]

For there shall be no night there. This tells us <u>Jesus,</u> is the <u>Light</u> of his <u>Kingdom,</u> see [Luke, 22: 30]. With the <u>Glory</u> of <u>God,</u> Shining through his <u>Glorified Body Forever,</u> verse (23) also [John, 17: 5].

26. And they shall bring the glory and honour of the nations into it.

Let's interpret, The pronoun "They" are these <u>Angels,</u> [Mat. 24: 31]. They shall bring the glory, and honour of the nations into it. The word nations shows us (People).

<u>Glory,</u> is <u>Praise</u> of a <u>Pure Heart</u>. "Sincere" <u>Honor</u> is "Admiration"

Respect, A Feeling of Great Delight. This is in the Glorified Body of the people of all nations of the earth that are saved. [1st. John, 3: 2] When Jesus, shall appear we shall be like him, for we shall see him as he is.

27. And there shall in no wise enter into it any thing that defileth, neither whatsoever worketh abomination, or maketh a lie: but they which are written in the Lamb's book of life.

Let's interpret, And there shall in no wise enter into it, anything that defileth. This is speaking of The Holy City, New Jerusalem.

Defile, is to make filthy, "Corrupt the Purity" This is impossible for this to get in to the Kingdom of Jesus.

These words are the works of the flesh. Defileth, Abomination, Lie, [Gal. 5: 19, 20, 21] But they which are written in the Lamb's book of life.

CHAPTER 22

1. And he showed me a pure river of water of life, clear as crystal, proceeding out of the throne of God and the Lamb,

Let's interpret, The Pure River of Water of Life, <u>Clear</u> as <u>Crystal,</u> proceeding out of the <u>Throne</u> of <u>God,</u> and the <u>Lamb.</u> Proceeding is continual.

The Pure River of Water of Life, is the <u>Holy Spirit</u> of <u>God,</u> and <u>Jesus.</u> It is Flowing out to the <u>People</u> on <u>Earth</u> today verse (17) shows us that. See [Mark, 1: 8] [Acts, 2: 3, 4].

This is the same <u>Living Water,</u> that Jesus, told the Samaritan woman at Jacob's Well, he would give her if she would have ask him [John, 4: 10]. Also this Living water <u>Jesus,</u> gives every one that are saved by <u>Grace</u> shall be in him a <u>Well</u> of <u>Water</u> springing up into <u>Everlasting Life</u> [John, 4: 14] also [John, 3: 16] <u>Everlasting Life!!</u>

This scripture depicts the Pure River of Water of Life see [Gen. 28: 12, 13, 17]. Jacob, saw this Holy Spirit, and called it a <u>Ladder.</u> It set up on the earth, and the top reached to heaven; And behold the <u>Lord,</u> stood above it, and said I am the <u>Lord God,</u> of <u>Abraham,</u> and the <u>God,</u> of <u>Isaac.</u> Jacob, said this is the <u>Gate</u> of <u>Heaven</u> [Gen. 28: 17]. The whole <u>Earth</u> is full of his <u>Glory</u> [Is. 6: 3]. Consider the <u>Sun</u> it's light shines on the earth day, and night; so does the Pure River of Water of Life, The Holy Spirit of God, and Jesus.

2. In the midst of the street of it, and on either side of the river, was there the tree of life, which bare twelve manner of fruits, and yielded her fruit every month: and the leaves of the tree were for the healing of the nations.

Let's interpret, In the midst of the street of it. This is in the (Middle or Center) of it. And on either side of the river.

Notice!! One side of the river is the Top Side Heaven where it started from. The other side of the river is the Bottom Side Earth where it came to. It is still with mankind on earth today. All that mankind on earth, has to do, is follow the instructions in verse (17) Take The Water of Life Freely Simple.

Was there the tree of life, The Tree of Life, is Jesus. In the midst of the river of Water of Life; and on either side Heaven, and Earth. Plainly written here [Gen. 2: 9] the Tree of Life in the Midst of the Garden of Eden., this is Jesus, see [Gen. 3: 22].

Which bare twelve manners of fruit. This is Jesus, and his Twelve Apostles, The Fruit is the Preached Gospel of the Kingdom of Jesus see [John, 15: 3, 4, 5].

And yielded her fruit every month. This is continually, Jesus, and the Apostles, Preached the Gospel of the Kingdom of God, every day they were on earth. And a month has (30 or 31) days in them.

And the leaves of the tree were for the healing of the nations. The leaves are (S/L) people that are saved by grace. The tree, is (S/L) Jesus. Healing of the nations are the righteous people in every nation on earth see [Acts, 10: 34. 35].

Notice!! This (S/L) Water of Life; Tree of Life; this is JESUS [John, 14: 6] he is the way the Truth, and the Life.

3. And there shall be no more curse: but the throne of God and of the Lamb shall be in it; and his servants shall serve him:

Let's interpret, And there shall be no more curse. This is to cause Harm, and Evil.

But the throne of God and of the Lamb shall be in it. This suggest the throne of God, and the Lamb, will be in the Holy City New Jerusalem.

This is the first indication we have of the Throne, of God, and of the Lamb, being in the Holy City, Verse (1) shows us that also

And his servants shall serve him, this let's us see we have something to do in the Kingdom of Jesus. The New Heaven, and New Earth, and the Holy City New Jerusalem.

4. And they shall see his face; and his name shall be in their foreheads.

Let's interpret, And they shall see his face. The pronoun <u>They</u> are all the children of <u>God,</u> and <u>Jesus,</u> in The New Heaven, and the New Earth ; And the Holy City New Jerusalem.

They shall see his face, This is see God's, face because no man has ever seen God's, face see [1ˢᵗ. John, 4: 12].

And his name shall be in their forehead. This is God's, Name, <u>Jehovah</u> [Ex. 6: 3].

We know what is going to be written upon us; when we enter that Holy City See [Rev. 3: 12] plain isn't is?

5. And there shall be no night there; and they need no candle, Neither light of the sun; for the Lord God giveth them light: and they shall reign for ever and ever.

Let's interpret, Notice! No night, no candle, no light of the sun. All of these fled away [Rev. 20: 11] for the former things are passed away see [Rev. 21: 4]. This is The New Heaven, and The New Earth [Rev. 21: 1].

This is referring to the Kingdom of Jesus. The New Heaven, and the New Earth, and the Holy City New Jerusalem. The Lord God, is Jesus. Remember God, and Jesus, are ONE [John, 10: 30]. The Lord God, giveth them light, see [Dan. 12; 3]. And they shall reign for ever, and ever. This assures us we will be working for Jesus. See this scripture [1ˢᵗ. Cor. 2: 9] plain isn't it?

6. And he said unto me, These sayings are faithful and true: and the Lord God of the holy prophets sent his angel to show unto his servants the things which must shortly be done.

Let's interpret, The pronoun (He) is the same pronoun (He) in verse (1), and verse (9). This is the Fellowservant Talking, with the instructions from the Angel in [Rev. 1:1].

And he said unto me, These sayings are faithful and true. Faithful, is firm in keeping promises. True, is completely loyalty, that can be relied on. This is a Perfect Picture of Jesus.

And the Lord God; The Lord God is Jesus, these two are one. Notice!! God, doesn't have an Angel. But Jesus, does see [Rev. 1: 1], and [Rev. 22: 16] (Proof).

Jesus, is the Lord God, of the holy prophets sent his angel to show unto his servants the things which must shortly be done, this Angel, is the one in [Rev. 1: 1].

To show unto his servants, This is today the righteous that are saved by Grace. Things which must shortly be done. This shows us we are near the End of Time.

7. Behold, I come quickly: blessed is he that keepeth the sayings of the prophecy of this book.

Let's interpret, Behold is to look or look upon. I come quickly, is in the twinkling of an eye see [1st. Cor. 15: 51, 52, 53] see also [Mat. 24: 27]. Blessed is he that keepeth the sayings of the prophecy of this book this is from [Rev. 1: 1 to Rev. 22: 21] the complete Book of Revelation Blessed is Enjoying Happiness.

8. And I John, saw these things, and heard them. And when I had heard and seen, I fell down to worship before the feet of the angel which showed me these things.

Let's interpret, And I John, saw these things, and heard them. John, is speaking from verse (1) to verse (8). John, is part of what he saw, and heard. In verse (2) the twelve manners of fruit are the twelve Apostles of Jesus, The Tree of Life.

And when I had heard and seen, I fell down to worship before the feet of the angel which showed me these things. We can see John, was Elated filled with joy; when he realized what he had seen and heard. He was so thankful that he would have worshipped the angel. Our answer is in verse (9), let's take a look.

9. Then saith he unto me, See thou do it not: for I am thy fellowservant, and of thy brethren the prophets, and of them which keep the sayings of this book worship God.

Let's interpret, Then saith he unto me, See thou do it not: for I am thy fellowservant "I work for Jesus, also". and of thy brethren the prophets. This shows us he is of, one of the tribes of Israel as John. He is also a Prophet. And of them which keep the sayings of this book, these are the Saints of God, This book is Revelation worship God. This is good advise from the Fellowservant.

The Fellowservant, that showed John, these things and talked with John. Was a natural man on earth, until God, called him to work for God. As God, Called Moses.

Now we find this Fellowservant, in his Glorified Flesh Body, Clothed with a Heavenly Garment. Working for God, and Jesus, in the Great Book of Revelation. Showing John, things of the Glorious Kingdom of Jesus, which John, is part of.

The Angel, in [Rev. 21: 9-thru-27] is working for Jesus, also. He talked with John, and showed him, the Bride the Lamb's Wife, (The Holy City New Jerusalem).

[Rev. 22: 1] the Fellowservant, started working for Jesus, and showing John, these things. "What a Marvelous piece of Work". All of this is under the directions of this Angel, [Rev. 1: 1], and [Rev. 22: 16], Very Plain isn't it?

10. And he saith unto me, Seal not the sayings of the prophecy of this book: for the time is at hand.

Let's interpret, The pronoun He is the Fellowservant. Seal not the sayings of the prophecy of this book. Notice! Seal not, this shows us the book of (Revelation) is open. Here is where it was opened see [Rev. 5: 5, 6, 7] Jesus. For the time is at hand. This is, it is time for the prophecy of this book (Revelation) to be Fulfilled. This is a Wonderful Book of Jesus Christ.

11. He that is unjust, let him be unjust still: and he which is filthy, let him be filthy still: and he that is righteous, let him be righteous still: and he that is holy, let him be holy still.

Let's interpret, He that is unjust, let him be unjust still: He that is filthy, let him be filthy still: This is a (State of being) of unrighteous people. At the time of the appearing or Jesus, verse (12) is proof of this. "For the time is at hand" this is now.

He that is righteous, let him be righteous still: He that is Holy let him be holy still this is a (State of Being) of righteous people. This also is at the appearing of Jesus.

The word (Still) is the end there are no changing at this time.

12. And, behold, I come quickly; and my reward is with me, to give every man according as his work shall be.

Let's interpret, Behold I come quickly; This is in a twinkling of an eye [1st. Cor. 15: 52] [Mat. 24: 27] and my reward is with me. This is the reward; to the Righteous, and Holy, a Crown of Life [Rev. 2: 10] [Rev. 21: 7]. The reward to the unjust, and filthy is this [Mat. 25: 41] everlasting punishment.

13. I am Alpha and Omega, the beginning and the end, the first and the last.

Let's interpret, All three of these titles are (S/L) of Jesus. Alpha is the first letter in the Greek alphabet, Omega is the last.

The beginning and the end is (S/L) Jesus, is the beginning of the creation of God, see [Prov. 8: 22, 23] [Rev. 3: 14]. Jesus, is also the end of every thing on earth see [Rev. 20: 11] [Rev. 21: 5, 6].

The First and the Last, is (S/L) of Jesus, he is the first born of every creature [Col. 1: 15]. [1ˢᵗ. Cor. 15;20] First risen from the dead. The last (S/L) of Jesus, is the last see [Act, 4: 12] There is none other <u>Name</u> under heaven <u>Given</u> among men, whereby we must be saved, but the name of Jesus. To sum up the First, and the Last see [John, 1: 14] The Only Begotten of The Father, Jesus, is the First, and the Last <u>Son</u> of <u>God.</u>

14. Blessed are they that do his commandments, that they may have right to the tree of life, and may enter in through the gates into the city.

Let's interpret, Blessed are they that do his commandments. Blessed is happiness; here are some of his commandments [John, 14: 15, 23] also [James, 1: 27] Pure religion and undefiled before God, see also [John, 8: 51]. If a man keep my sayings he shall never see death. Do his commandments are these. Keep the Sabbath, feed the hungry, cloth the naked, visit the sick, widows and orphans. The New Testament is full of his Commandments, most of all, Be Faithful unto death. I will give thee a crown of life see [Rev. 2: 10] proof.

Without faith it is impossible to please God see [Heb. 11: 6] also [James, 2: 18] I will shew thee my faith by my works. This is do his Commandments.

By these we have the right to the <u>Tree</u> of <u>Life,</u> and enter in through the gates into the city. This is the Holy City New Jerusalem. The commandments of God, Started here [Gen. 2: 16, 17] the Tree of <u>Knowledge</u> <u>Good</u> and <u>Evil.</u> We must choose (Good).

15. For without are dogs, and sorcerers, and whoremongers, and murders, and idolaters, and whosoever loveth and maketh a lie.

Let's interpret, All of this verse is <u>Works</u> of the <u>Flesh</u> unrighteous people. Proof see [Gal. 5: 19, 20, 21]. They that do such things shall not inherit the Kingdom of God.

The word (Dogs) is (S/L) people that will do anything; as the nature of a wild dog. They have no respect for anything. We find these kind of people all through the Bible. See [Gen. 6: 5] [John, 8: 44, 47]. The Book of Jude, Teaches us all about these kind of people.

16. I Jesus have sent mine angel to testify unto you these things in the churches. I am the root and the offspring of David, and the bright and morning star.

Let's interpret, I Jesus, Have sent <u>Mine Angel,</u> to testify unto you these things in the churches. This is the angel in [Rev. 1: 1]. The word testify, is a true statement, and it is for us the world of mankind.

We can see this Angel, working for Jesus. Showed John, the good and bad things in each of the Seven Churches; and told them how to correct their problems. He spoke the words that Jesus, gave him to speak, and John, wrote them in this book of Revelation. For all the world to read, we find this here [Rev. 1: 3].

If we go back and read (Chapter-2, and 3) we can understand what this Angel, is Testifying about, and testifying of Jesus.

(Example) See [Rev. 2: 1] Unto the angel of the church of Ephesus write; These things <u>(Saith He)</u> These two words, show us the <u>Angel,</u> is speaking for Jesus. that holdeth the seven stars in his right hand, who walketh in the midst of the seven golden candlesticks. A huge book could be written on this subject,

I am the root and the offspring of David, see [Rev. 5: 5] [Luke, 1: 32] [Mark, 10: 47, 48]. The lineage of the family of King David, these scriptures confirm this [Luke, 2: 4, 5, 6, 7, 10].

And the bright and morning star. Notice! And the <u>Bright</u> and <u>Morning Star,</u> a natural star doesn't shine in the day, but Jesus, does see [2nd. Peter I: 19] [John. 8: 12] I am the <u>Light</u> of the <u>World.</u> This

Bright, and Morning Star, shines Day, and Night it is still shining today Jesus. There is no other star like the Morning Star. He out shines them all.

17. And the Spirit and the bride say, Come. And let him that heareth say, Come. And let him that is athirst come. And whosoever will, let him take the water of life freely.

Let's interpret, The Spirit, is the Holy Spirit, [Rev. 3: 22]. And the Bride is the Real Church they both say the same thing. The bride is referring to the Holy City New Jerusalem [Rev. 21: 9, 10] which is the real church see [2nd. Peter 3: 13] this is why it is called (Holy).

And let him that heareth say, Come. This is the real Preacher that Jesus, called and sent, see [Rom. 10: 13, 14, 15]. And let him that is athirst come. See [Mat. 5: 6] and whosoever will, let him take the water of life freely, this is a Divine Invitation. From Jesus, through his Angel. This is the Pure River of Water of Life Clear as Crystal, verse (1).

18. For I testify unto every man that heareth the words of the prophecy of this book, If any man shall add unto these things, God shall add unto him the plagues that are written in this book:

Let's interpret, For I testify the pronoun I, shows us this is the Angel, in verse (16), He is in charge of the Book of Revelation.

(Here is what the Angel, is testifying) Unto every man that heareth the words of the prophecy of this book. If any man shall add unto these things, God shall add unto him the plaques that are written in this book.

There is nothing here that says; the book of Revelation can't be interpreted. We change nothing of the book of Revelation. But it is interpreted by the Holy Spirit.

This is why these words are written (He that Hath an ear let him hear what the Spirit saith unto the churches), this is to understand. Without the Holy Spirit, nothing in this Holy Bible can be understood.

God, shall add unto him the plagues that are written in this book. This is a <u>Warning</u>! Don't change <u>Anything Accept</u> the <u>Book</u> of <u>Revelation,</u> as it is <u>Written</u>. And use these scriptures, see [James, 1: 5], and [Mat. 7: 7, 8] very plain.

19. And if any man shall take away from the words of the book of this prophecy, God, shall take away his part out of the book of life, and out of the holy city, and from the things which are written in this book.

Let's interpret, This is the Angel, in verse (16) testifying. Again we Accept the Book of Revelation as it is Written. We acknowledge the Warning from the Angel.

And if any man shall take away from the words of the book of this prophecy. The book is Revelation, and it is a Book of Prophecy [Rev. 1: 3]. God, shall take away his part out of the book of life. The book of life is Jesus. The part of man in the book of Life, is his name written therein see [Rev. 3: 5] [Rev. 20: 15].

And out of the Holy City, this is New Jerusalem, see [Rev. 21: 2]. And from the things which are written in this book. To sum this up see [Rev. 21:7]. He that overcometh shall inherit all things. Mankind will loose everything if they take away anything that is written in the book of Revelation. Believe it as it is, and ask for wisdom to understand it.

20. He which testifieth these things saith, Surely I come quickly. Amen. Even so, come, Lord Jesus.

Let's interpret, He which testifieth these things saith. Surely I come quickly. This is <u>Jesus,</u> Verse (12) confirms, this. <u>Jesus,</u> is the only one to come, and he is coming from Heaven.

These scriptures show us how <u>Quickly Jesus,</u> will come see

[Mat. 24: 27] and [1st. Cor. 15: 52]. The word <u>Amen,</u> is I agree with the words in this verse. These words are the words of John. (Even so, come, Lord Jesus) These words are of John, also. At this time John, is still on earth with the saints of God. All of the saints of God, are tired of this world of sin..

21. The grace of our Lord Jesus Christ be with you all. Amen.

Let's interpret, <u>Grace,</u> is given to people by <u>God,</u> and <u>Jesus.</u> It is Favor, Help, Freedom, Joy, by Divine Grace, Pure Love.

Fear not, little flock; for it is your Father's good pleasure to give you the kingdom [Luke, 12: 32]. This is Joy Unspeakable. The word Amen, is agreeable to what is said in this verse, and the entire <u>BOOK</u> of <u>REVELATION</u> of <u>Jesus Christ.</u>

I Pastor, Bob Stidham, Am Lost For Words To Explain To You How Elated I Am That <u>JESUS,</u> Has Blessed Me To Interpret His Book The <u>Revelation,</u> of <u>Jesus Christ.</u>

THANK YOU JESUS,

Copyright, Author Pastor Bob Stidham, February 23, 2019
Only Pastor Bob Stidham, has the authority
to Grant anyone Permission
To copy any of this written material, or Electronically record it.
Easter Sunday Morning, April 15th. 2001. The Holy Spirit
of God, Spoke these words to Pastor Bob Stidham.
<u>**God, has a good excuse to ignore you.**</u>
<u>**The same one you gave him.**</u>
Please see these scriptures [Luke, 19: 22] Out
of thy own mouth will I judge thee.
[Job, 15: 6] Thine own lips testify against thee.
[Galatians, 6: 7] For whatsoever a man
soweth, that he shall also reap.
Amen

Printed in the United States
By Bookmasters